SYZYGIES

capturing the hiding sun

THREE ECLIPSES

The 2017 Great American Eclipse
The 2019 Chilean Sunset Eclipse
The 2023 Australian Hybrid Eclipse

Glenn W. Sturm

CEO,
Author, Creator,
Director &
First Principal Photographer

Brittany Lunsford Kurz

Executive Vice-President,
Director of Photography &
Technical Operations,
Post-production Artist, &
Second Principal Photographer

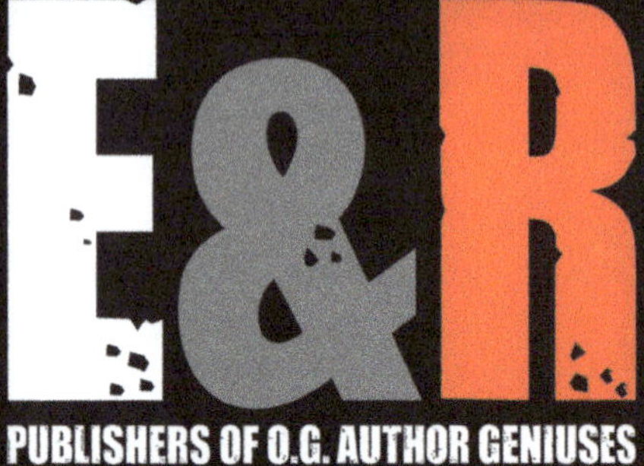

Published by E&R Publishers
New York, NY USA

An imprint of MillsoCo Publishing, USA
www.EandR.pub

Copyright: © 2024 Glenn W. Sturm. All rights reserved.

Your guarantee of quality

As publishers, we strive to produce every book to the highest commercial standards. The printing and binding have been planned to ensure a sturdy, attractive publication that should give years of enjoyment. If your copy fails to meet our high standards, please inform us and we will gladly replace it.

admin@millsi.co

ISBN: 9781945674952 (Hardcover)
ISBN: 9781945674969 (Softcover)
ISBN: 9781945674976 (Ebook)
Library of Congress Control Number: 2024930590

First Edition

TABLE OF CONTENTS

There is one set of terms that are used throughout this book. They are:

1. C1 or First Contact. (Start of the partial eclipse)
2. C2 or Second Contact (Start of the total eclipse)
3. Maximum Totality
4. C3 or Third Contact (End of the total eclipse)
5. C4 or Fourth Contact. (End of the partial eclipse)

DEDICATION

To Linda LaRue, whose spirit, concern for others, and efforts to improve our world have left the people, places, and our world better than she found them.

INTRODUCTION

In 2015, I first learned a total solar eclipse would pass over my Jackson, Wyoming home in August of 2017. Brittany and I started discussing the eclipse almost immediately. The eclipse project started as a simple idea and turned into a major undertaking because of the passion it inspired in all of us. The preparation consumed weeks and months of our time, and was worth every second we devoted to it.

Neither Brit nor I had any experience shooting eclipses, but we are both dedicated to photography and love studying. Since the eclipse was nearly 18 months away, we believed that we had plenty of time to identify and learn how to use all the necessary equipment and find the perfect location to shoot it. We looked everywhere. The most memorable hike that we took looking for the best location to shoot the eclipse was aptly named "Death Canyon Trail." The length of the trail is approximately 10.5 miles long with an elevation gain of approximately 3,000 feet. The hike was difficult and we made it even more difficult because we ran out of water, which was not great planning on our parts.

The toughest part of the eclipse preparation turned out to be picking the perfect location, though I had thought this would be the easiest. There are so many beautiful settings in Jackson. That said, I had simply been wrong. As it has turned out, no matter how much work we put into it, choosing the "perfect location" is the hardest part of every eclipse shoot. In Jackson, after spending over two years preparing for the shoot, we ended up choosing the final shoot site at 7:00 a.m. on August 21, 2017, the day of the eclipse.

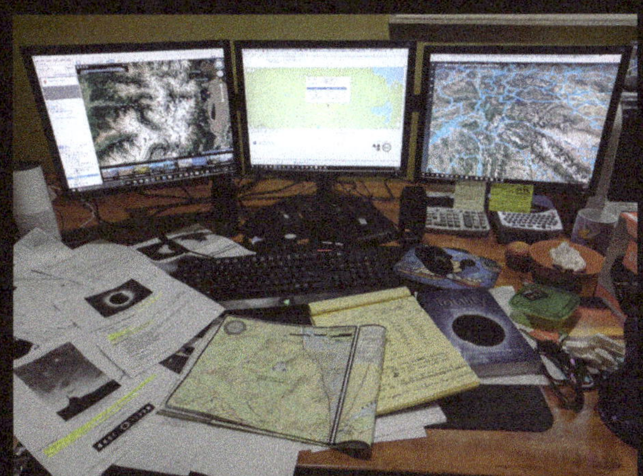

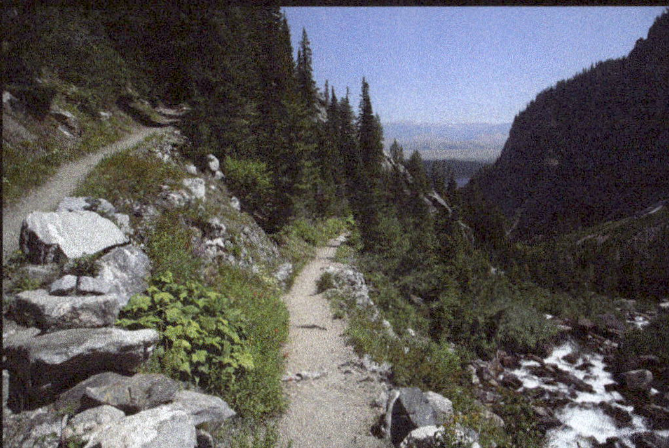

We photographed the 2017 eclipse with nine cameras, four of them shooting five-stop brackets every five minutes during the partial phases and as many shots as we could capture manually during the two minutes and eleven seconds of totality.

When the shoot was over, we were both relieved, drained, and excited. An eclipse is a wonderful, emotional, and moving event. However, when we were finished shooting the eclipse, we didn't know if we had gotten a single good shot. We all went to my house for something to drink and to relax. Since I have no patience, I pulled out one of the memory cards to see if we had taken any good pictures. This is the first one I saw:

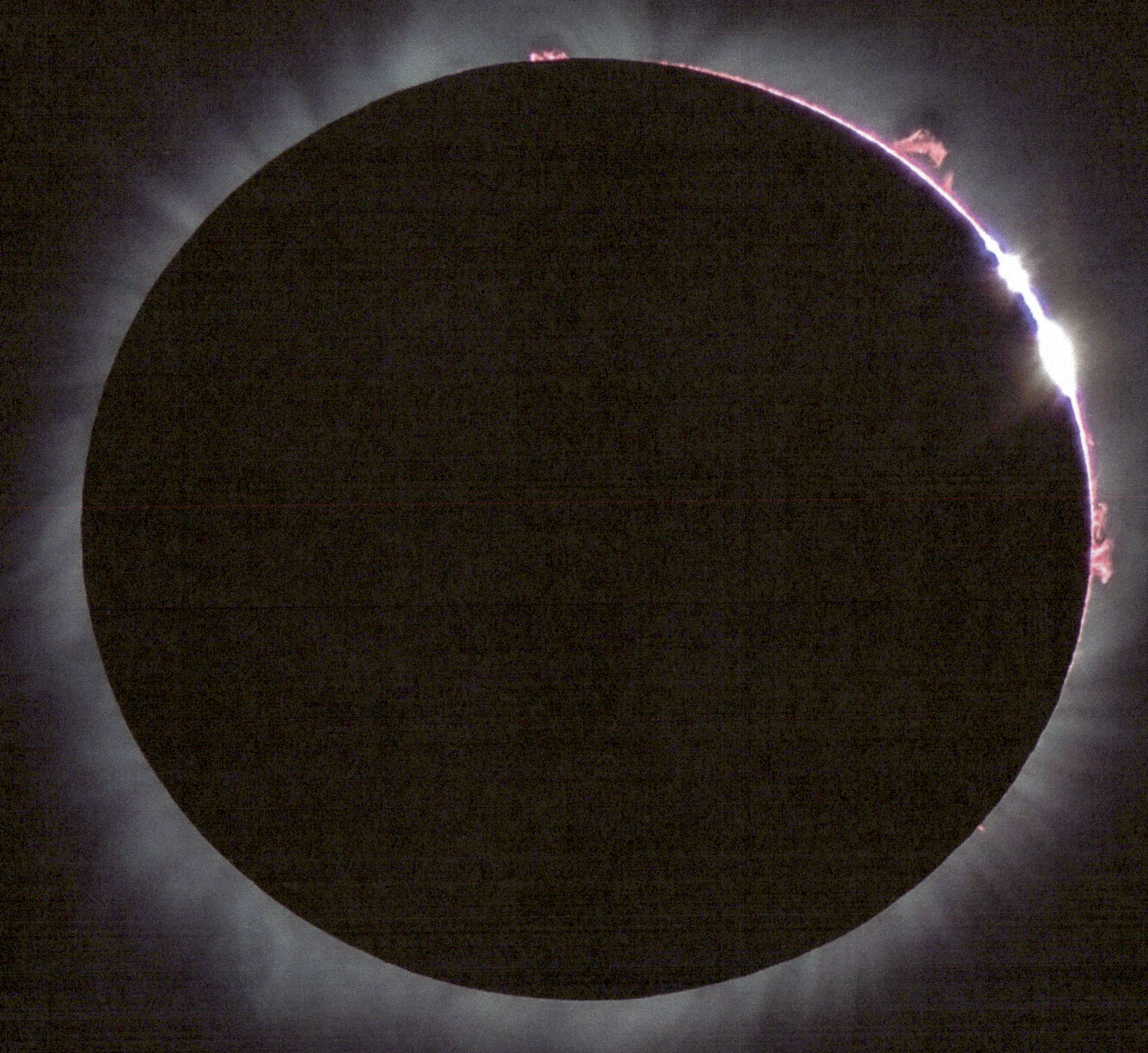

After seeing this image, I knew I was hooked. We started going through the pictures, and we couldn't stop looking at them. They were overwhelming. We had shot approximately 9,400 images. Most of them were great, and some were outstanding.

Immediately, we started talking about two things. First, we decided that we were going to shoot the next eclipse that we knew about, in the Patagonia region of Argentina. Second, I was determined to write a book about eclipses which would be comprised of images of three eclipses, a narrative that was written in layman's terms for people who wanted to shoot eclipses, and the complete metadata associated with each picture. We hoped to finish the book in late 2020 or early 2021, shortly after the 2020 eclipse in Patagonia. At the time, I was so excited about the Patagonia eclipse that the upcoming 2019 eclipse in Chile was inadvertently overlooked.

Upon realizing our oversight surrounding the Chilean eclipse, we immediately started planning that shoot. The event was a sunset eclipse on the west coast in 2019. Following Chile, the next eclipse would be in Argentina on December 14, 2020, and that day just happens to be my birthday. Shooting an eclipse on an already special day was the best birthday gift I could have received.

With the work that we had accomplished so far, meeting our objective to publish the book in 2021 appeared achievable. We didn't know, however, that COVID was coming and that we wouldn't be able to shoot the upcoming eclipses in Argentina or Greenland. As a result, we waited over three years for the April 20, 2023, eclipse near Exmouth in Western Australia.

Glenn W. Sturm

ACKNOWLEDGMENTS

Brittany ("Brit") Lunsford Kurz is the author of the Raw and White Balance sections. She owns the copywrite on these sections. I want to thank her for permission to include the sections in the book and acknowledge her help throughout. Thanks for your work, your teamwork, and your talent. You have been a wonderful teammate on all the projects.

Mark Littmann, Fred Espenak, and Ken Willcox. We wanted to say thank you again for this wonderful resource. We wouldn't have had our success without your wonderful book. Please buy a copy. You will get your money's worth.

Dr. Simon Mills. Without your help, guidance, and creativity, this book would never have come to fruition. You are one of the most talented individuals I have ever met. Thank you, Simon, for your wizardry.

Kristin Hooten, while new to our team, you are indispensable. You are one of the best editors that I have ever encountered. Without your logistics for the team and setting up the Easter Island Eclipse while we are all working on the April 8, 2024 project, we'd never get it all done. Thank you, Kristin.

Linda LaRue, a new member of our team, dedicated a significant amount of time to enhancing the quality of our book "Syzygies." During the last few weeks of her life, she diligently edited and reorganized various sections of the book. Upon completion of her work, we collectively spent around four hours reviewing her suggestions. The morning, I finalized the edits based on Linda's contributions, I was filled with pride at the outcome. Shortly after finishing my work, I ran into Linda's husband and learned of Linda's passing. The magnitude of loss I experienced was immeasurable. Her impactful work will remain an integral part of our team's work on this book and all our future work. I gained invaluable knowledge from Linda, and her absence will be deeply felt.

PART I

The 2017 Great American Eclipse

Brittany and I started discussing shooting the 2017 eclipse in 2015. That was before her first daughter Kahlan, was born and before I owned a fine camera. It started as a simple idea and turned into a passion which consumed numerous days and weeks of preparation. During those years of preparation, we explored multiple locations to shoot the eclipse before settling on our final site the morning of the eclipse.

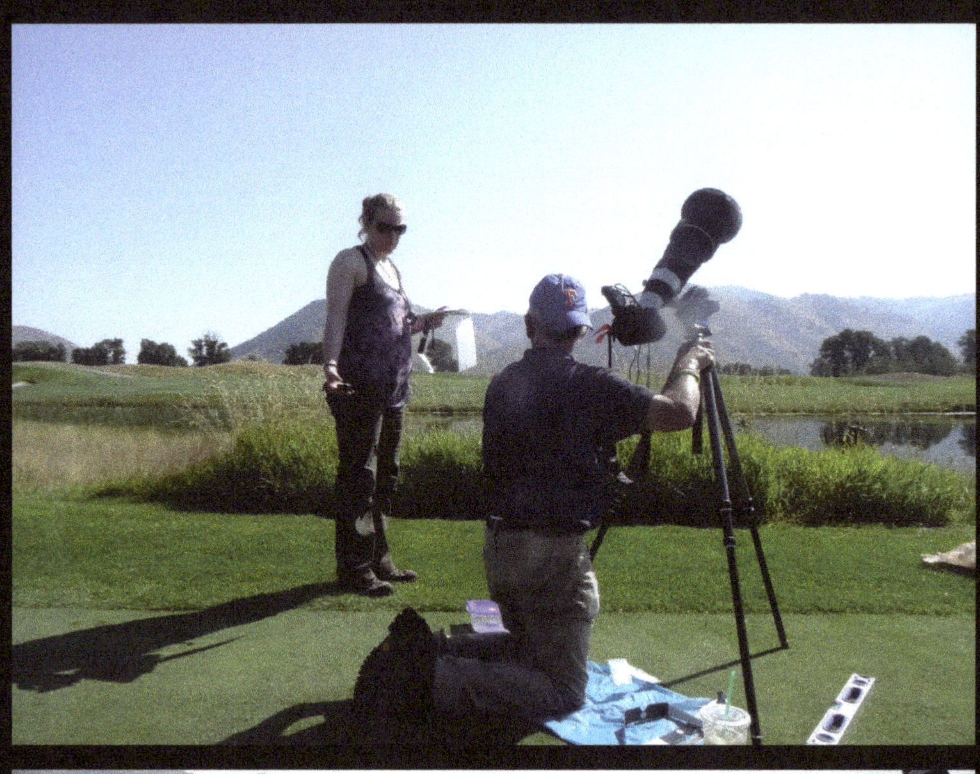

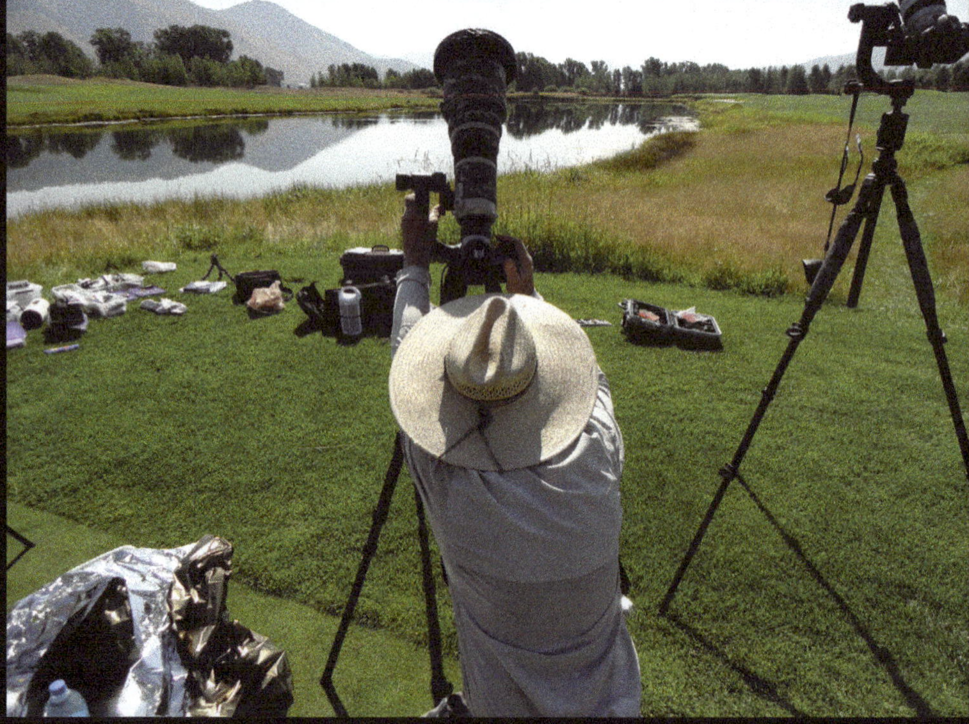

Below is the Sun as it appeared unobstructed at 10:15 a.m., just before first contact, the beginning of the eclipse, at 10:17 a.m. Several sunspots are visible. Sunspot activity plays a large role in the shape and appearance of the ever-changing corona, the outermost region of the Sun's atmosphere which can only be seen during a total eclipse. The orange cast of the photosphere is not a natural occurrence but rather the result of the properties of some common types of solar filters.

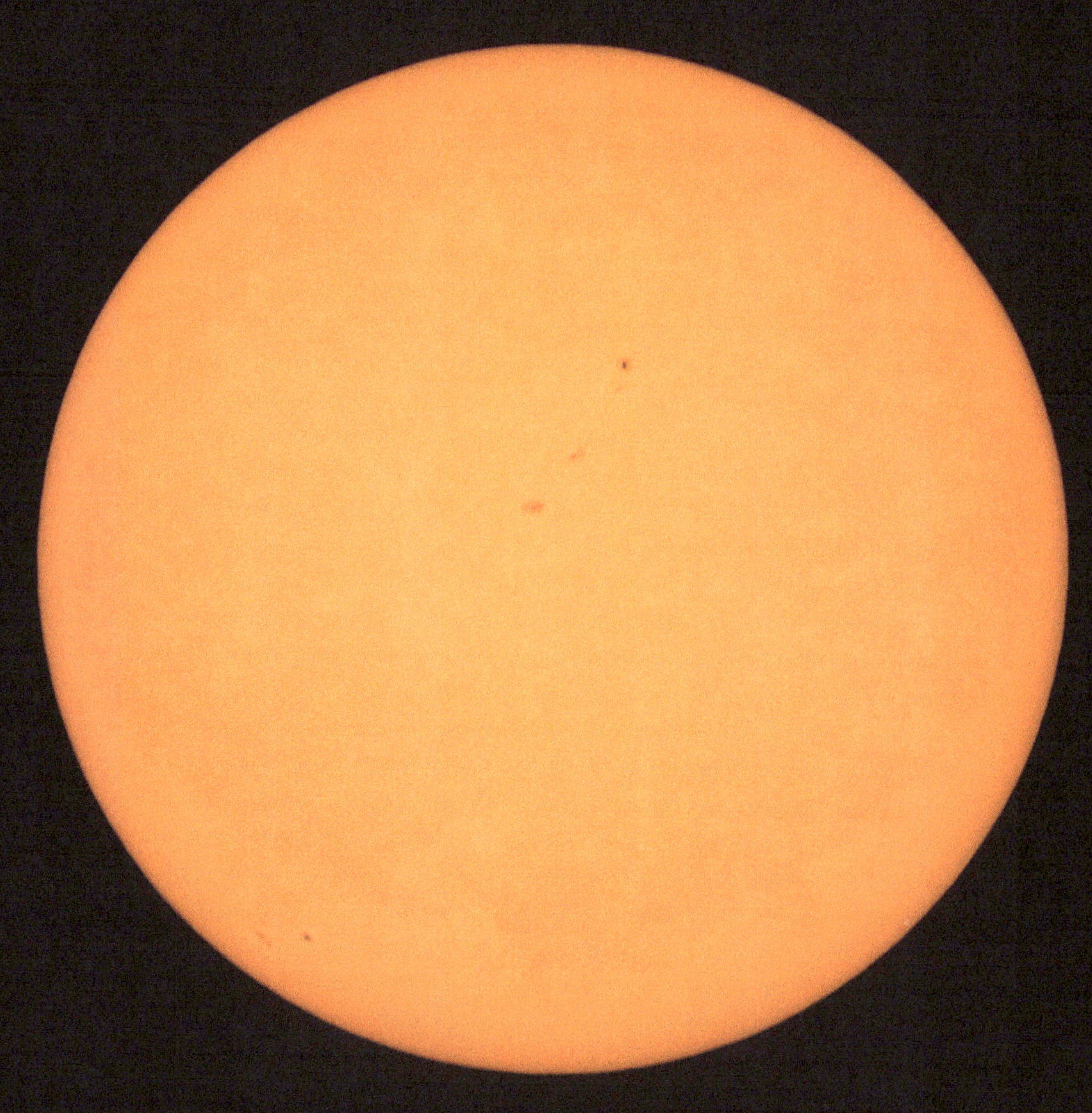

At 10:16:38 a.m. on August 21, 2017, the total solar eclipse began over Jackson, Wyoming. Less than one minute after first contact, the top right edge of the Sun's photosphere has already begun to slip behind the Moon.

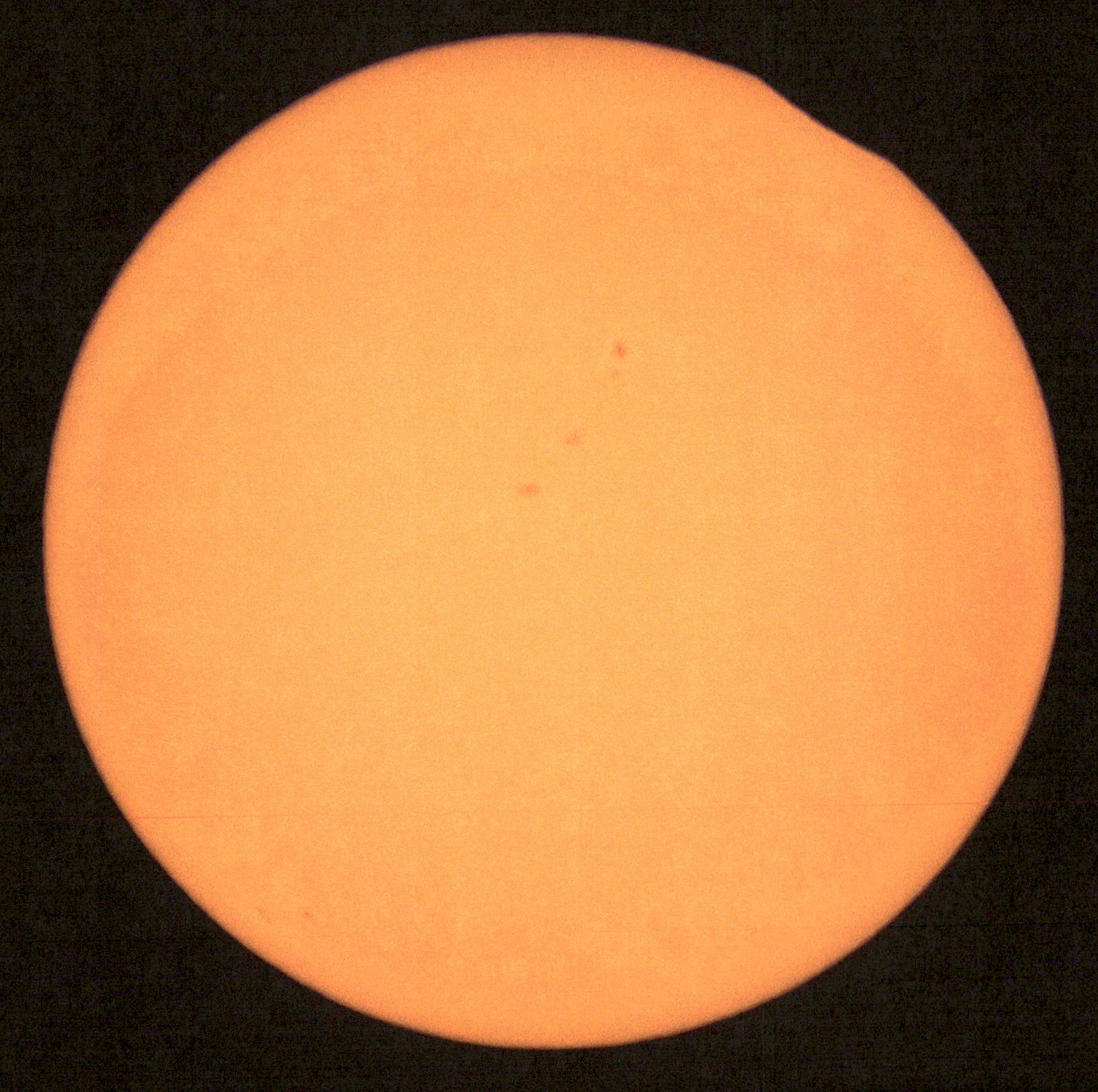

Five minutes into the eclipse, the encroaching shadow of the Moon is clearly pronounced. The images in this series were captured with a Canon EF 500mm f/4 IS II USM and a Canon Extender EF 2X III on a Canon EOS 5DS R body set to an aperture of f/8, a shutter speed of 1/250 of a second, and ISO of 100.

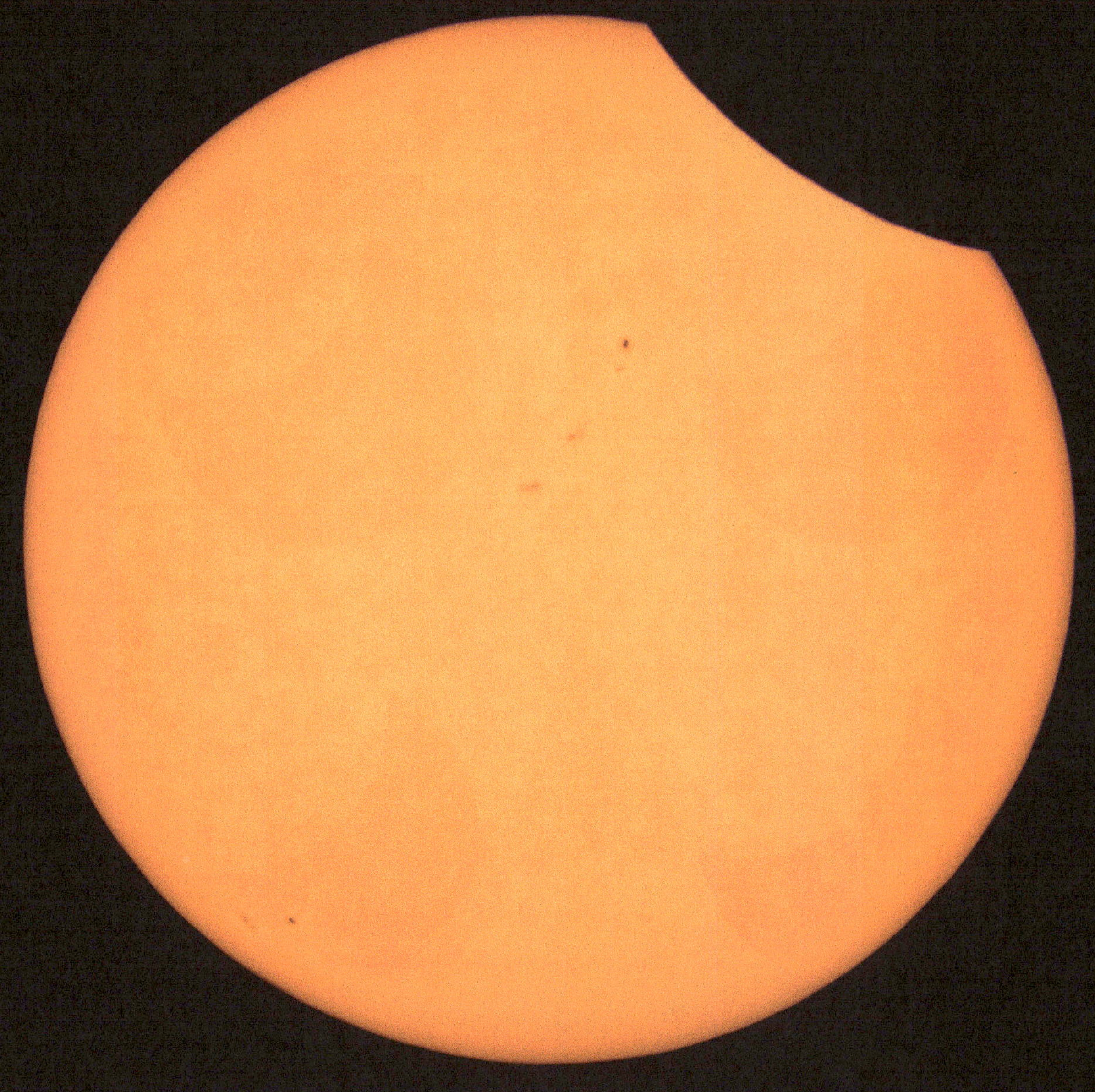

Over the first hour and ten minutes between first and second contact, we shot a five-shot bracket of photos every five minutes to illustrate the Sun's steady progression through the partial phases of the eclipse.

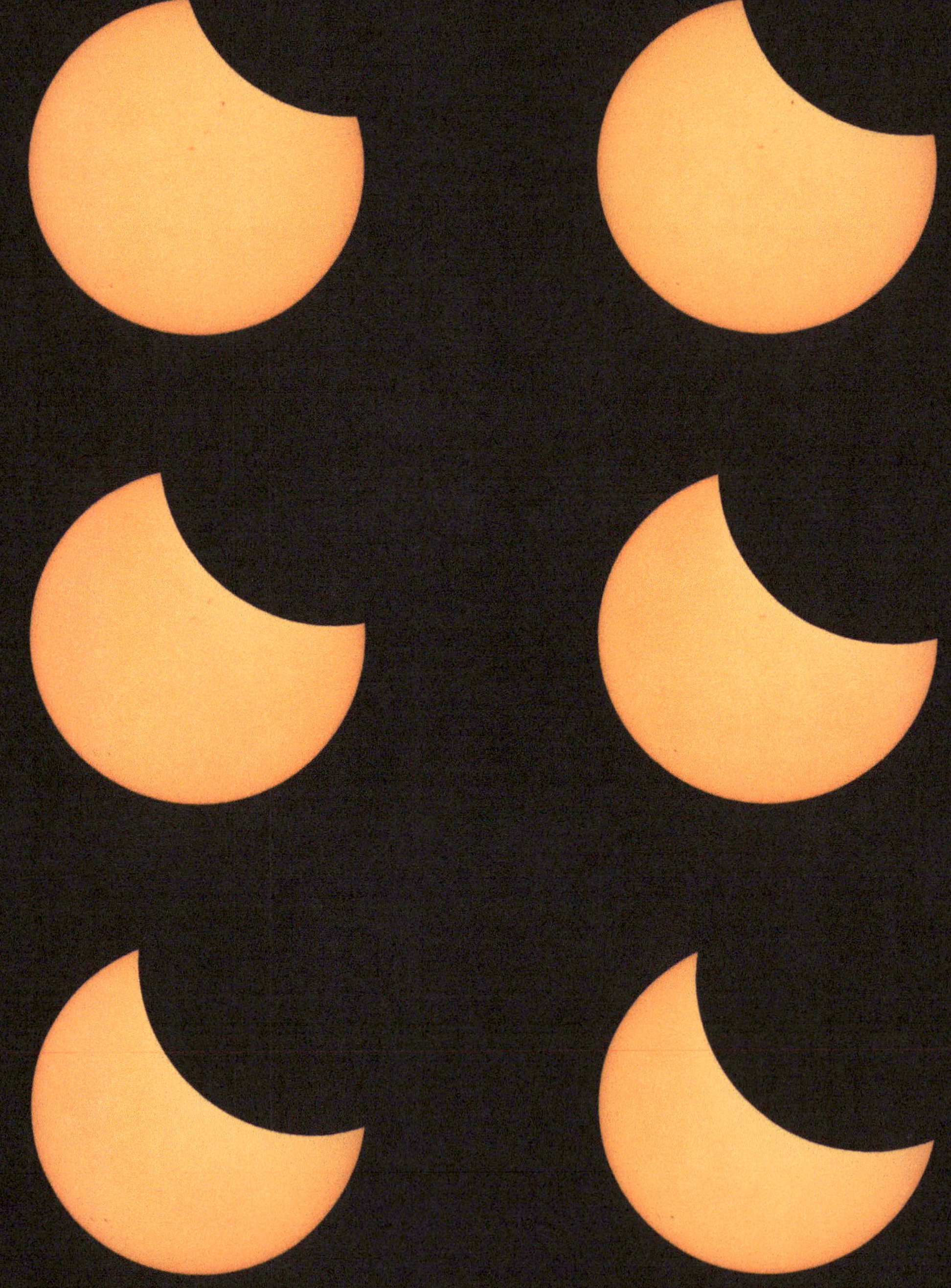

Not until the majority of the Sun's disk was obscured did the sky and landscape begin to take on a darkening steely blue cast. We donned our jackets as the temperature dropped significantly and the shadow of the Moon rapidly approached over the western horizon.

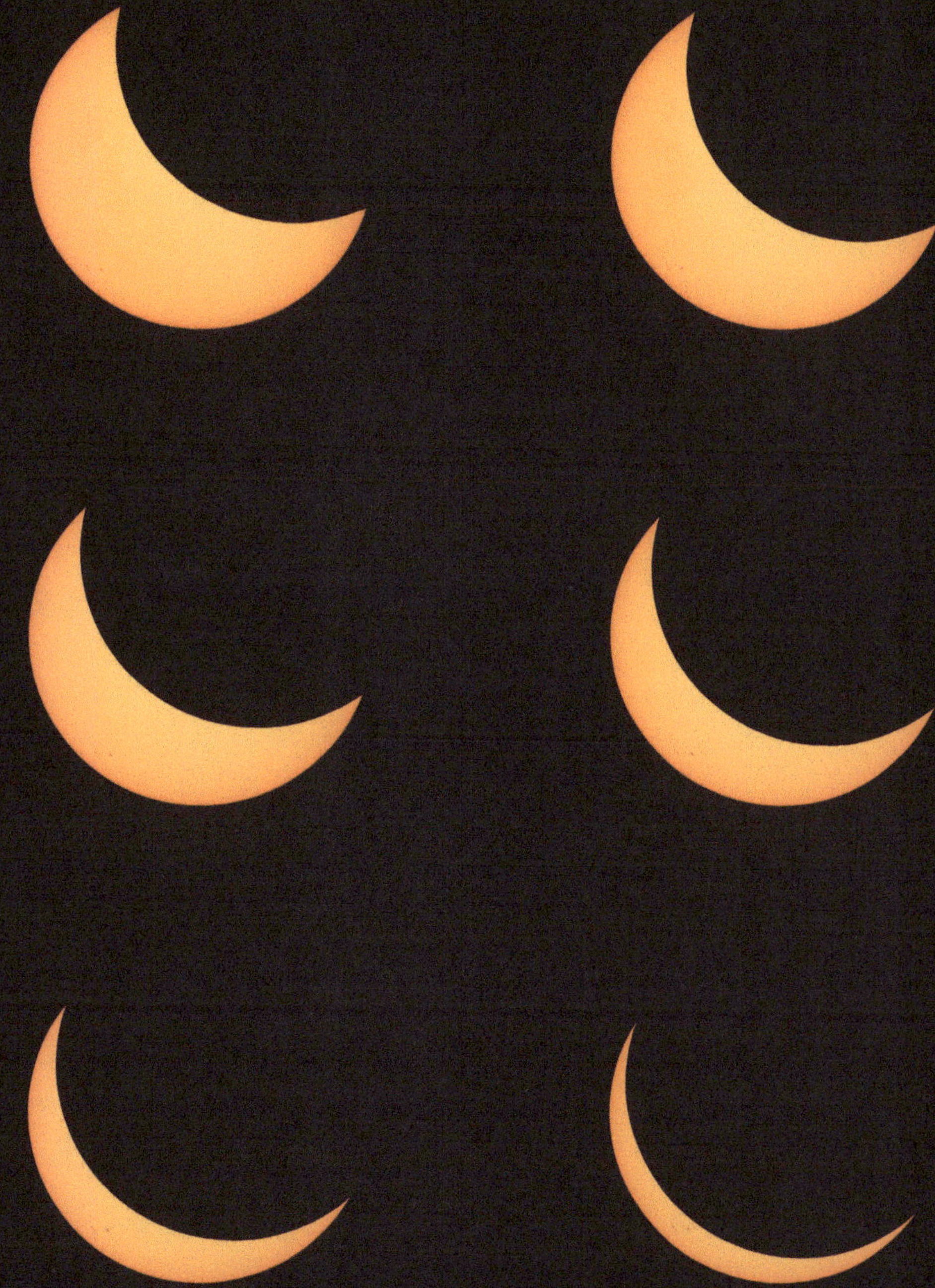

Seven minutes before the second contact (start of totality), we took our final filtered photos of the waning Sun. We then removed the solar filters to prepare for the diamond ring and Baily's beads*.

*Baily's beads are named for the English astronomer and four-term President of the Royal Astronomical Society, Francis Baily (1774-1884) who observed and described the phenomenon.

Each of these events lasted no more than ten seconds. The crescent Sun is shown below as it appeared at 11:27 a.m., followed by our team preparing for the spectacles surrounding second contact.

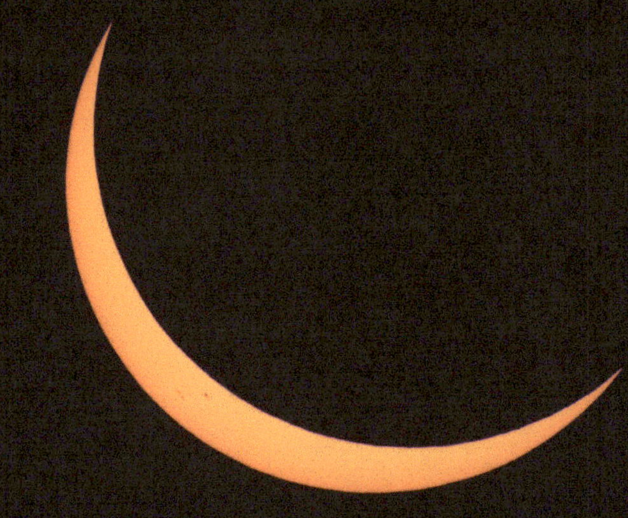

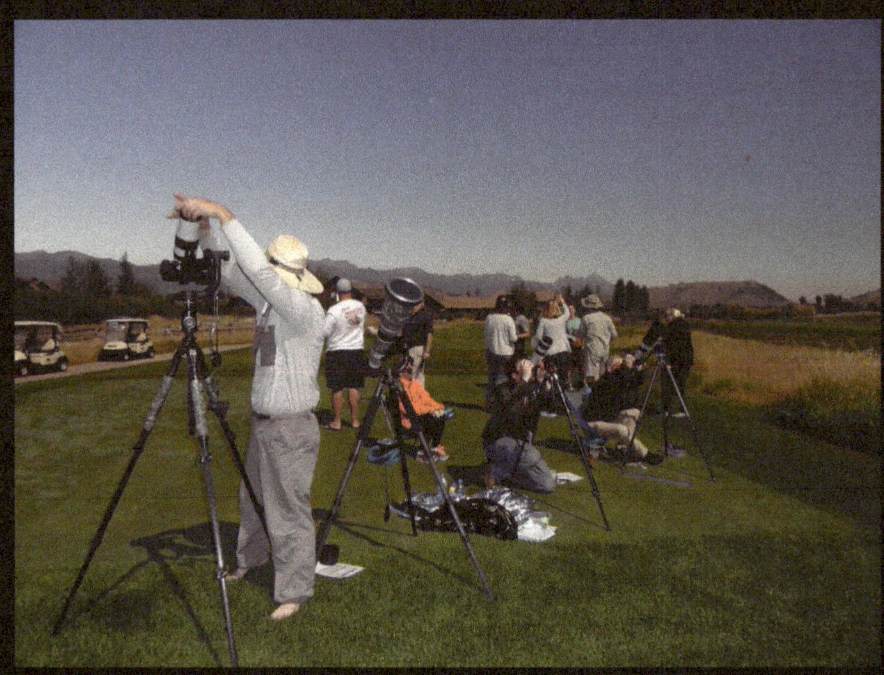

The following two striking shots, captured just before the first diamond ring, are the accidental result of lens flare. Lens flare is generally stray light that is reflected and refracted between individual glass elements of the lens. The more glass elements the lens contains, the more likely this effect. This is one of the reasons we use high quality prime (non-zoom) lenses. Zoom lenses tend to contain more elements which have a higher likelihood of causing these results. Prime lenses also generally produce sharper outcomes. These two photos were taken with a Canon EF 70-200 f/2.8 L IS II USM zoom using a Canon EF 2x extender.

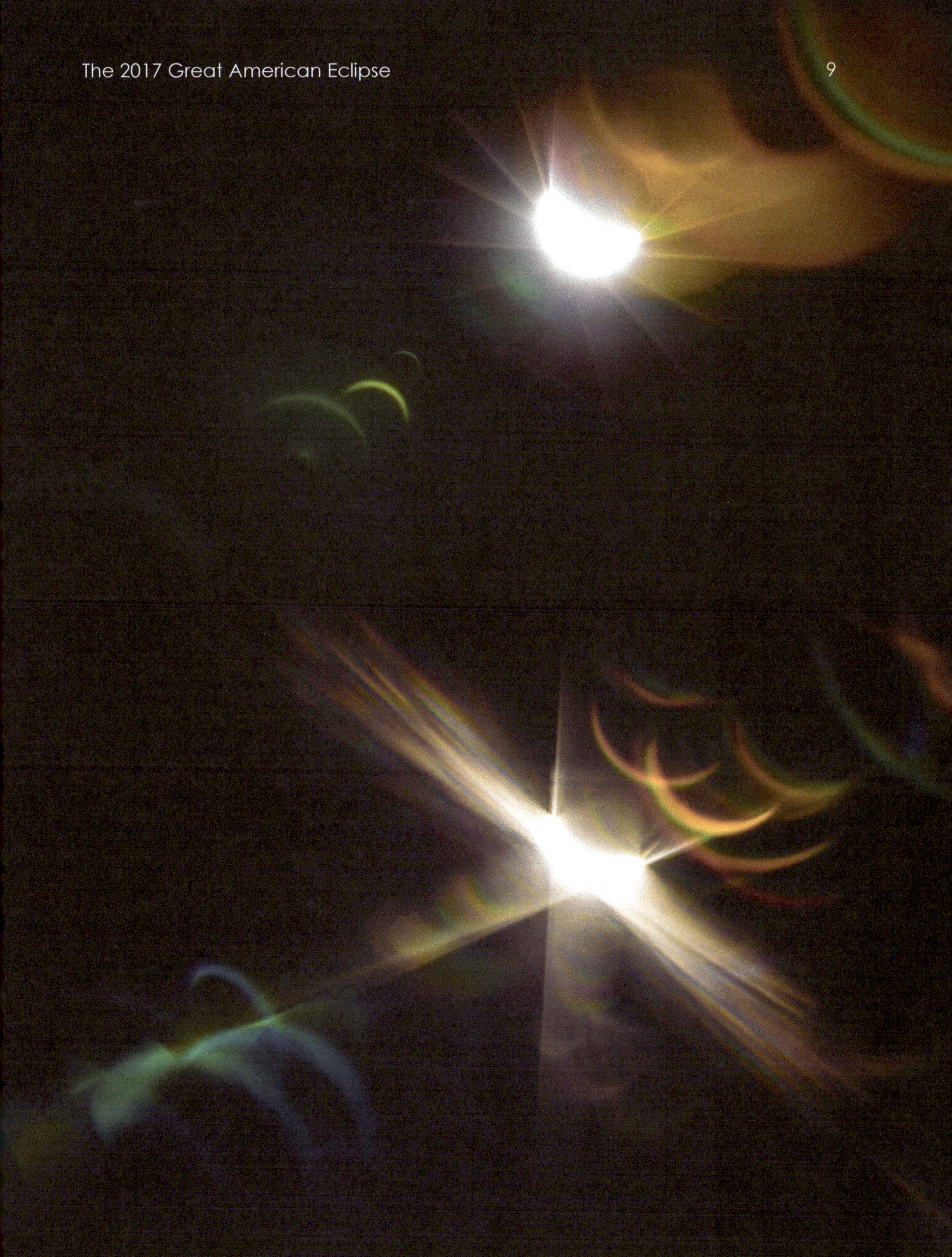

This series of images, taken seconds apart, showcases some of the final moments preceding totality. The diamond ring dramatically bursts forth before being completely extinguished by the Moon's shadow. These photos also illustrate the effect of the bracketed exposure techniques necessary to capture the fleeting features of the eclipse event, specifically during totality and the moments surrounding it.

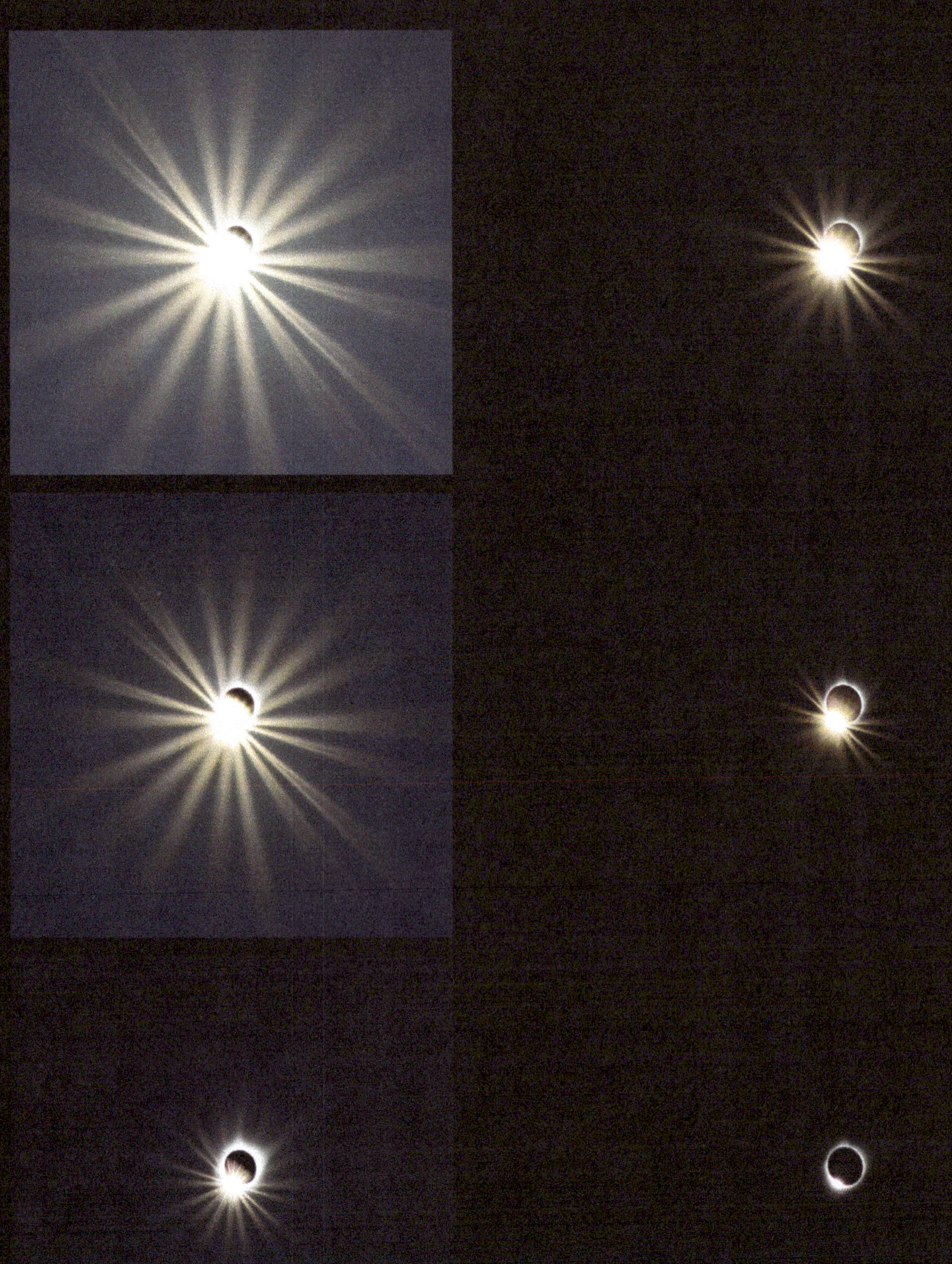

The following pages show the images our team recorded of Baily's beads, the diamond ring, and totality. The images of these elusive moments were captured in a variety of ways and are the result of the different cameras and lenses, as well as the creativity of the individual photographers.

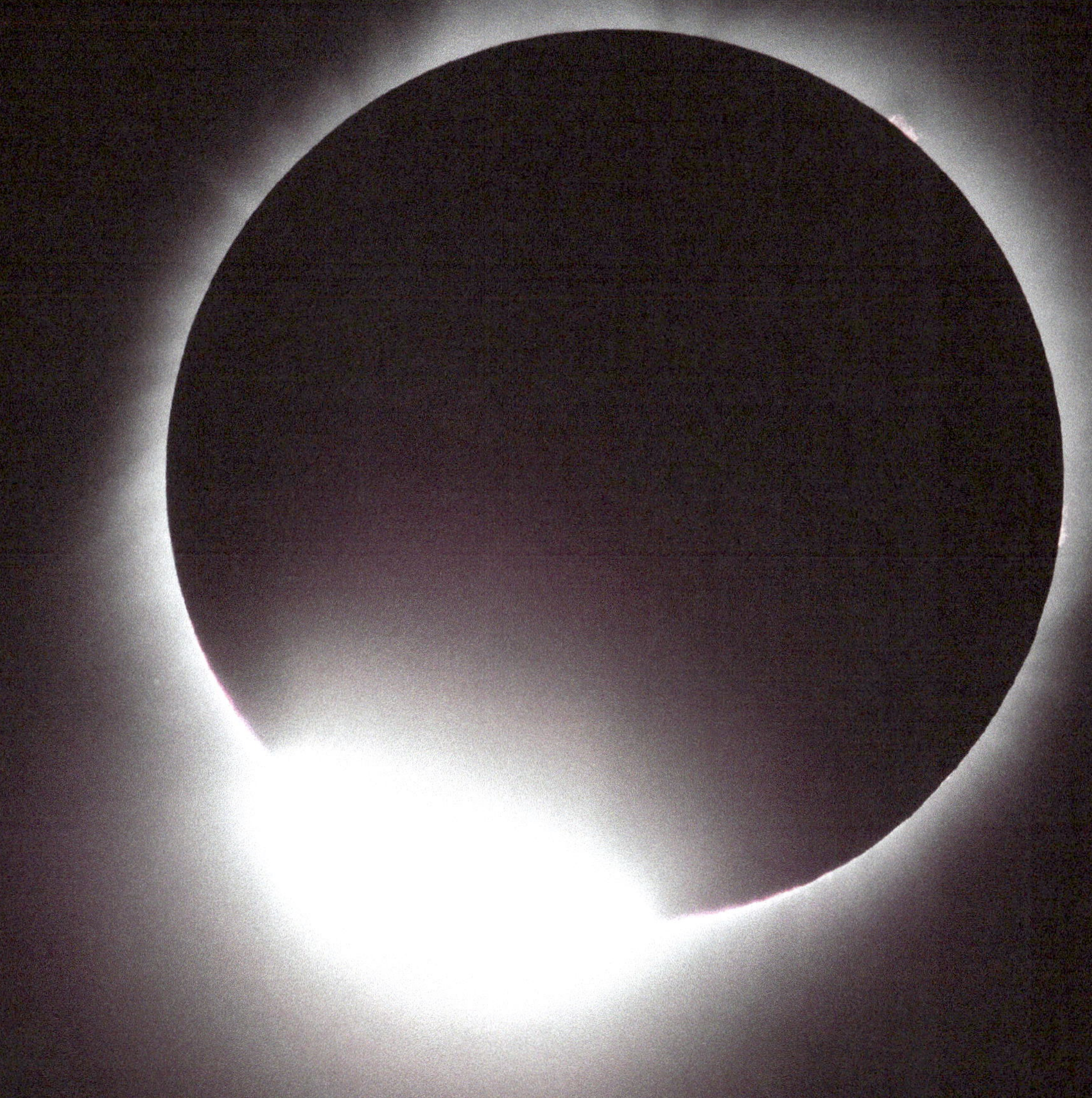

This shot of the diamond ring preceding second contact was taken with a Canon EOS 5DS R, Canon EF 500mm f/4L IS II USM, and Canon Extender EF 2X III.

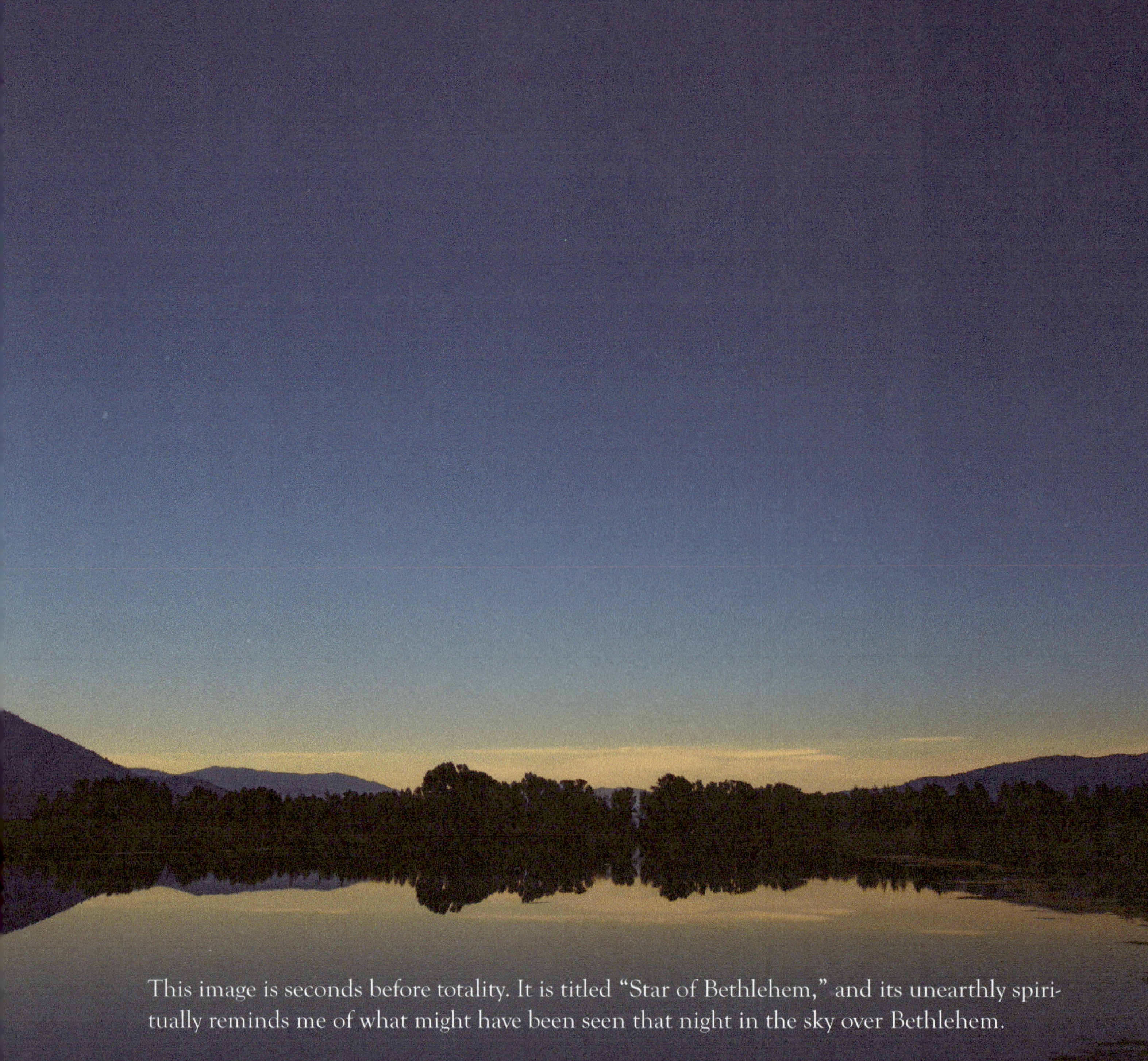

This image is seconds before totality. It is titled "Star of Bethlehem," and its unearthly spiritually reminds me of what might have been seen that night in the sky over Bethlehem.

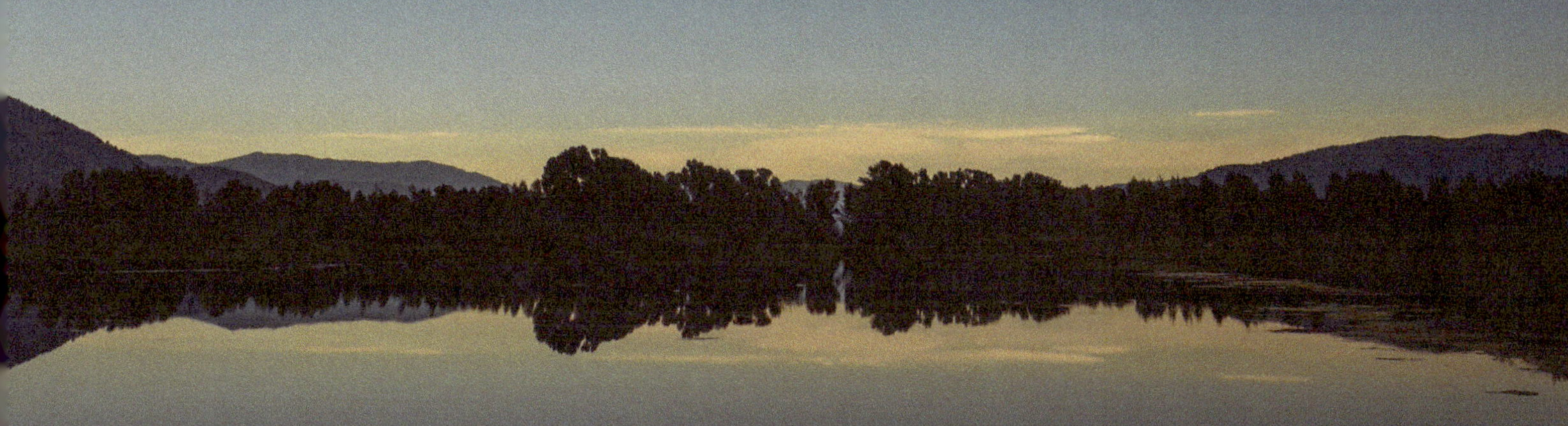

Totality was imminent with the shadow of the Moon as it approached from the west at a thousand miles per hour.

The Moon's shadow cast a darkening column across the sky, falling like a curtain over the western horizon.

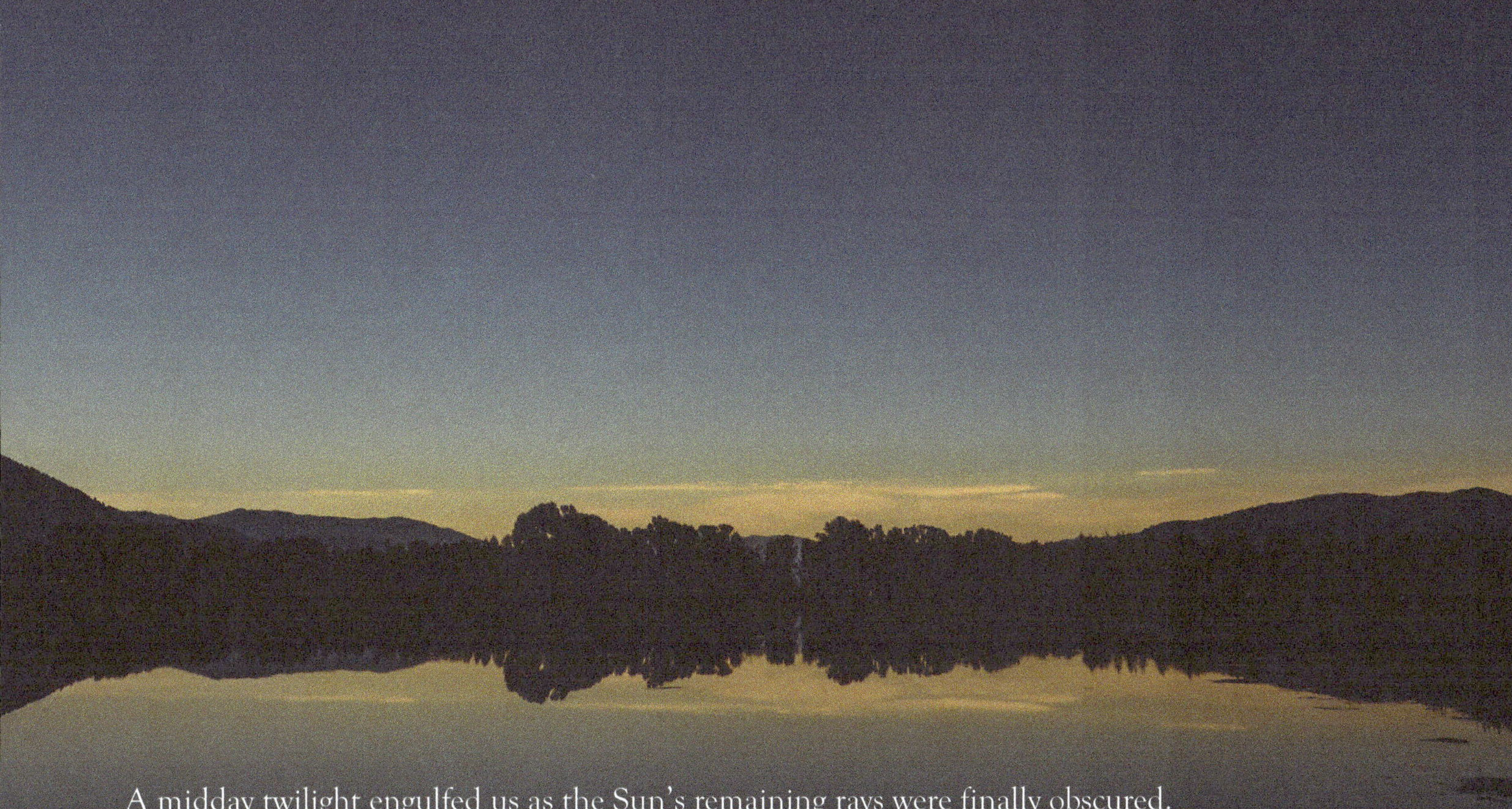

A midday twilight engulfed us as the Sun's remaining rays were finally obscured.

Totality would bring an unparalleled two minutes and eleven seconds.

Just before totality, the diamond ring split into smaller beads of light. Known as Baily's beads, this phenomenon occurs as the final rays of sunlight filter through the Moon's irregular terrain.

The beads fluctuate rapidly in appearance before blinking out of existence.

Left: Baily's beads seconds before totality begins.

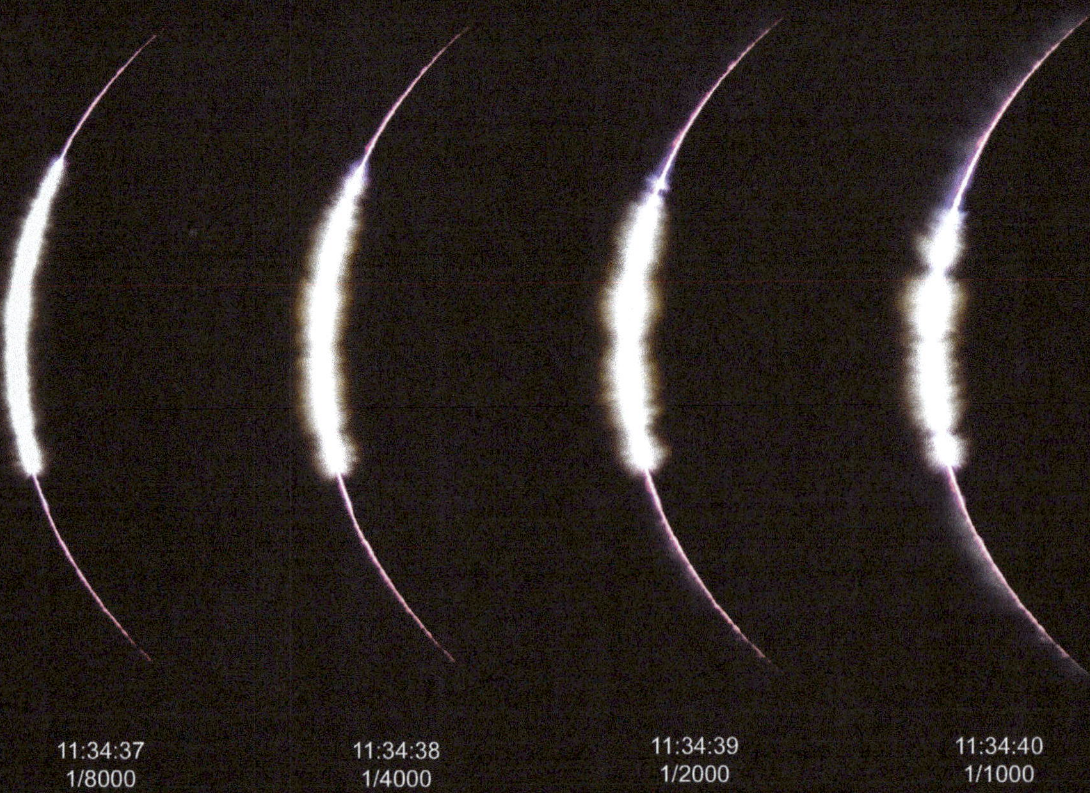

Right: Maximum totality occurs at 11:35:38 a.m.

Below: Eight photos document the full duration of Baily's beads in the final seven seconds before totality. Bracketing allowed us to capture various details of this fleeting spectacle (bracketing will be explained in Part IV). This phase of the eclipse moves very quickly. Note that each image is exactly one second apart.

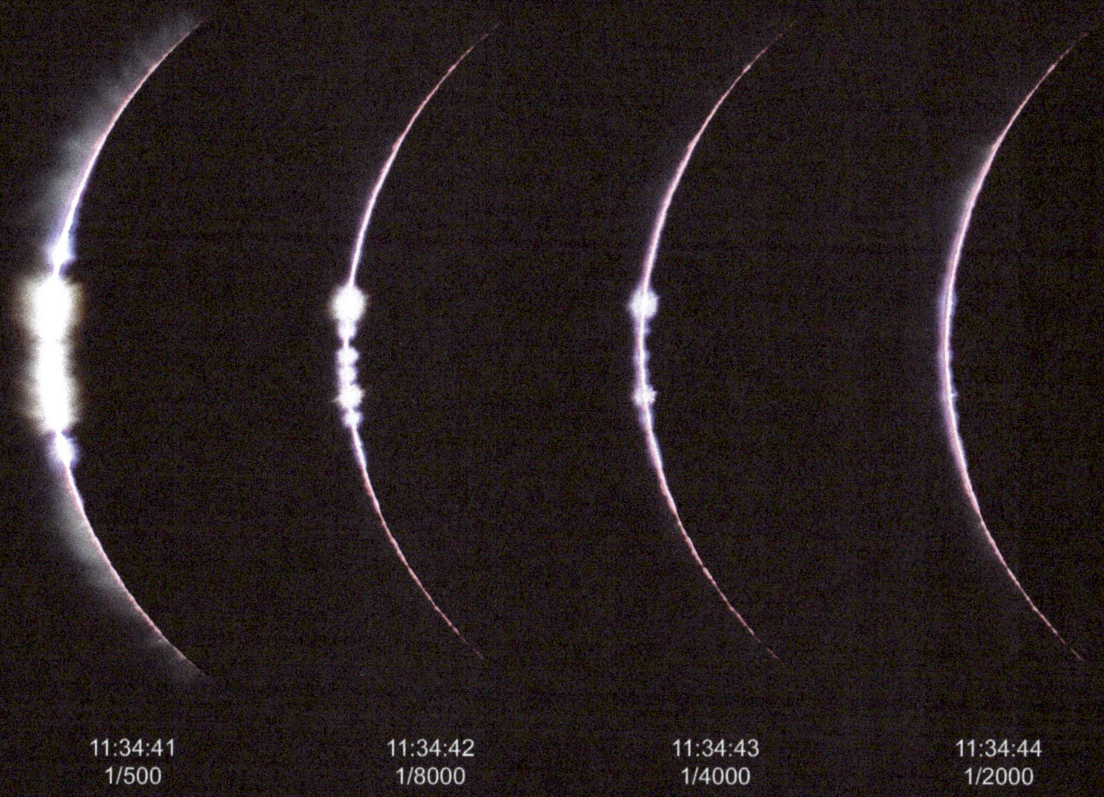

This process happens in reverse following the conclusion of totality (third contact).

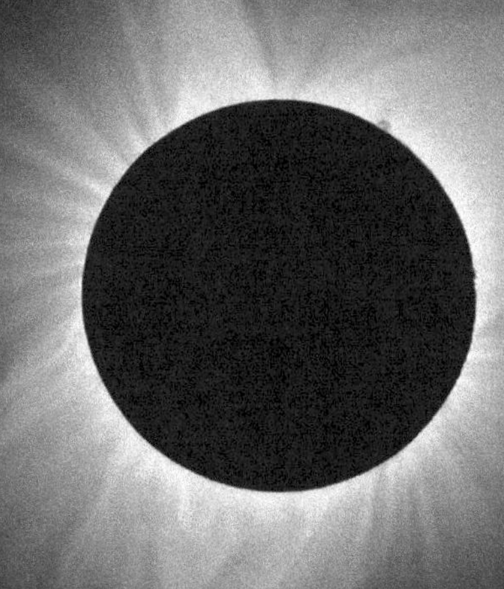

At 11:34:50 a.m., the total eclipse began over Jackson. This photograph of the corona was taken with a Canon EF 70-200mm f/2.8L IS II USM and Canon Extender EF 2X III on a Canon EOS 5D Mark IV and composited with various adjustments to the raw file to tease out the details of the corona's structure. The corona is twisted, stretched, and bent by the powerful electromagnetic currents at work within the Sun. It contains plasma heated beyond even the temperatures of the chromosphere much closer to the Sun's surface. The corona of each eclipse is like a fingerprint; no two are ever the same. Red prominences can be seen along the upper right edge of the Moon, and the dot at the bottom left is likely the International Space Station.

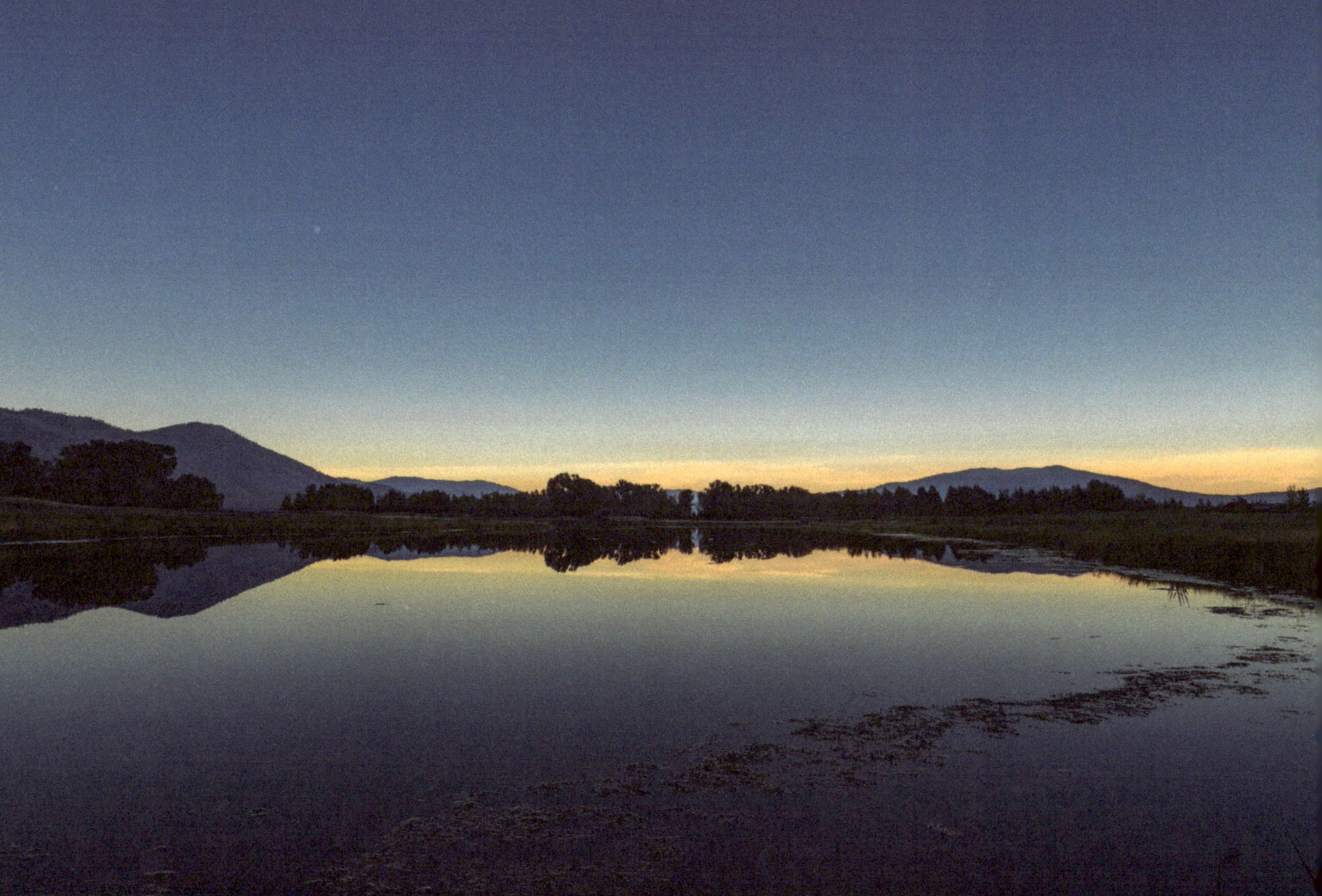

This composite image was created from a Canon EOS 5DS R with Zeiss Distagon T* f/2.8 15mm. We placed the camera in a stationary position to capture the eclipse's entire progression - nearly three hours. The final resulting image was constructed using thirty-three individual photos of the partial phases that were shot in five-minute intervals as well as eleven different exposures taken during totality and two overall exposures for sky and landscape.

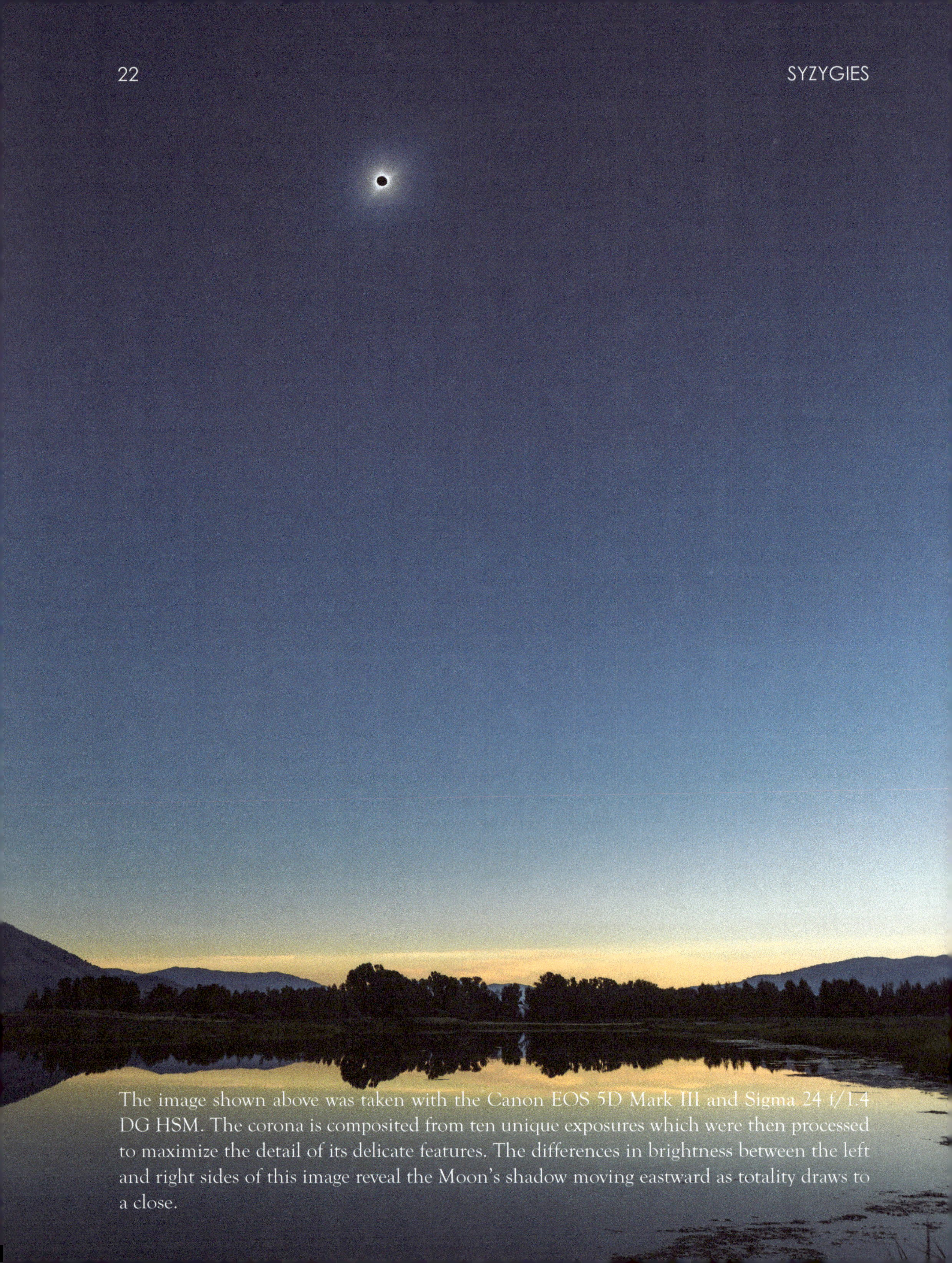

The image shown above was taken with the Canon EOS 5D Mark III and Sigma 24 f/1.4 DG HSM. The corona is composited from ten unique exposures which were then processed to maximize the detail of its delicate features. The differences in brightness between the left and right sides of this image reveal the Moon's shadow moving eastward as totality draws to a close.

The photograph shown above documents the rare illusion of a 360-degree sunset while the Sun continues to illuminate the surrounding landscape beyond the Moon's shadow. This full panorama was captured with a Google Pixel smart phone as a member of our team took a moment to appreciate the radical changes to our surroundings during totality.

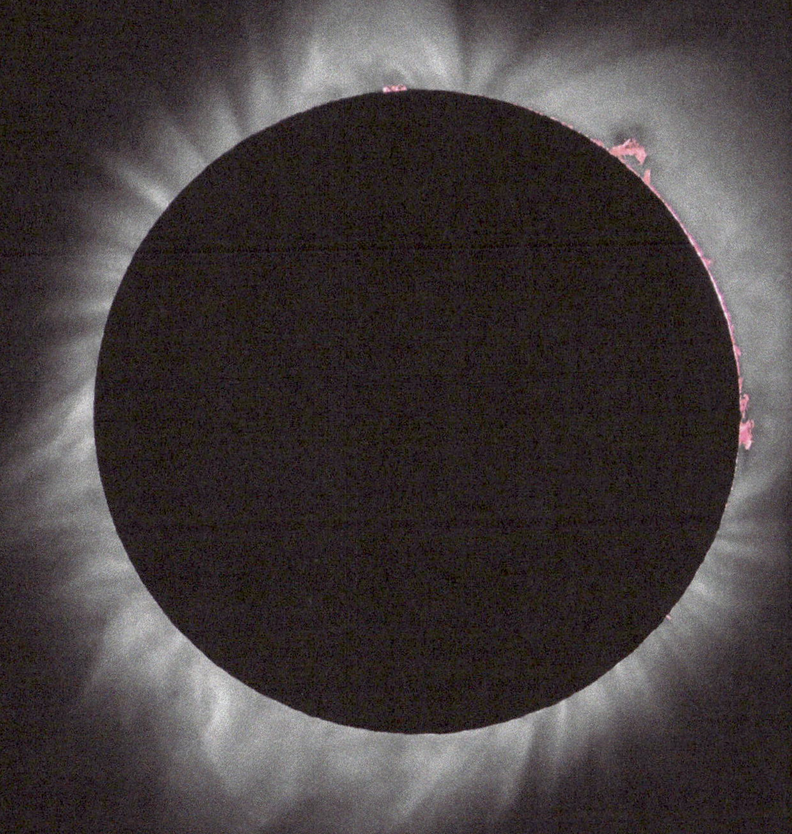

The image shown above is a composite of multiple adjustments made to a single shot from the Canon EOS 5DS R with a Canon EF 500mm f/4.0 IS II USM and a Canon Extender EF 2X III. This is the moment just before third contact as the Sun reemerges from its obscuration. The pinkish red outline along the top right rim of the Moon is the Sun's chromosphere (named for its reddish hue) coming into view.

The series of images below records the corona, the prominences of the chromosphere, and Baily's beads in the moments during third contact. The camera's timestamps and shutter speeds are listed.

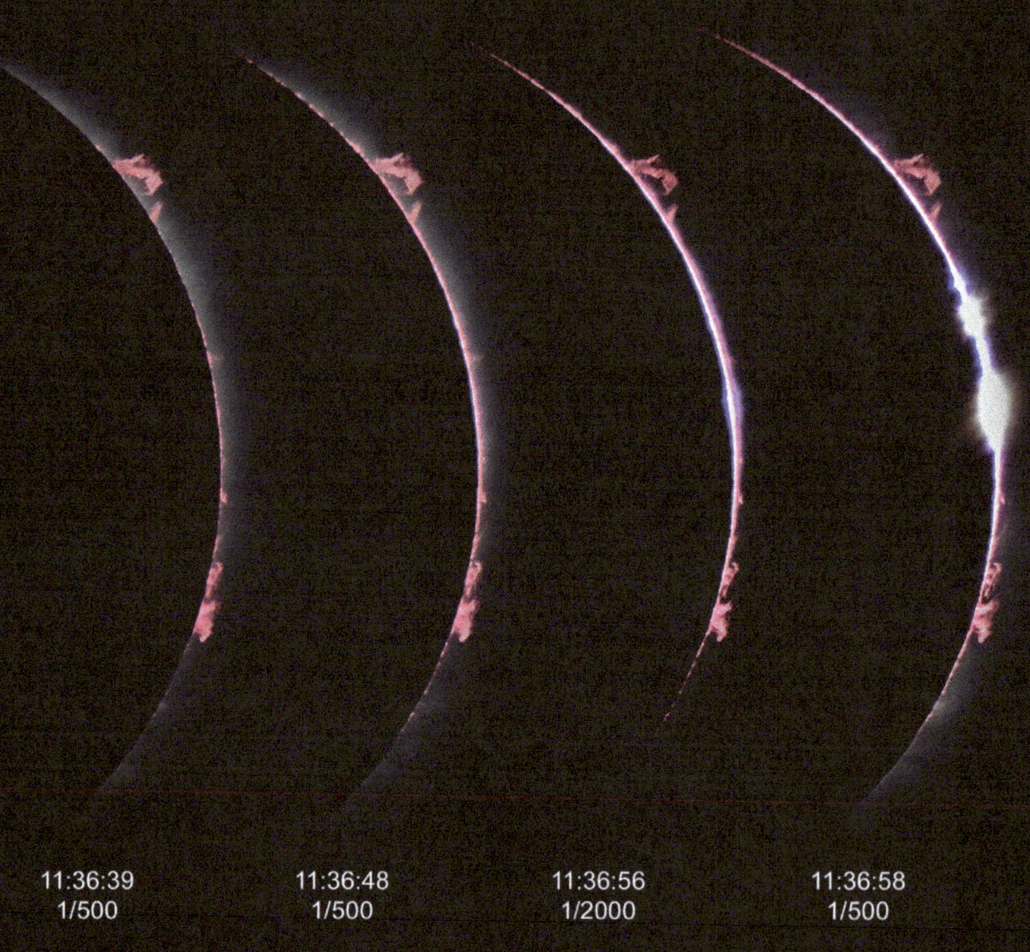

This composite of multiple variations of a single exposure is a breathtaking moment just after third contact when the corona, the prominences of the chromosphere, and the photosphere (in the form of Baily's beads) are all on beautiful display.

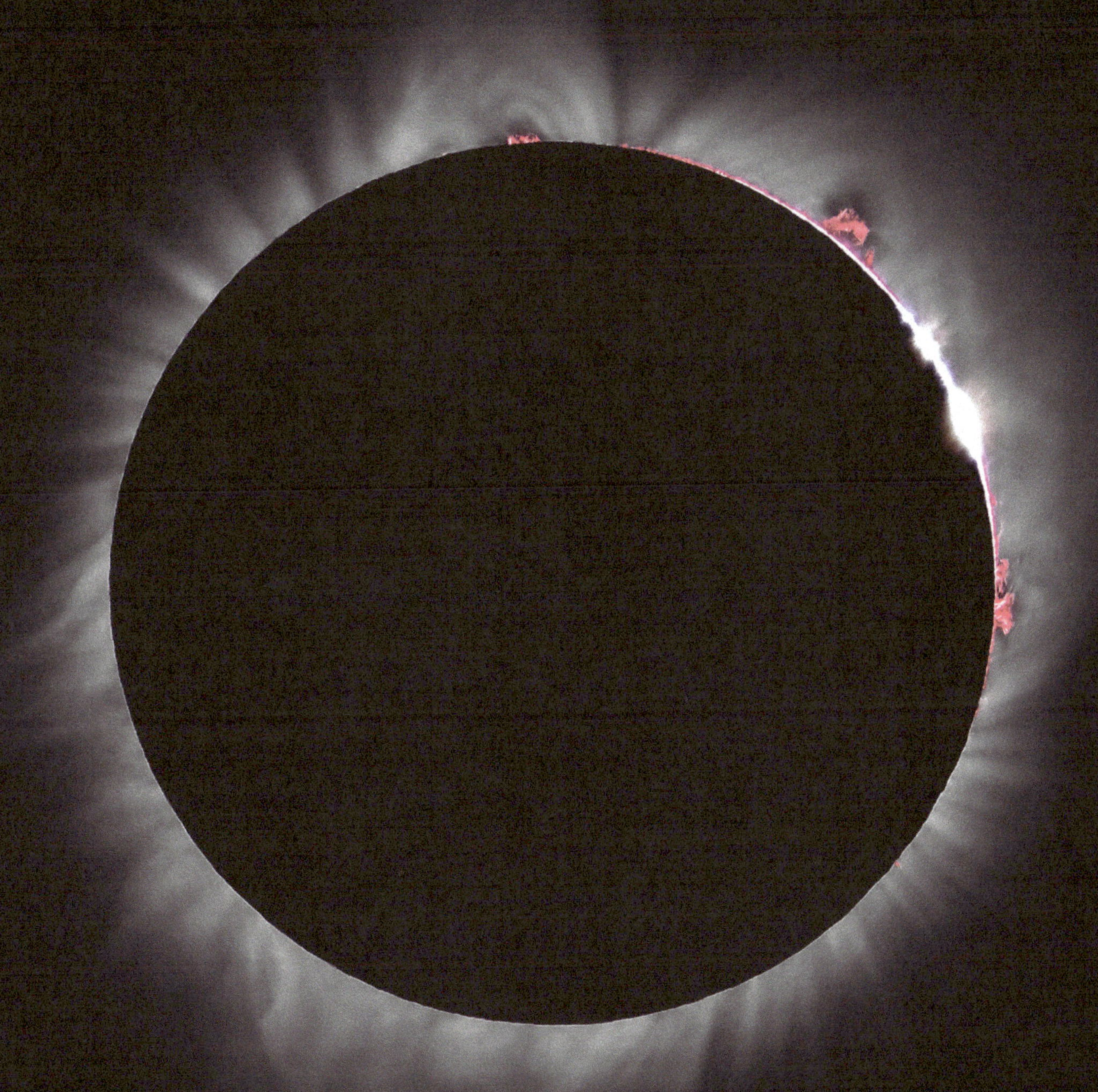

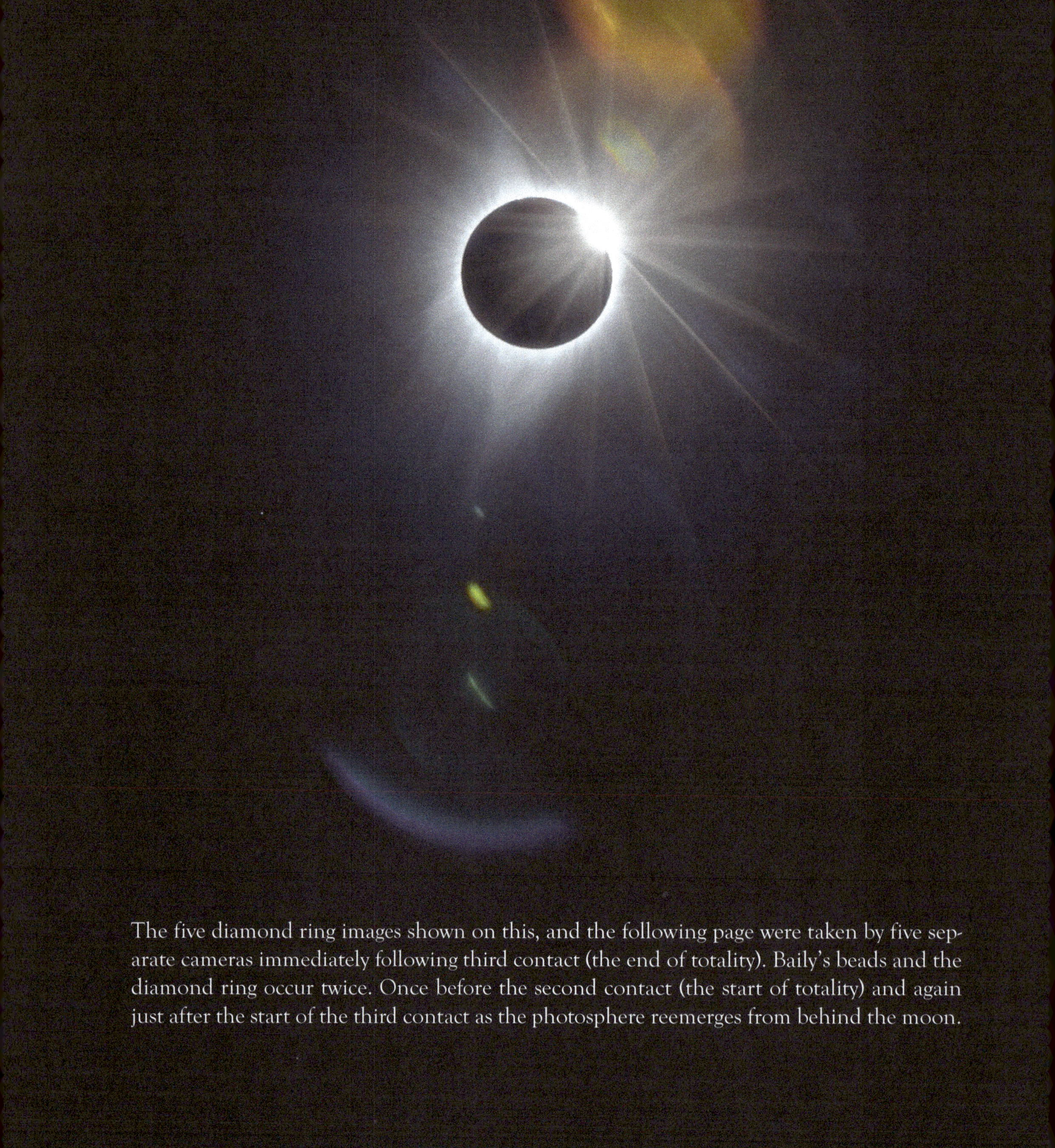

The five diamond ring images shown on this, and the following page were taken by five separate cameras immediately following third contact (the end of totality). Baily's beads and the diamond ring occur twice. Once before the second contact (the start of totality) and again just after the start of the third contact as the photosphere reemerges from behind the moon.

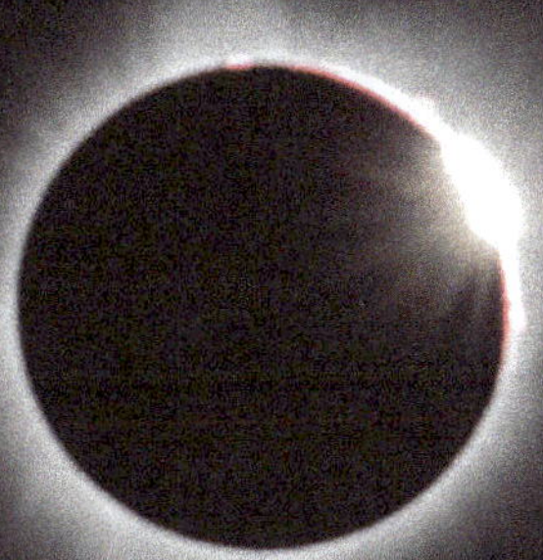

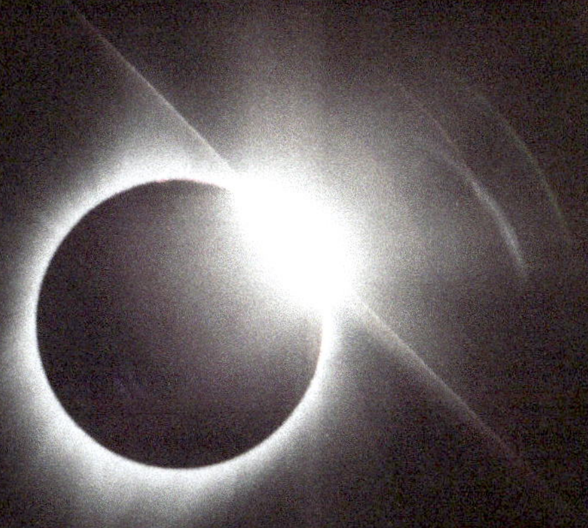

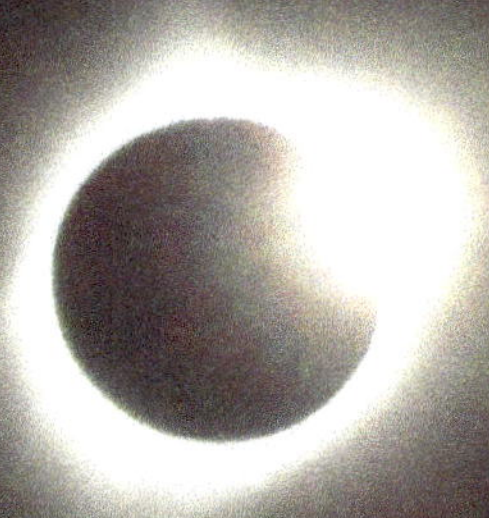

We replaced our solar filters after the second diamond ring. We then resumed our regular intervals of bracketed exposures until the conclusion of the eclipse.

One of our photographers decided to take an early picture. That's the first one at left. The rest of the shots were taken at five-minute intervals, beginning seven minutes after third contact through to the conclusion of the eclipse.

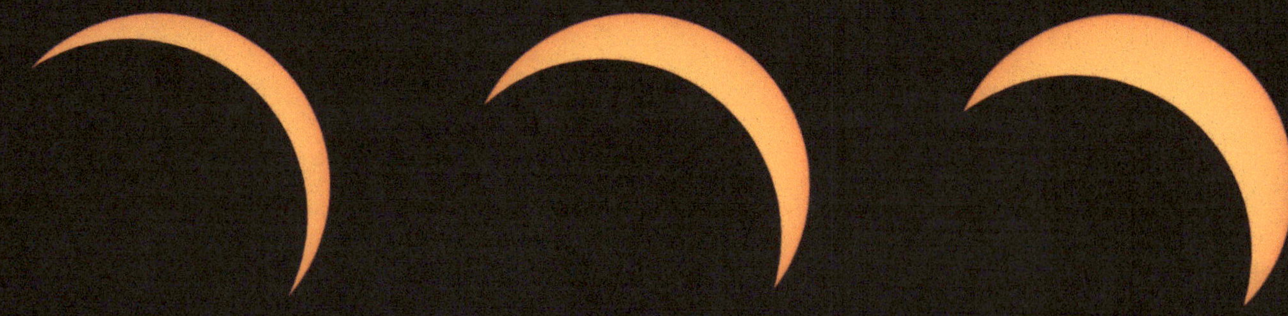

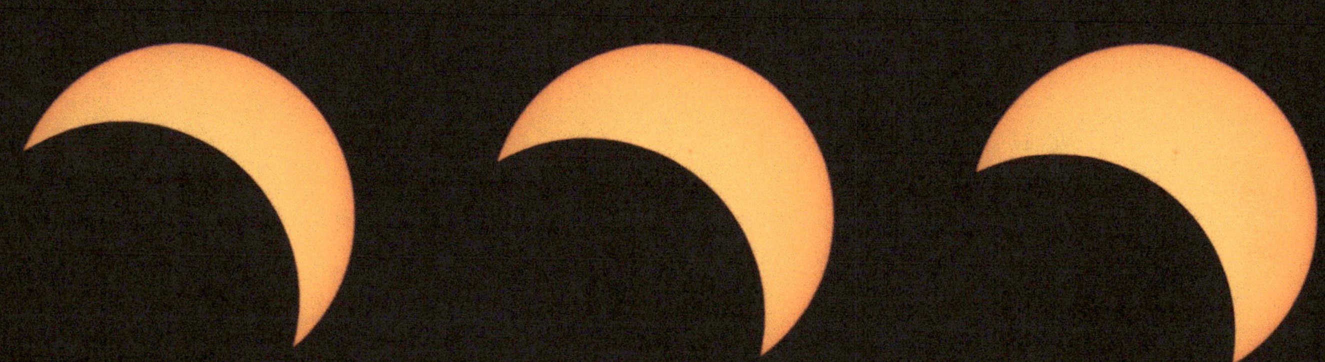

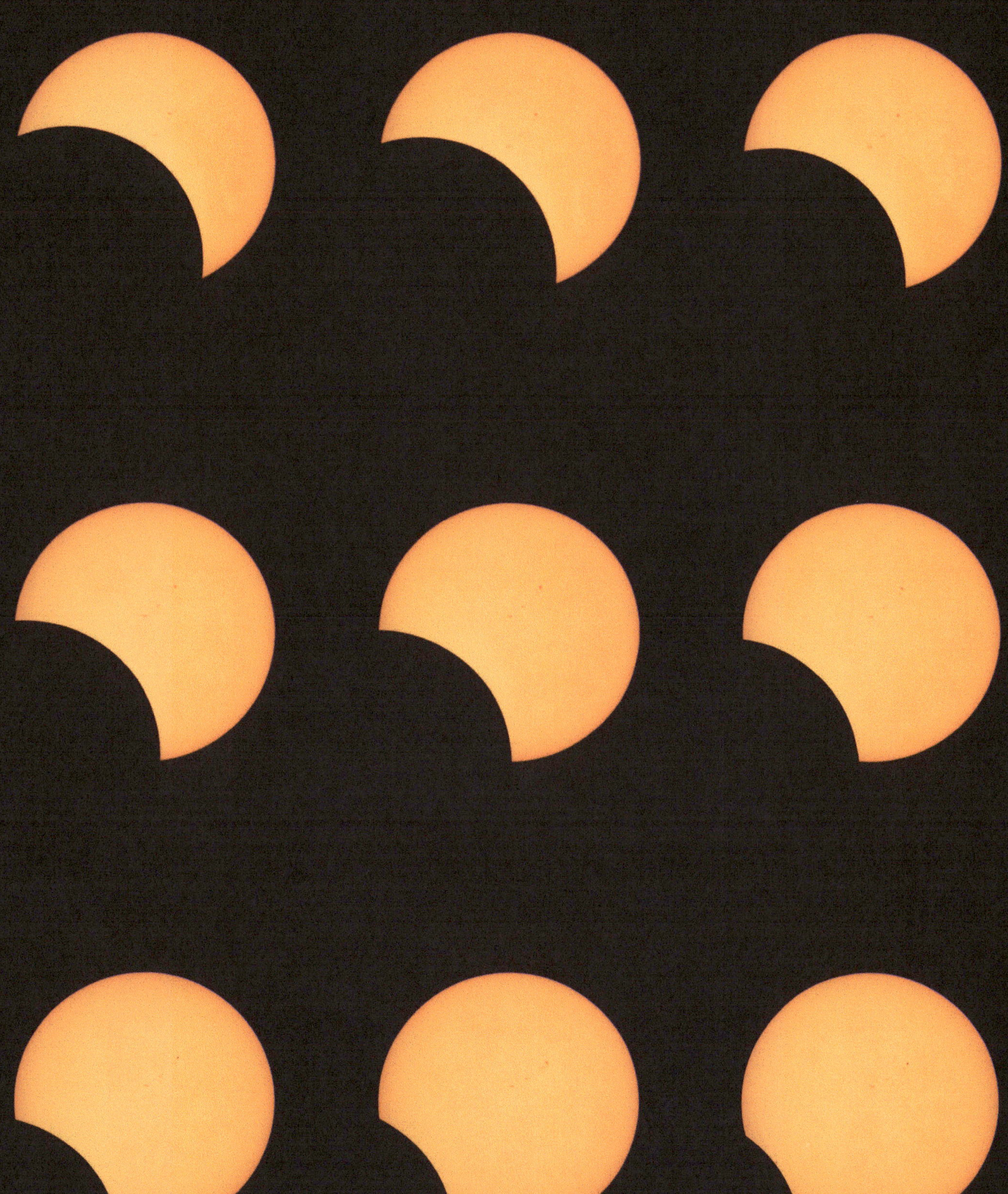

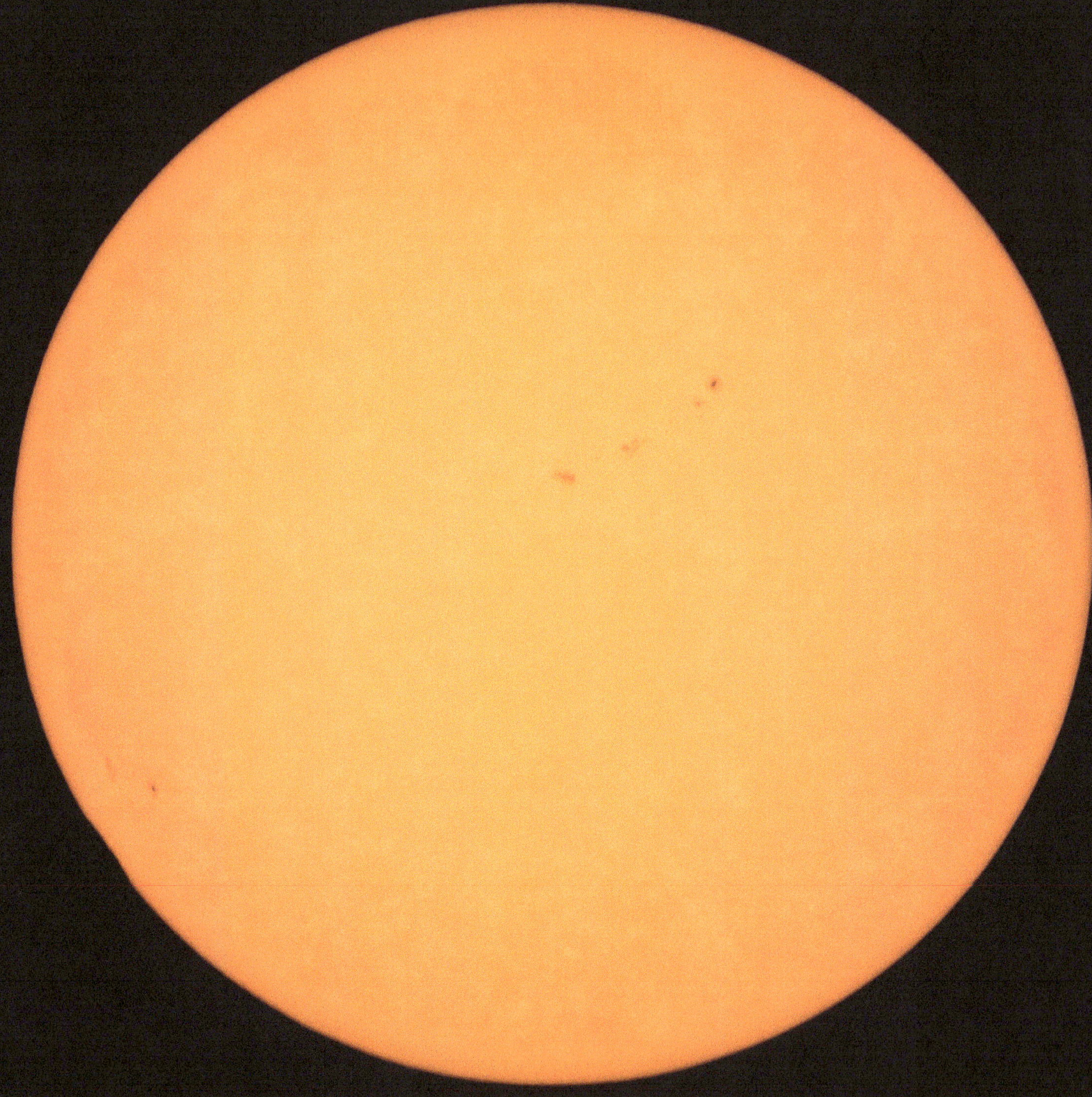

At 1:00 p.m., fourth contact signals the end of the Great American Eclipse and the culmination of months of painstaking planning and research.

The last tiny sliver of the Moon is visible in the lower left of this image as it just barely grazes the edge of the photosphere.

Another one of the wonderful aspects of an eclipse is that they always occur on the date of a new Moon. This means that there is always a dark night and, weather permitting, amazing photographs of the night sky can be captured. We obtained wonderful images of the Milky Way on the evening of the 2017 eclipse.

THE BEGINNING

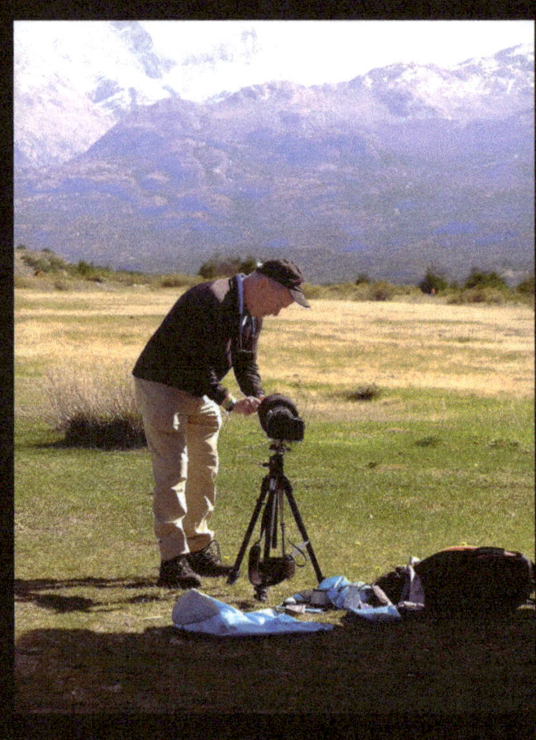

As the day ended on August 21, 2017, I thought I was finished with shooting eclipses. Brittany looked at me and asked if I had had fun. I am sure she could feel my energy and the team's energy. It was clear to me that I had caught the eclipse-chasing bug. She had too.

Since 2017, apart from the duration of Covid when we were unable to travel, we have planned and shot every total solar eclipse. We shot the Chilean eclipse, the Australian eclipse, and most recently the 2023 Annular eclipse that crossed the United States.

As it stands now, we plan on shooting the 2024 Easter Island Annular eclipse, Spain's 2026 Sunset eclipse, and the 2027 Egyptian eclipse.

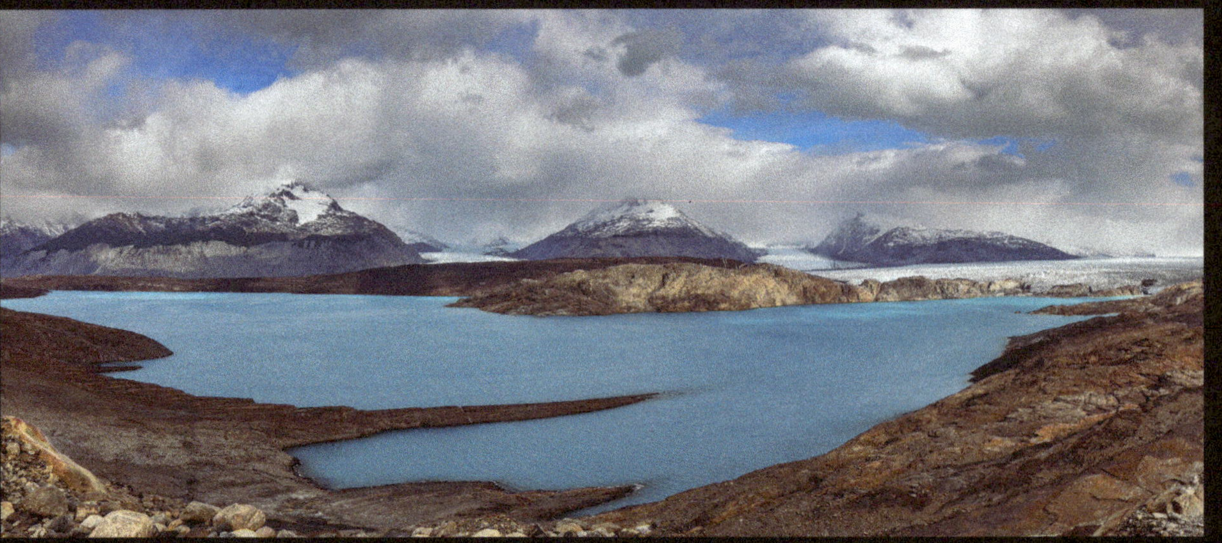

PART II

2019 Chilean Sunset Eclipse

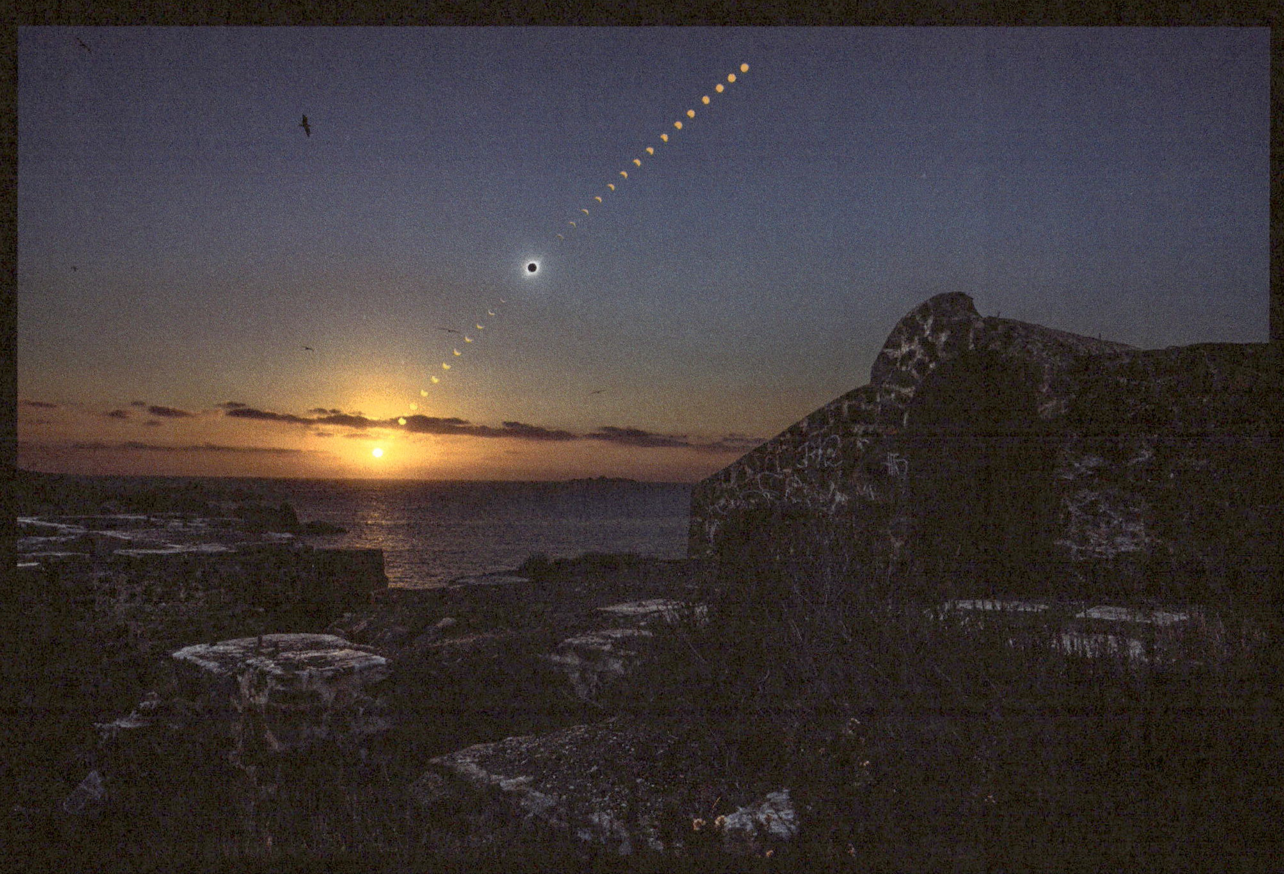

Chilean Sunset Eclipse Shoot Site

Puerto Cruz Grand, Chungungo Chile

July 2, 2019

INTRODUCTION

Like the first eclipse, we spent a lot of time planning for the Chilean Eclipse. By this point, Brittany was pregnant with her second daughter, Kara Luna, but still able to travel. We made our base in La Serena, Chile, a 350-mile drive from the Santiago Airport and well within the bounds of the path of totality. From La Serena, we visited approximately 18 locations that we had researched and previewed virtually. The sites ranged from uninteresting to quite picturesque. One of the places we scouted was Tololo Observatory in Vicuña, a town known for its dark skies and multiple observatories.

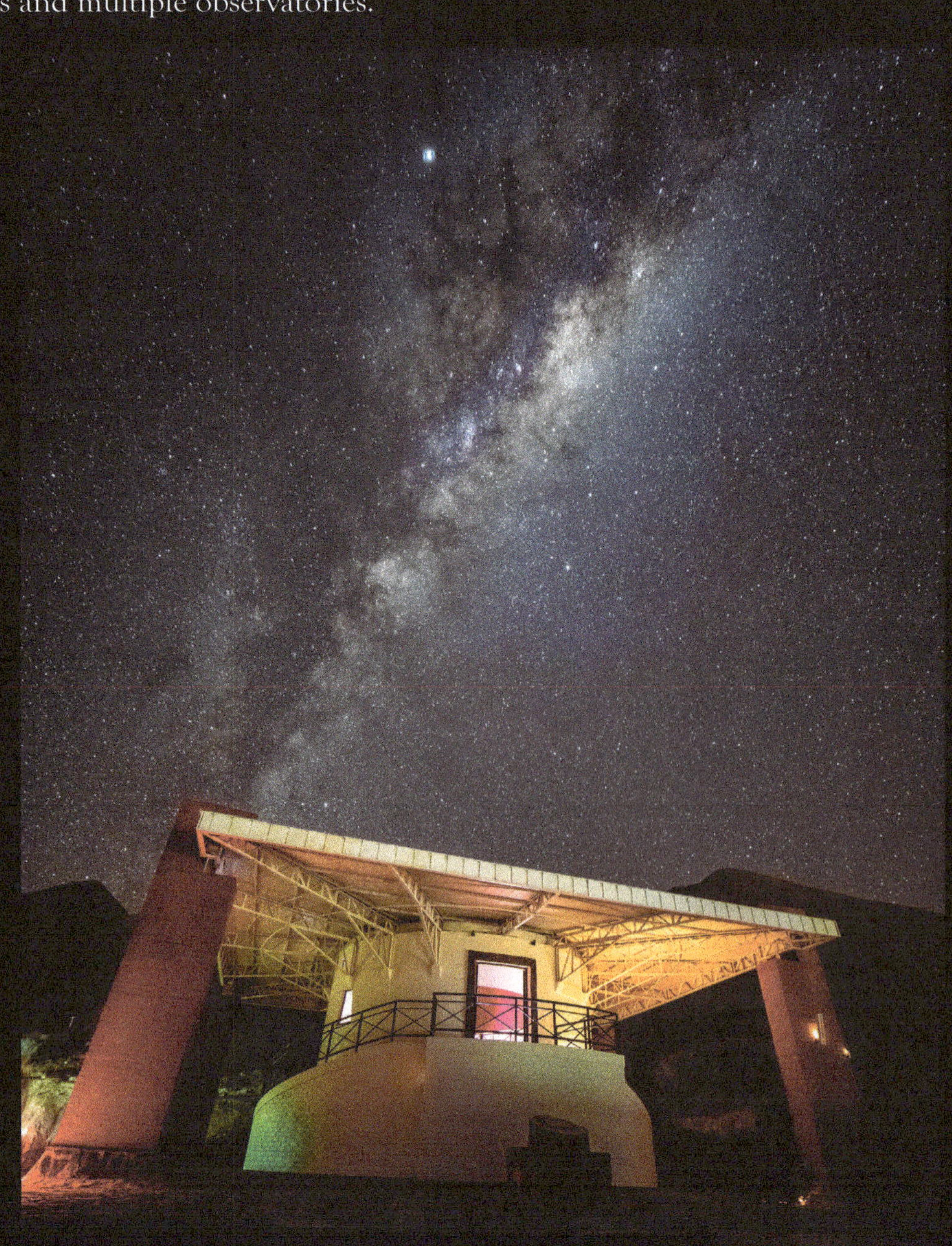

After visiting the last viable shoot location, we headed towards our hotel. While traveling, we chatted about a coastal town that was slightly out of the way. The town of Chungungo, Chile, is north of La Serena and seemed like it might have potential. The scouting mission to this tiny town sent us on a 28+ mile trek on a dirt path. Along the way, we encountered some mules who appeared to have never previously seen a car or human beings.

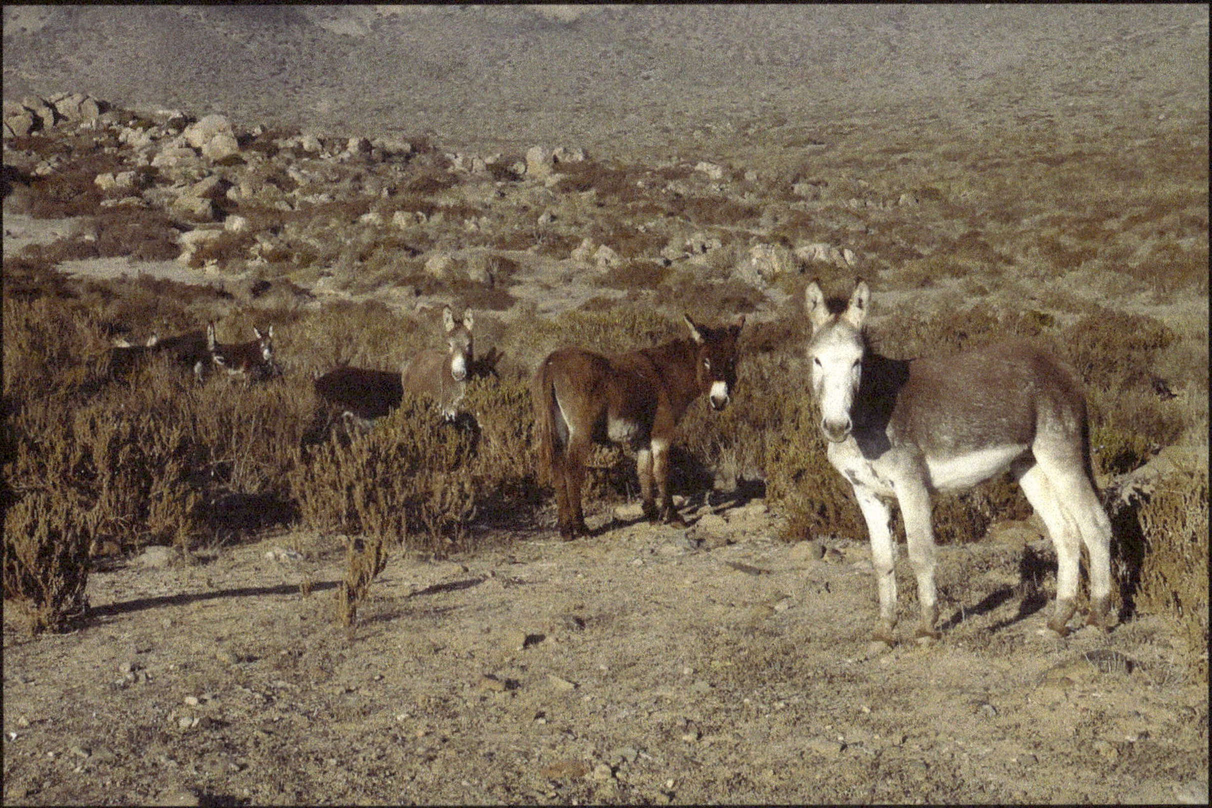

We stopped for a few minutes to observe at these beautiful mules as they gazed back seeming to say, "What's going on? Why are all these people bothering us? Please leave."

When we finally arrived in Chungungo, we found a quiet town with wide dirt roads and a wonderful restaurant. The residents were welcoming, kind, and very supportive of our project.

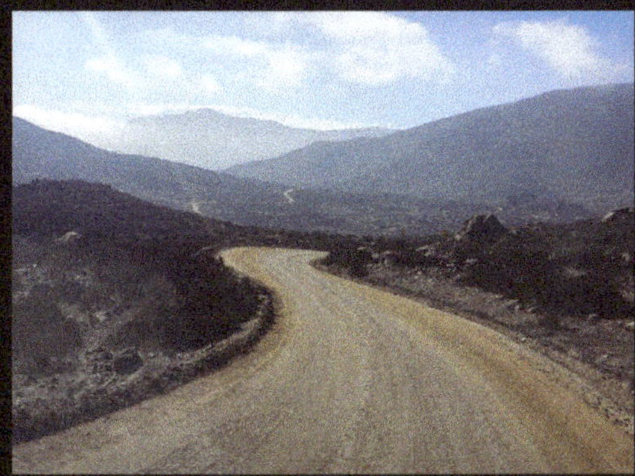

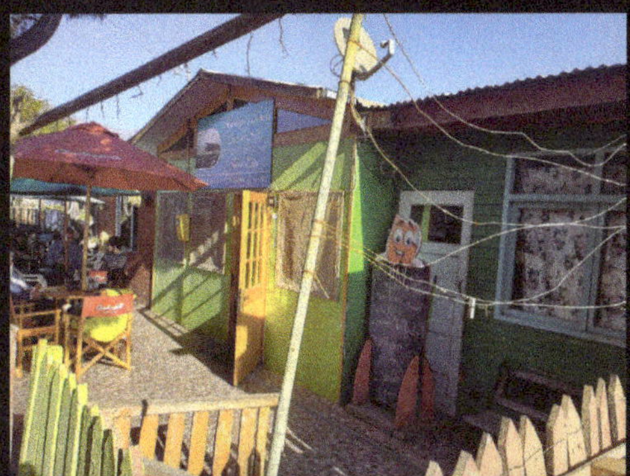

Chungungo and the nearby ruins of its once thriving mining complex was one of the most picturesque locations we had ever seen. Chungungo is now a small fishing village and is in the Atacama Desert of north-central Chile. Previously, the village was home to a thriving iron ore mining industry. The El Tofo mine was part of the huge Tofo – Cruz Grande mining complex operated by Bethlehem Steel from 1916 to 1971. The mine was a critical part of Bethlehem Steel's efforts during WWII. What made the location so striking was the ruin of the Cruz Grande iron ore port shown in the pictures below.

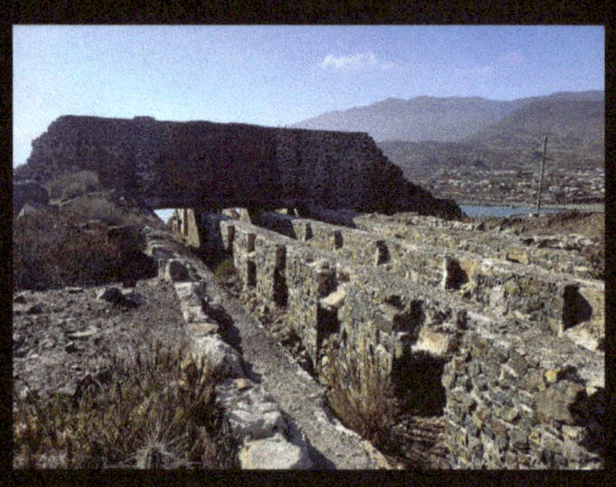

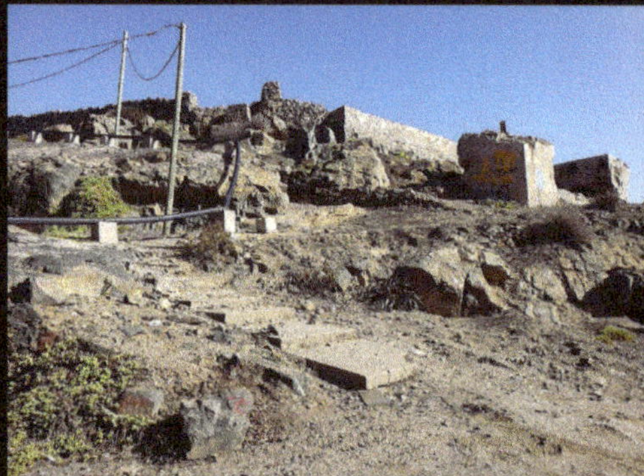

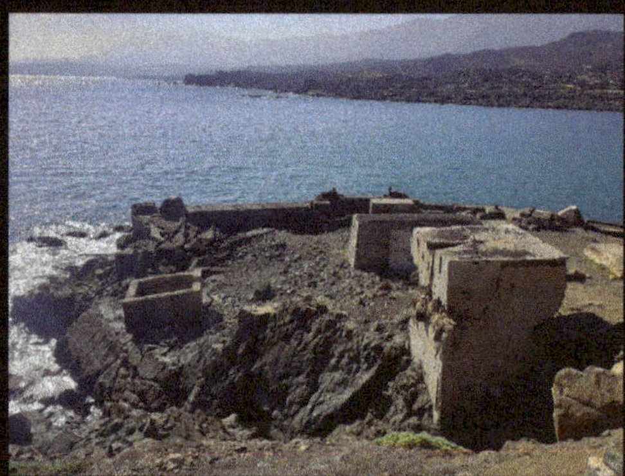

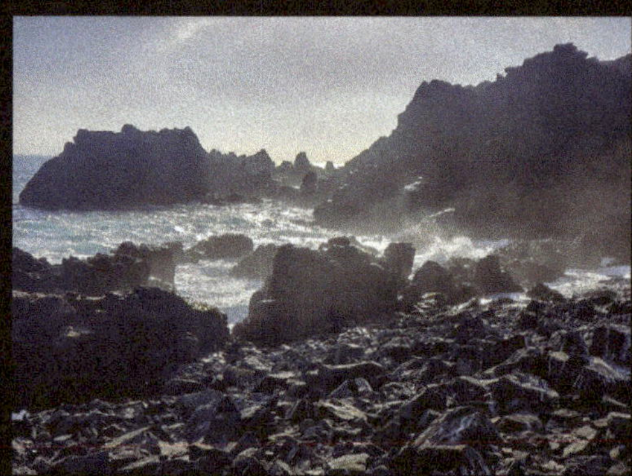

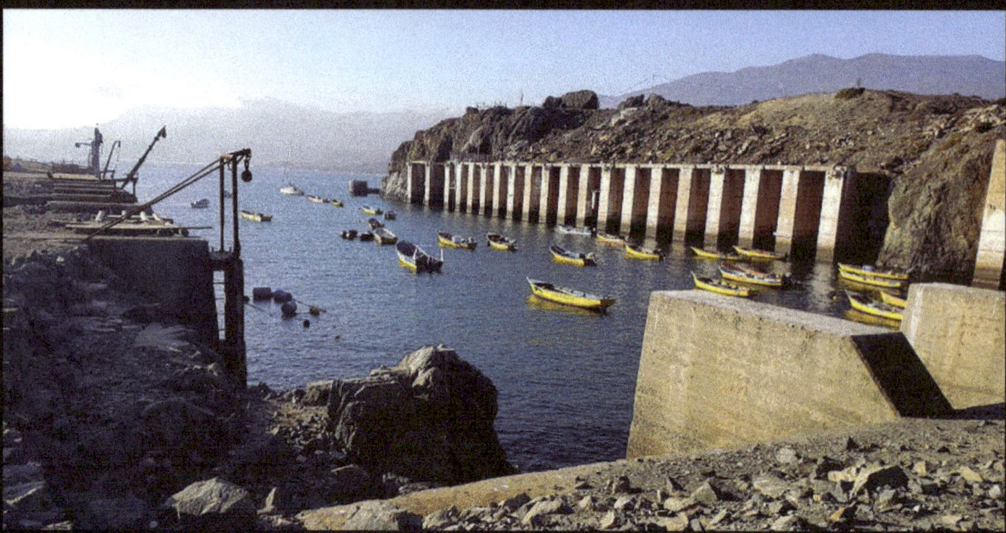

On the right side of the picture on the bottom of the previous page, remnants of the facility where iron ore was loaded directly from trains onto ships can be seen.

After finding this harbor, we spent the next few hours touring the ruins and searching for the best view from which to shoot the eclipse. The scale of the port and loading facility was amazingly large. The rawness of the location combined with the beauty of the ocean made choosing the perfect spot a challenge.

We finally settled on a place at the top of the iron ore transit area between the port and the mine.

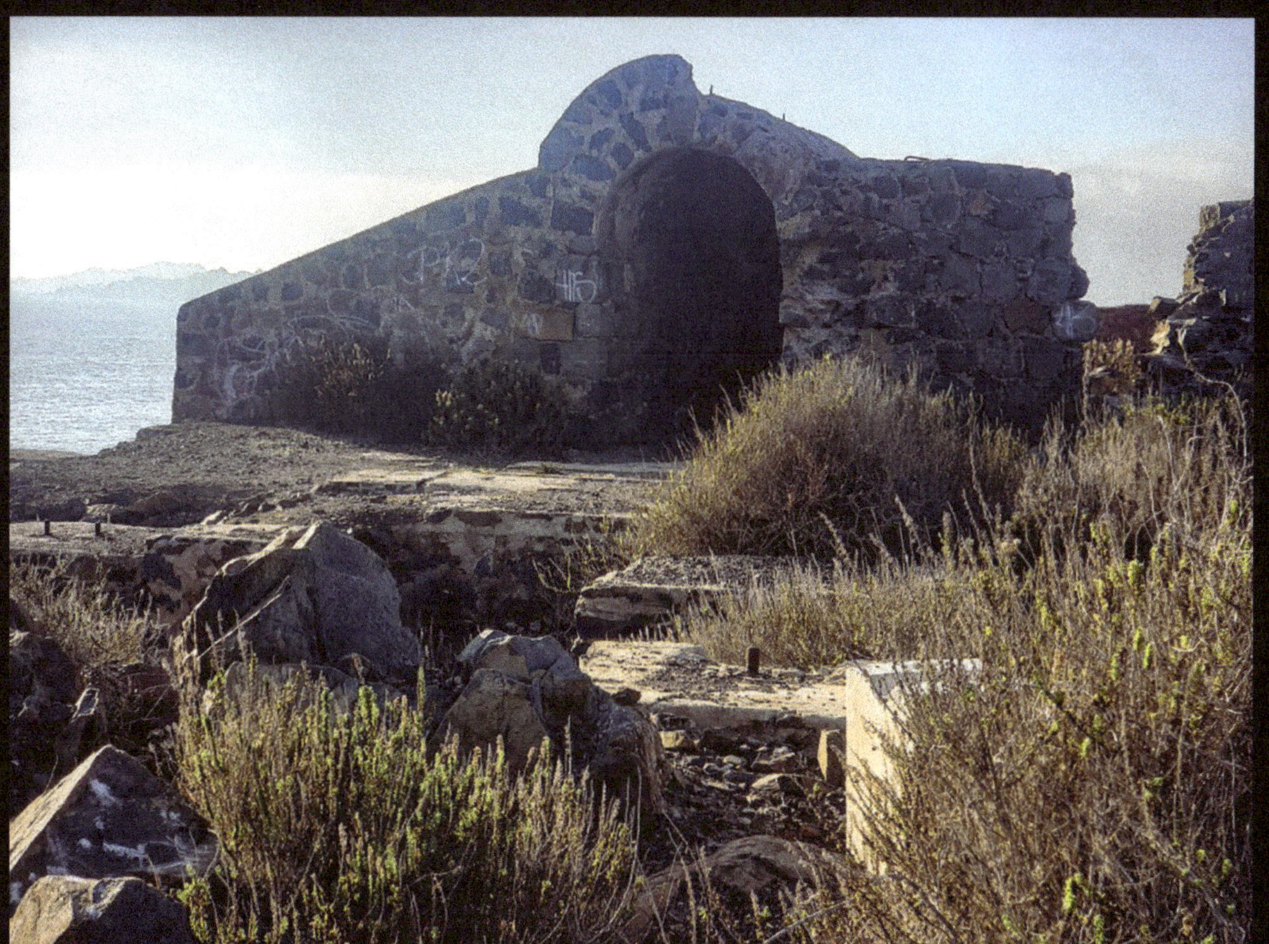

It was a long day, but we were convinced we had found a wonderful and unique setting for the impending eclipse shoot.

ECLIPSE DAY

The eclipse began at 3:22:45 p.m. on July 2, 2019, and lasted approximately two hours and twenty-four minutes. The shot at left below was taken at approximately 3:18:04 p.m., a little over four minutes before first contact (C1). The picture to the right was taken at 3:23:23 p.m., approximately 40 seconds after C1. A very small indentation can be seen on the Sun at the bottom left which is the first indication that the Sun's photosphere has begun to slip behind the Moon.

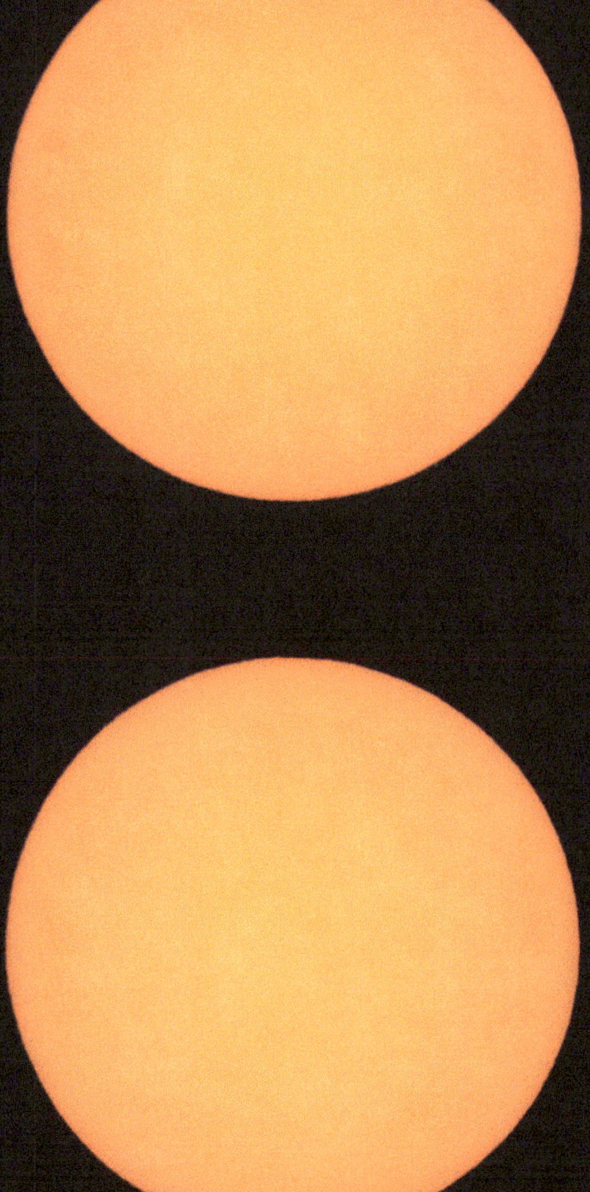

By 3:27:29 PM, the first partial portion of the eclipse has become apparent.

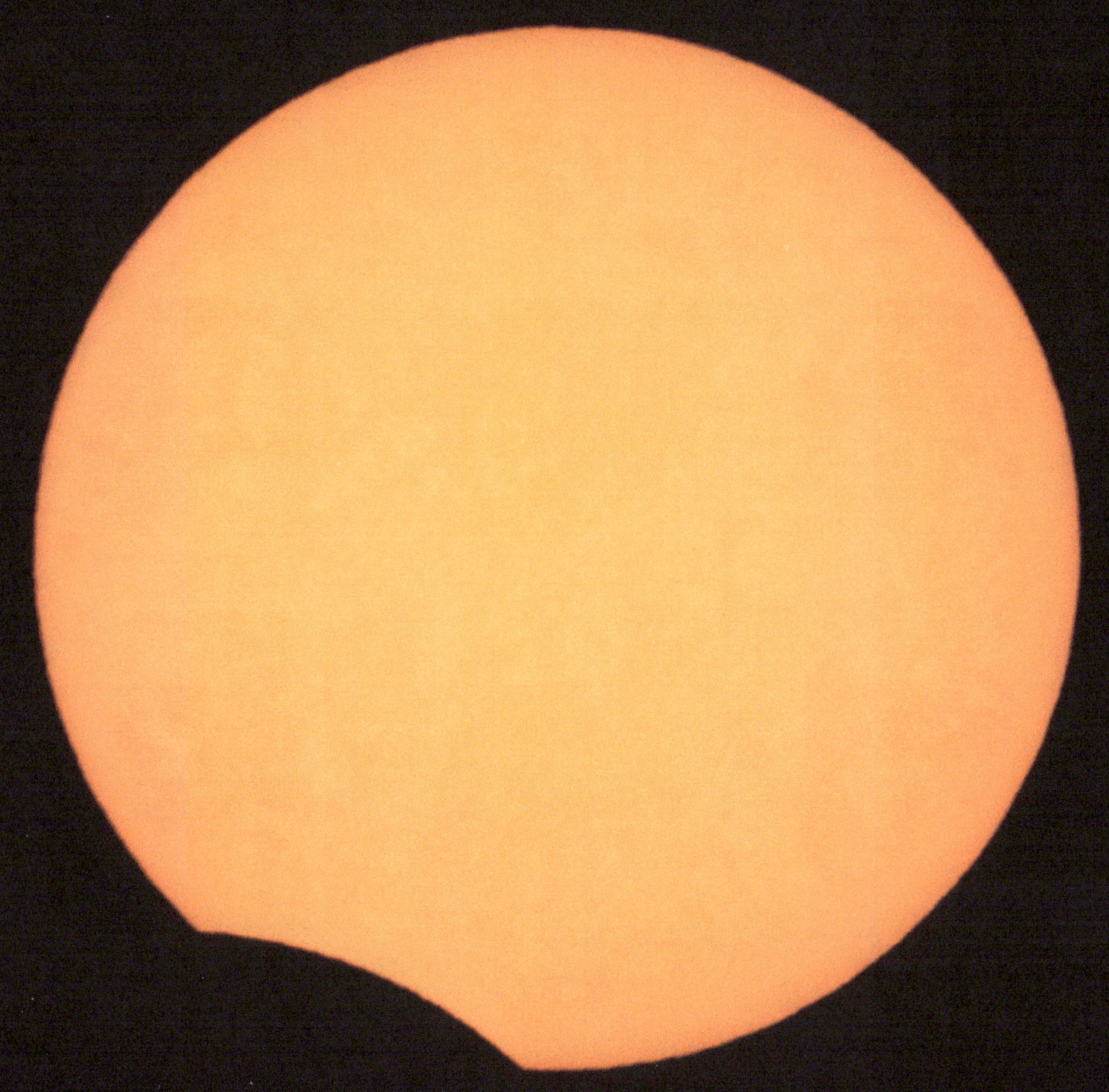

The close-up images of the partial phases from C1 to the start of totality (C2) were captured with a Canon EOS 5DS R and Canon 500mm lens with a 2x extender, effectively a 1000mm focal length. The base settings for our bracket were f/8.0, ISO 100, and 1/250 shutter speed. All camera settings are shown in Part V, which also contains the complete metadata for every eclipse picture in this book.

As in 2017, during partial phases of the eclipse, we shot a bracketed series of photos every five minutes to illustrate the Sun's steady progression towards totality.

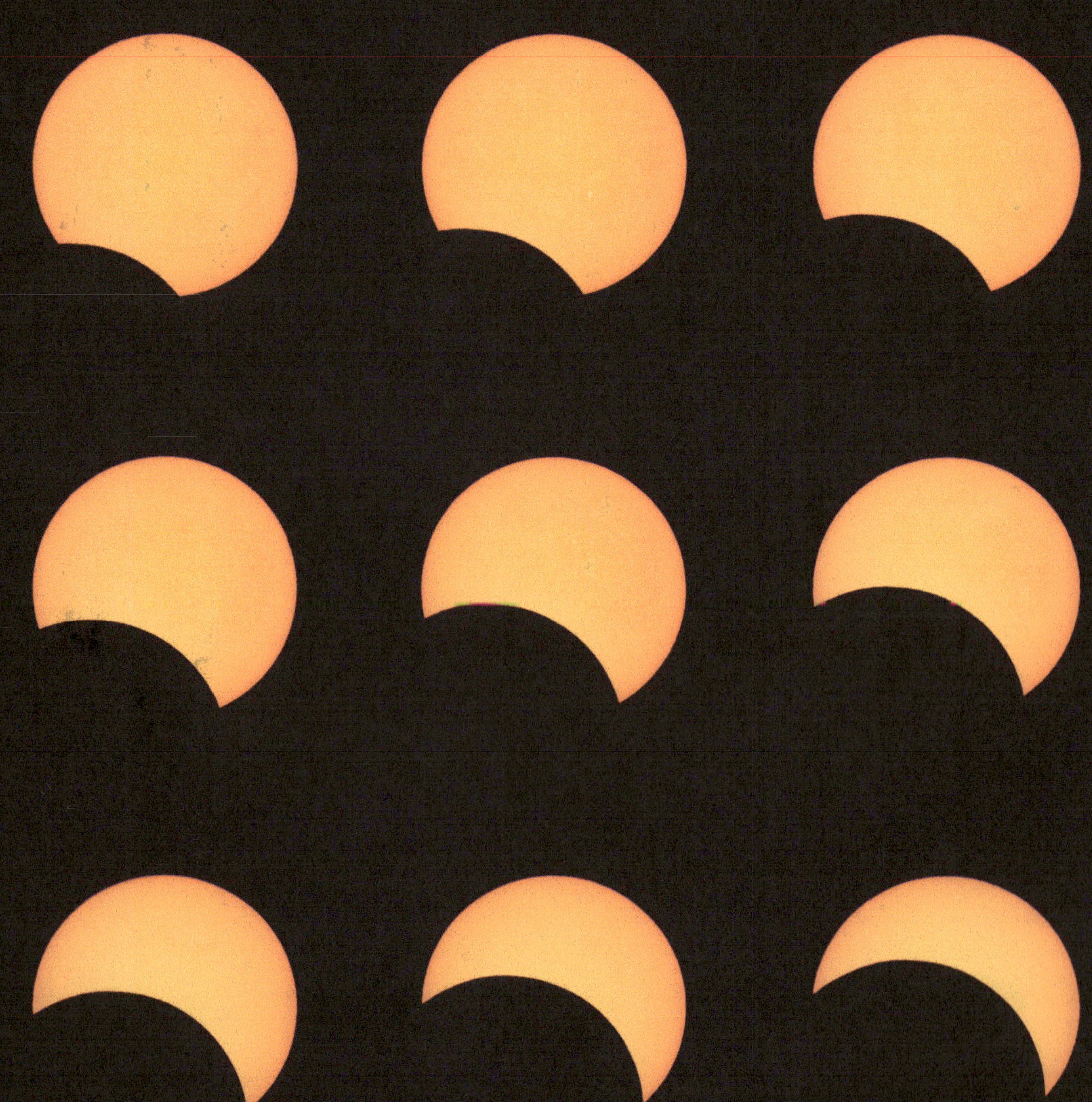

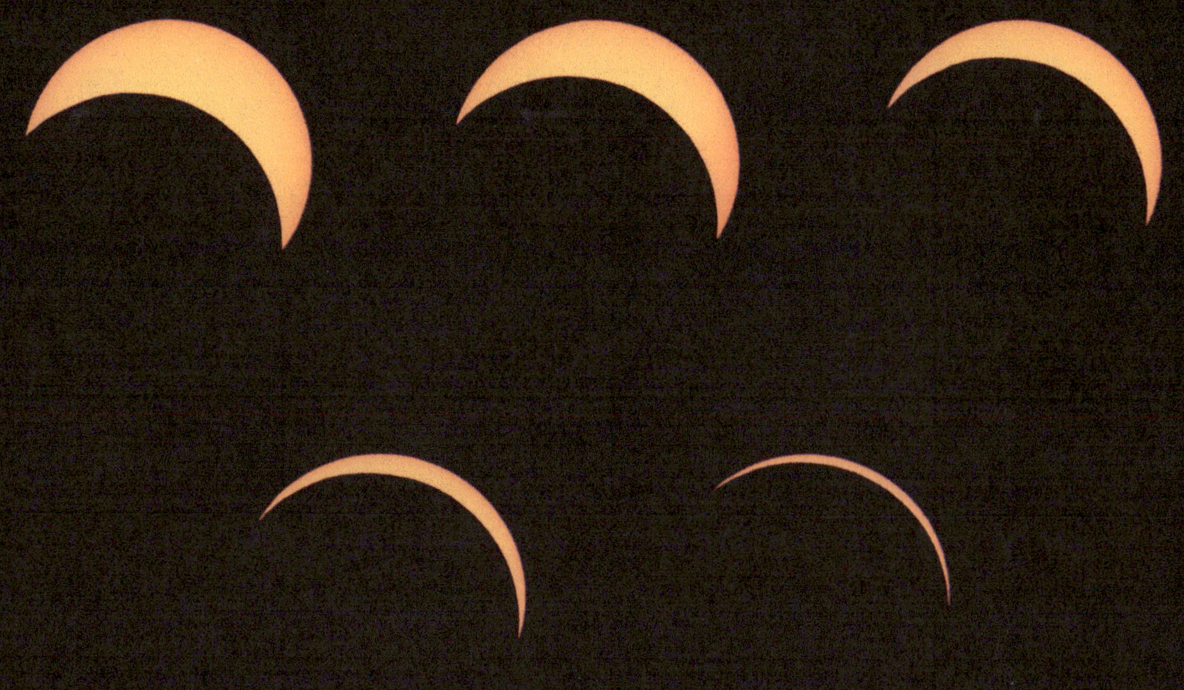

As the Sun waned, our excitement mounted about the coming diamond ring, Baily's beads, prominences, and the corona. We couldn't wait to see how the unique corona of this eclipse would present itself.

Our excitement was justified by the capture of some amazing images just prior to totality. The diamond ring is very easily recognizable on the first two images on the next page.

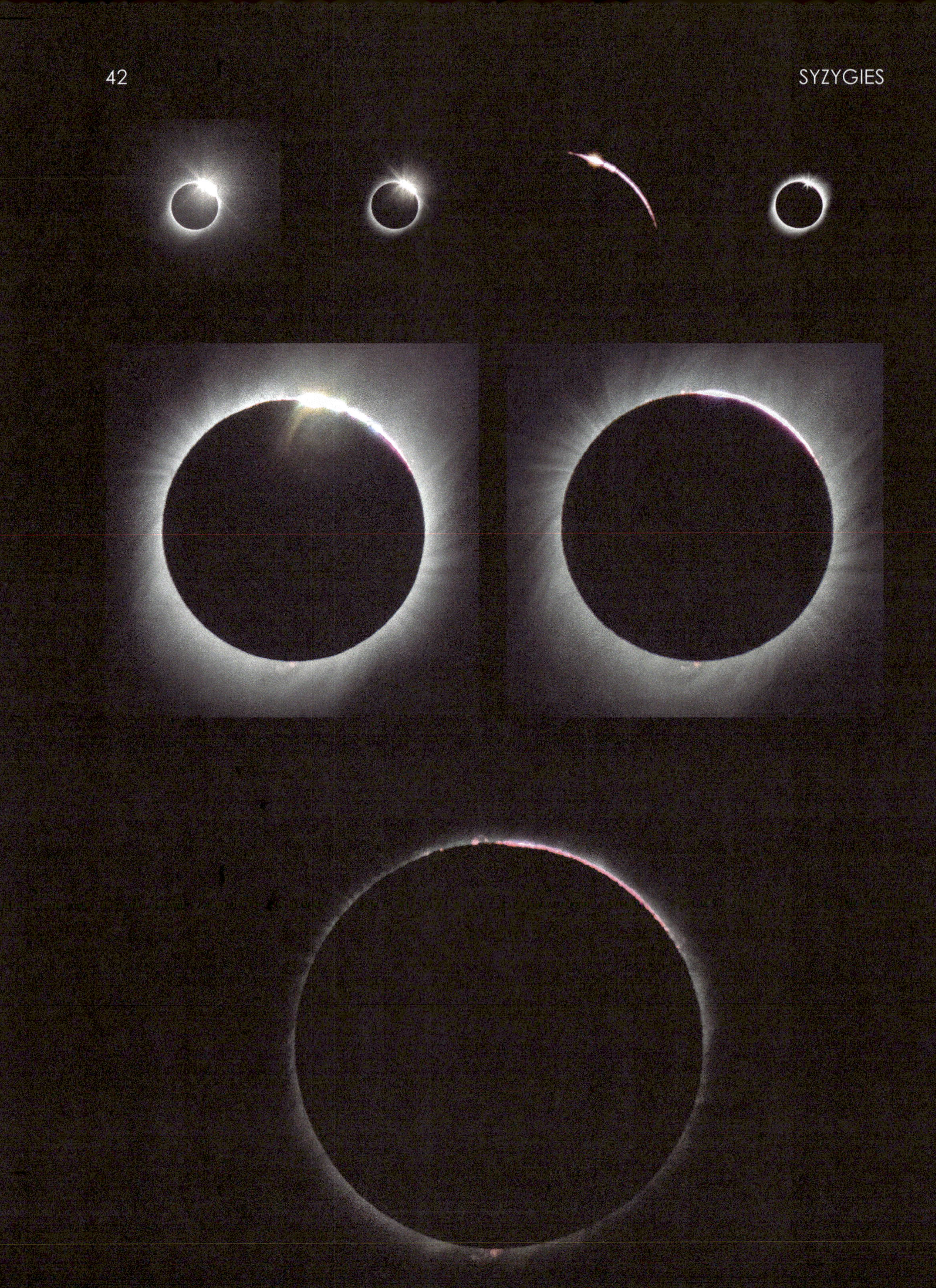

Totality occurred at approximately 4:38:21 p.m. local time in Chungungo with maximum totality at 4:39:39 p.m. It was a beautifully serene experience. The wind died down; the animals all became quiet. People standing on the shore cheered and applauded. While totality only lasted for two minutes and thirty-six seconds, it was an experience we will never forget.

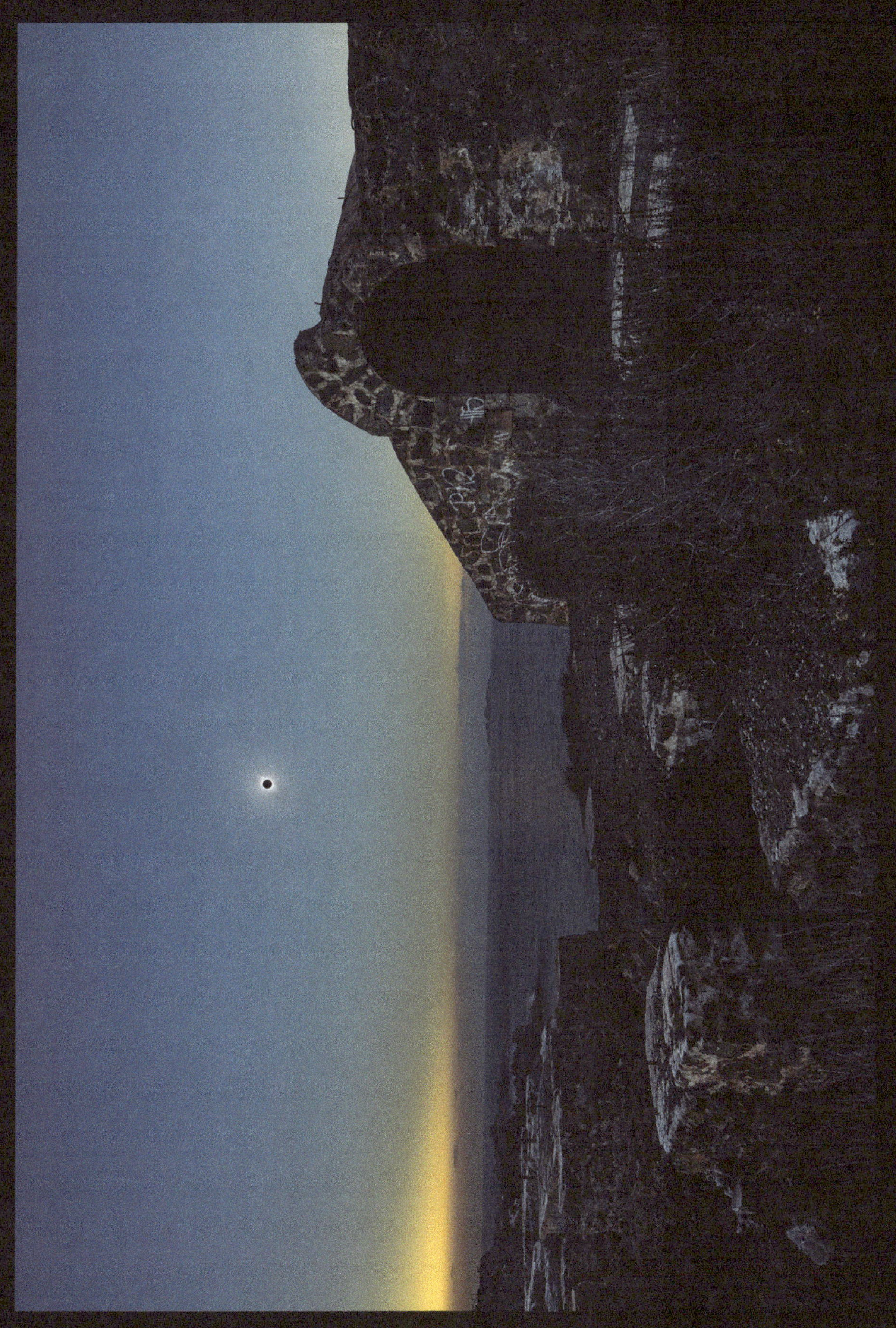

The end of the total eclipse (C3) occurred at 4:40:57 p.m. As totality ended, sunlight began to peek through the geographic edges of the Moon's topography. In a reverse of the events leading up to C2, first came the irregular edge of the red chromosphere. Next Baily's beads reappeared and then merged to form the second diamond ring. The following image illustrates the red prominences of the chromosphere as well as Baily's beads as the photosphere re-emerges from behind the Moon.

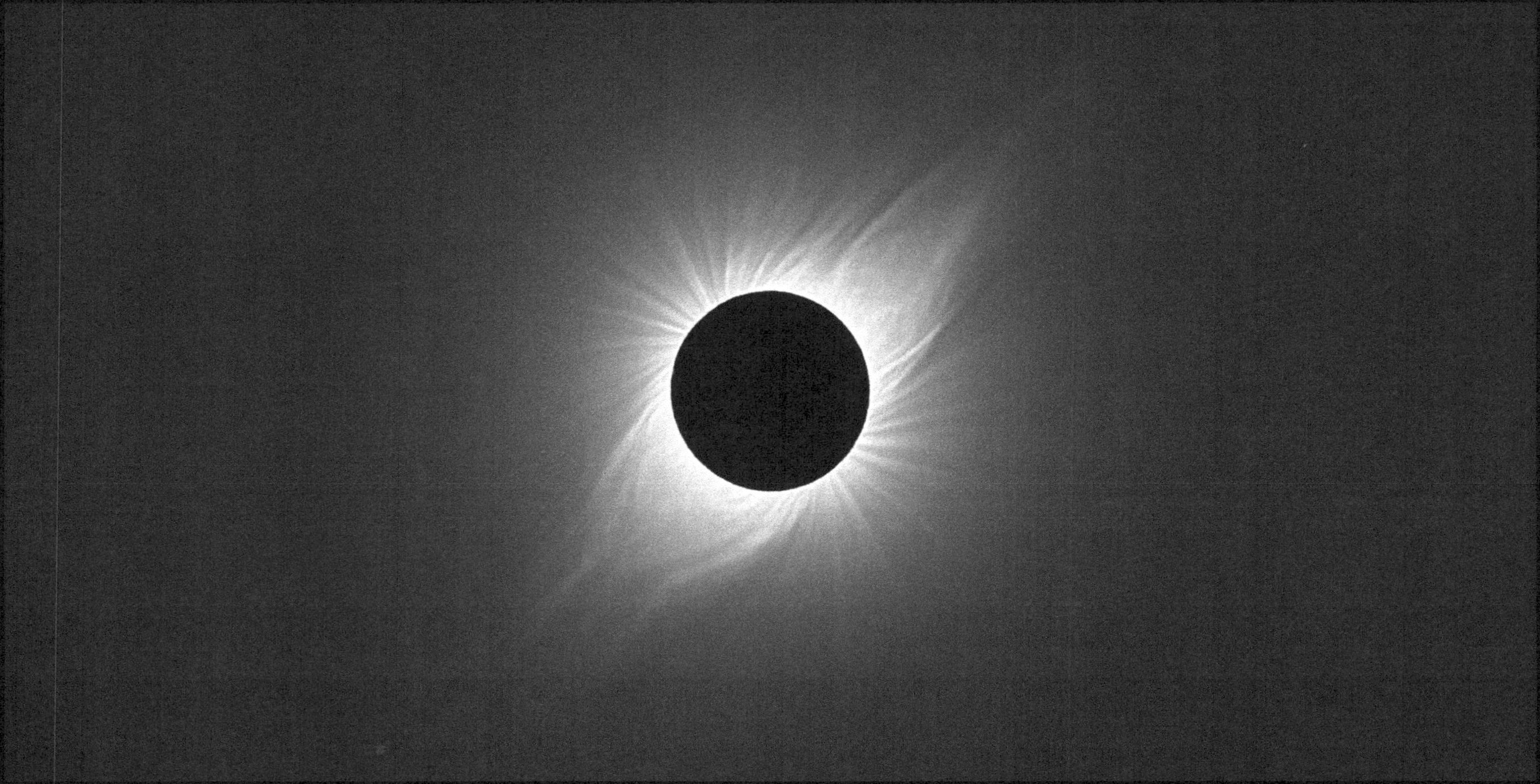

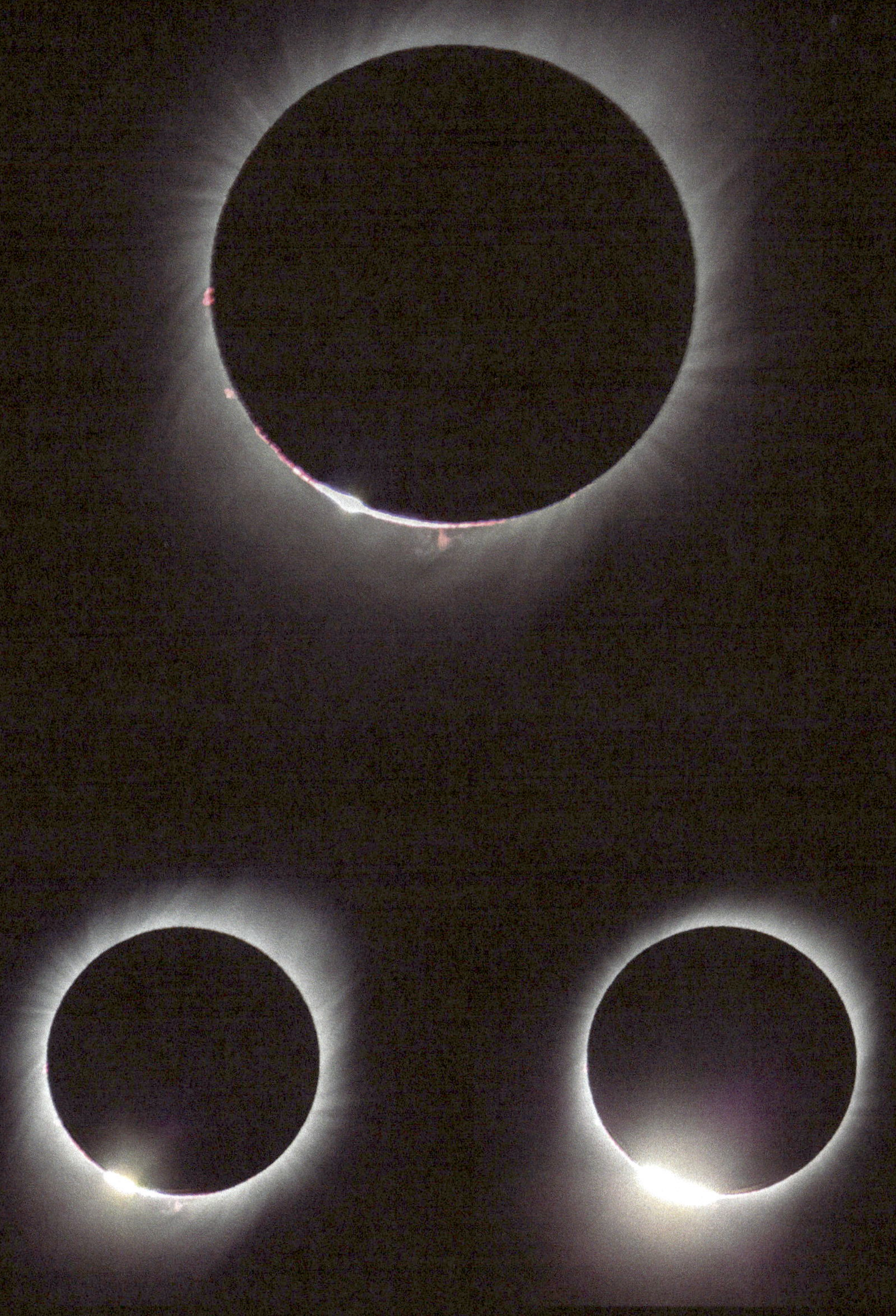

After the diamond ring, we replaced our solar filters and resumed shooting the partial phases of the second half of the eclipse in five-minute intervals.

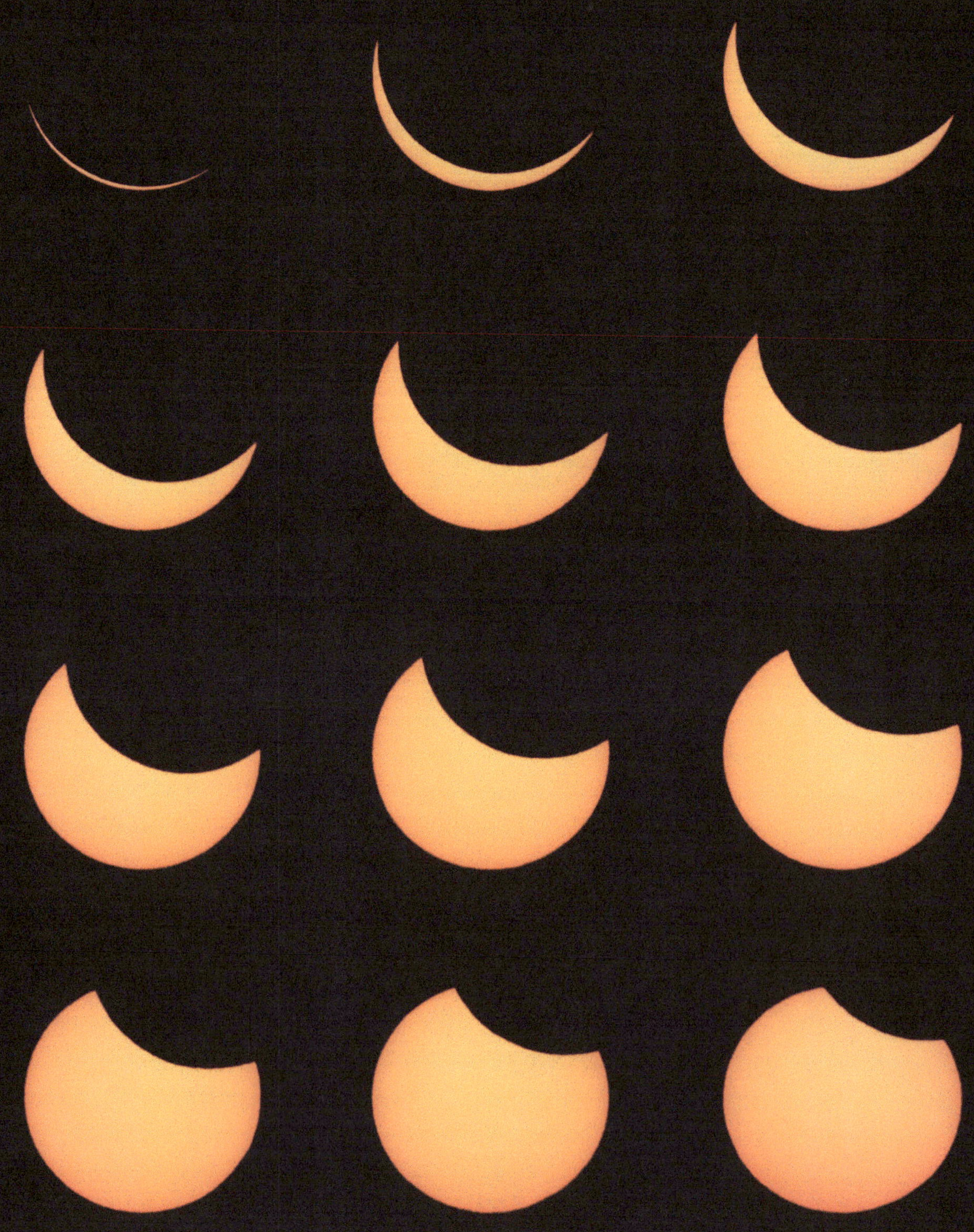

Towards the end of the eclipse, the Sun slipped into a cloud bank on the horizon. Initially, we were concerned; however, the resulting images were breathtaking.

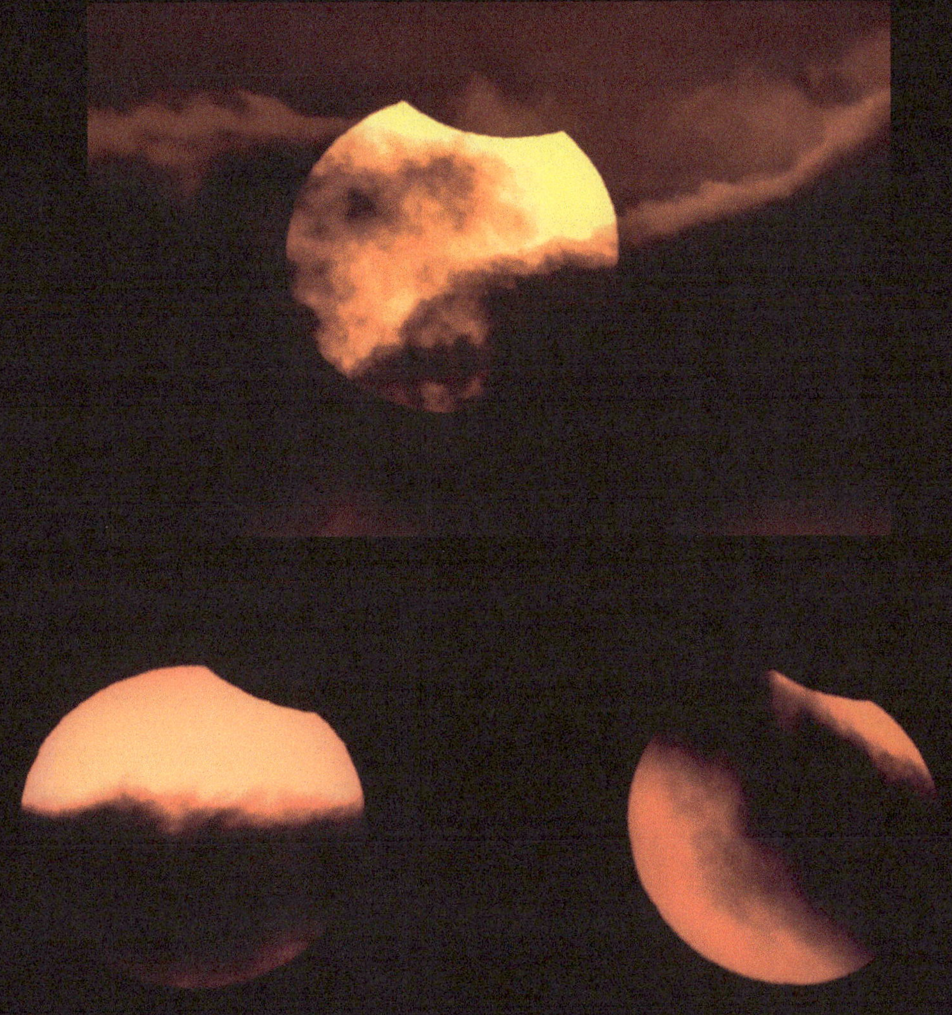

The white image of the Sun at right above and the picture below are unfiltered shots. We experimented with various settings and took some unfiltered shots as the Sun dimmed at the end of the day.

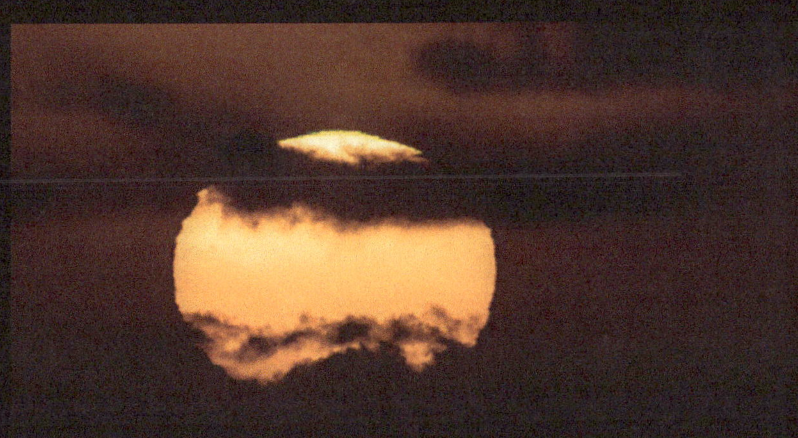

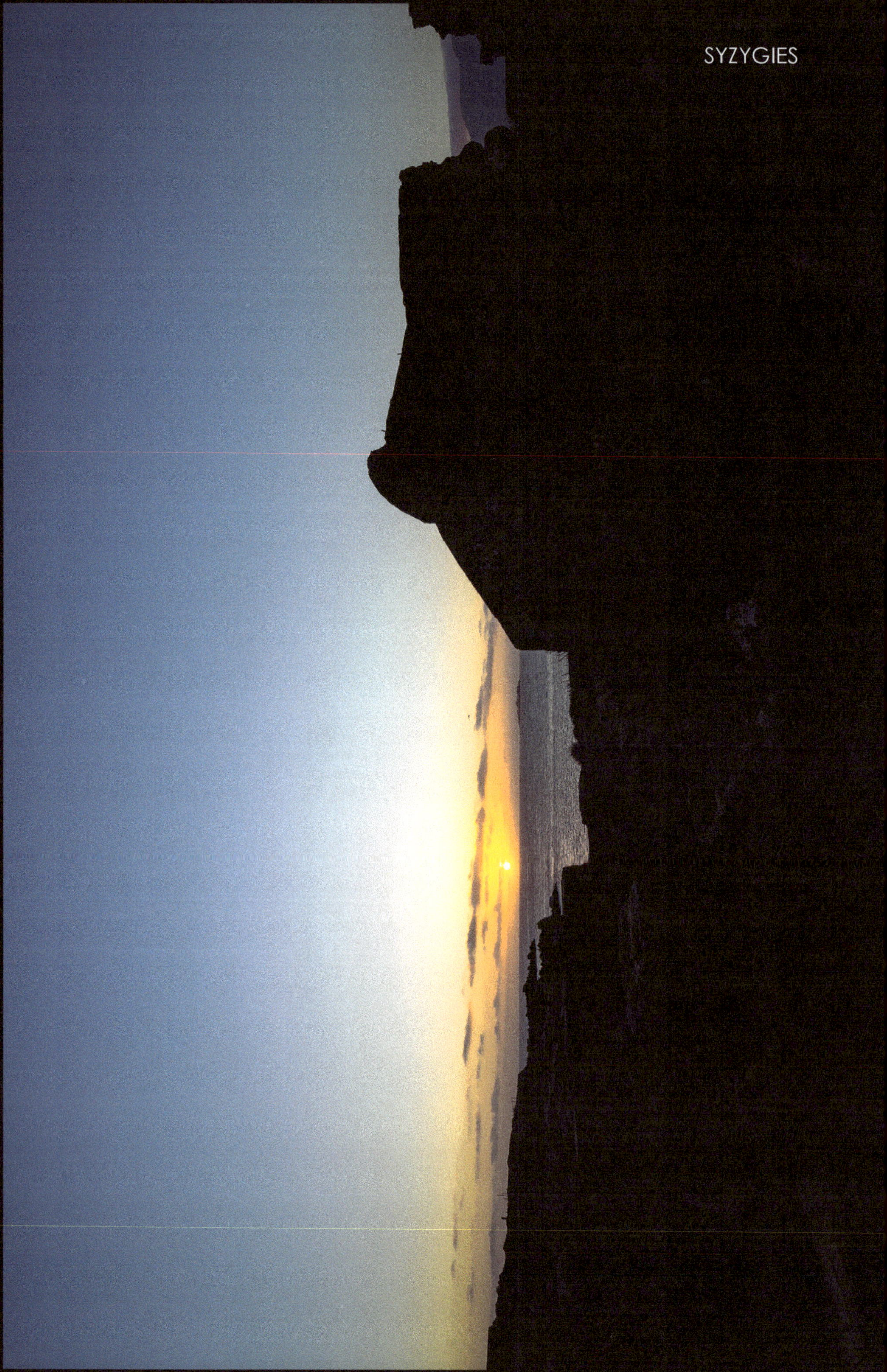

The eclipse concluded with a wonderful sunset as the Sun and Moon slipped below the horizon.

We saved our two favorite and most unique images from the Chilean eclipse for the end of this section. The first image was taken on July 2, 2023, at approximately 4:41 p.m. That was the start of the second portion of the partial eclipse. The photograph was taken with a Canon 500mm lens and a 2x Extender and initially processed with Aurora HDR software.

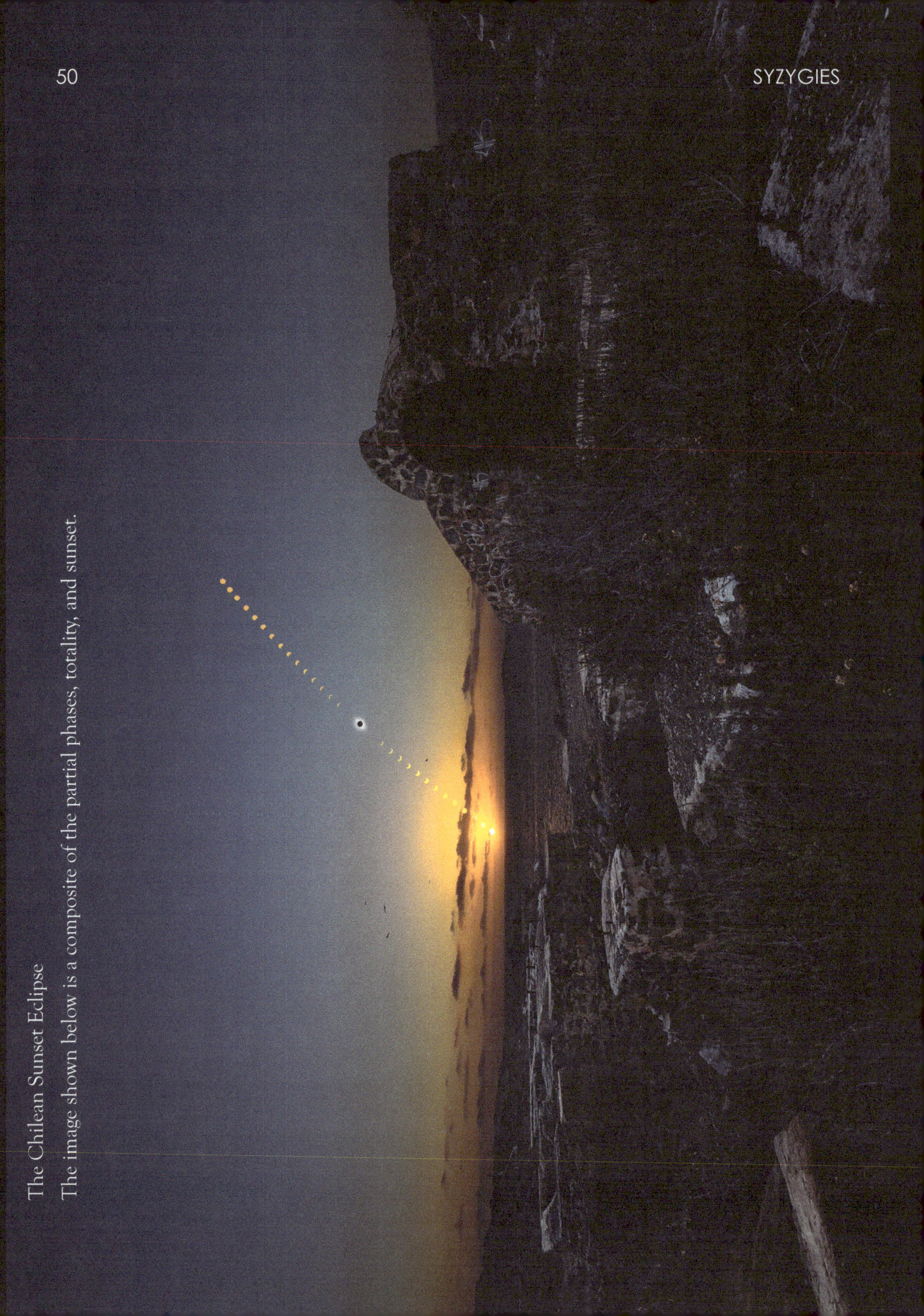

The Chilean Sunset Eclipse

The image shown below is a composite of the partial phases, totality, and sunset.

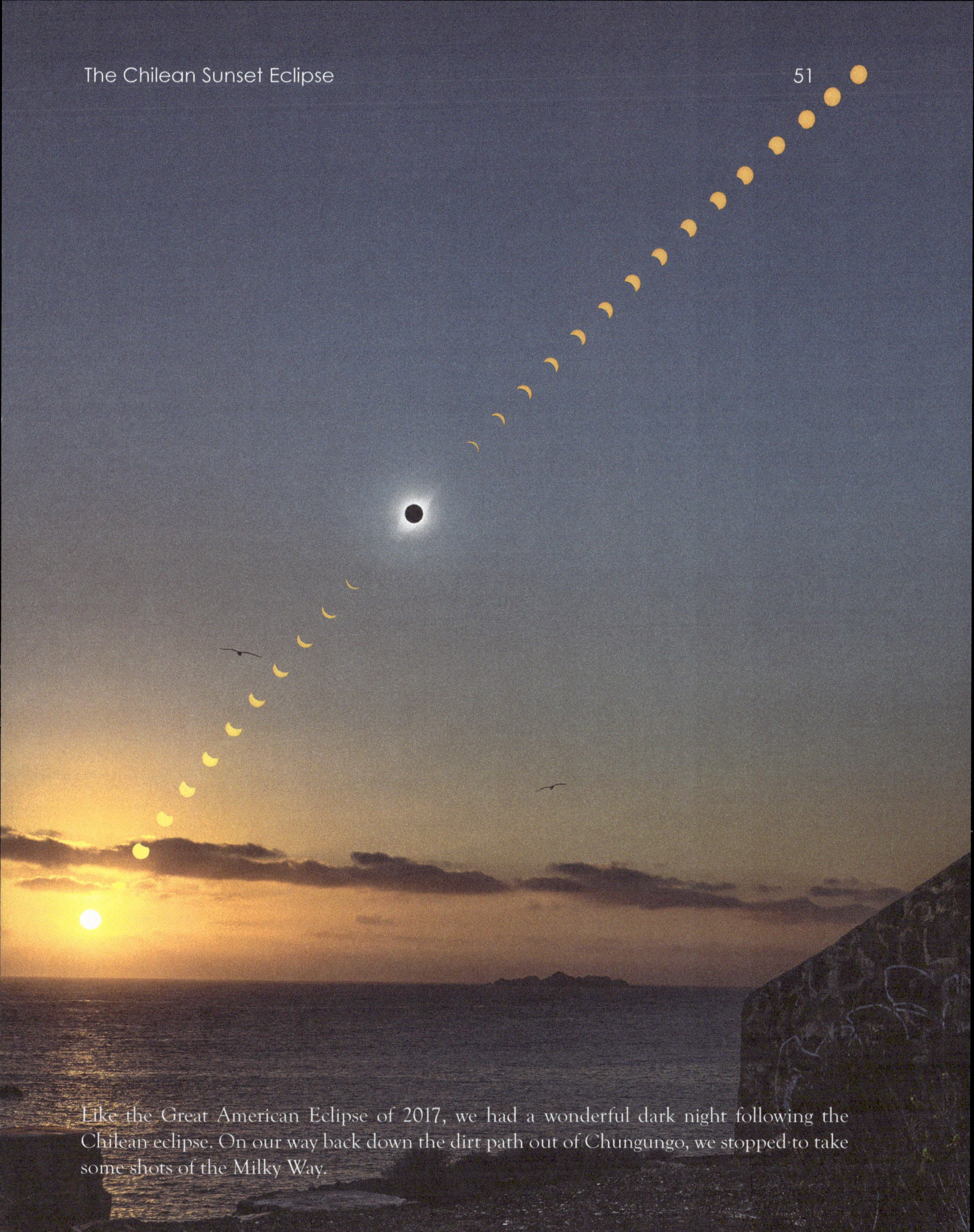

Like the Great American Eclipse of 2017, we had a wonderful dark night following the Chilean eclipse. On our way back down the dirt path out of Chungungo, we stopped to take some shots of the Milky Way.

Here are some of the friends that we met in Chile. We are forever thankful to them for finding all the things we forgot to bring.

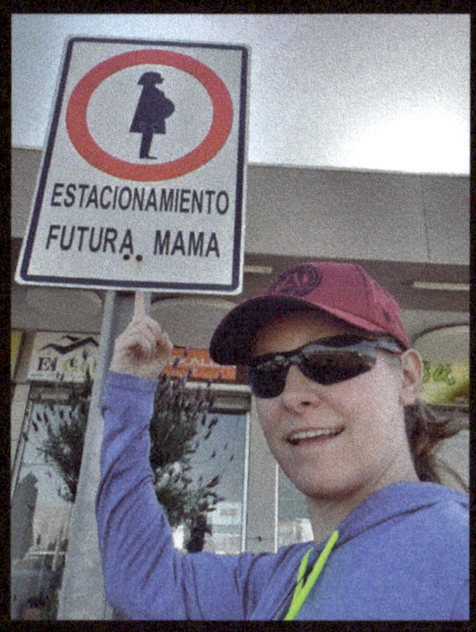

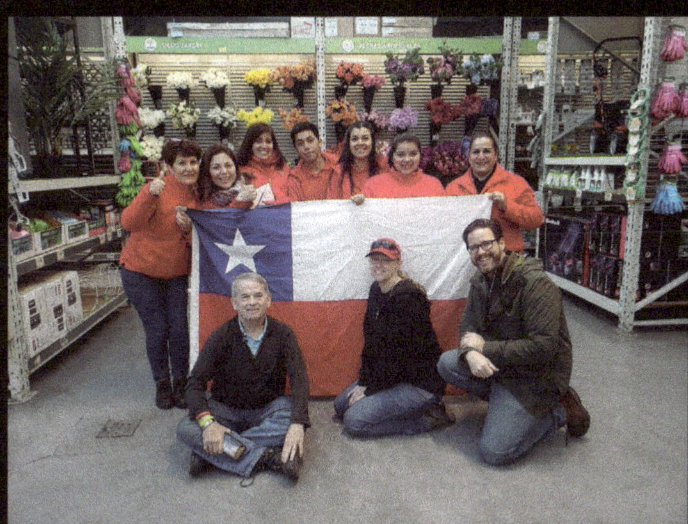

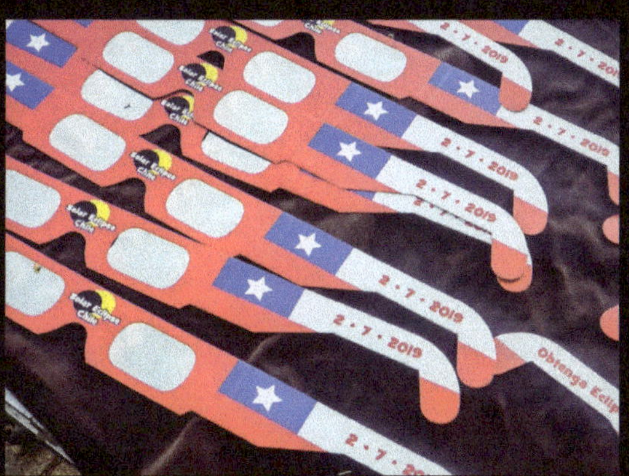

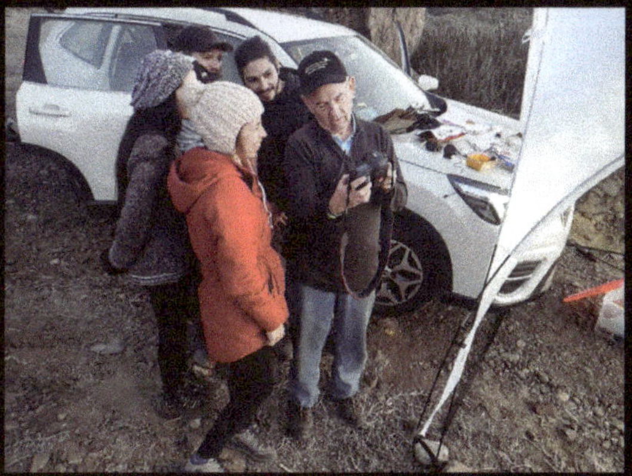

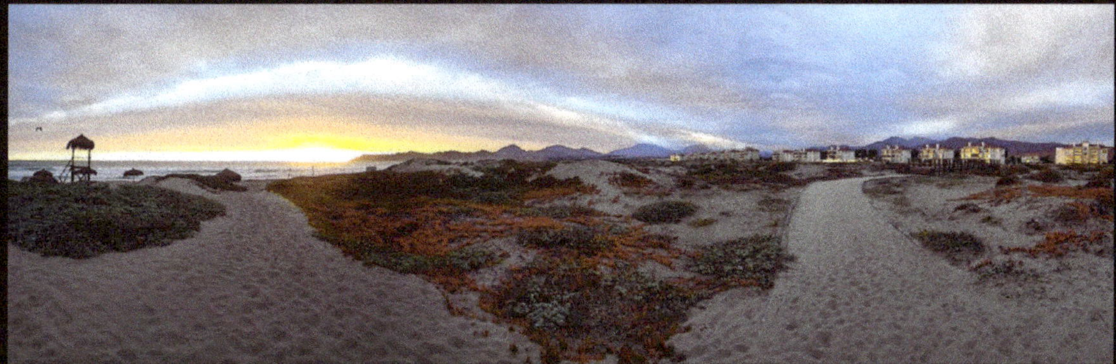

PART III

2023 Australian Hybrid Eclipse

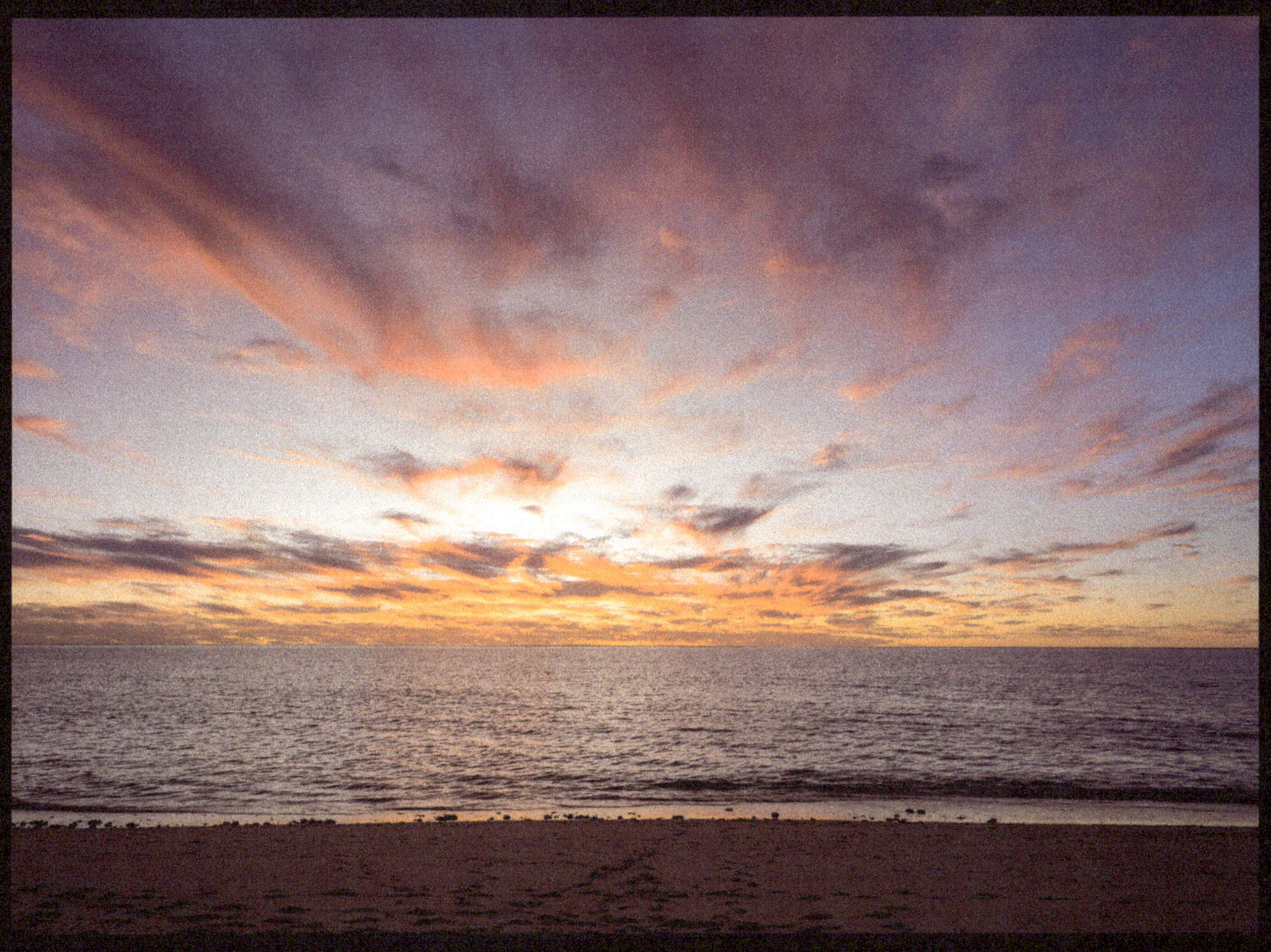

Australian Eclipse Shoot Site

Yardie Creek, Cape Range National Park, WA, Australia

April 19, 2023

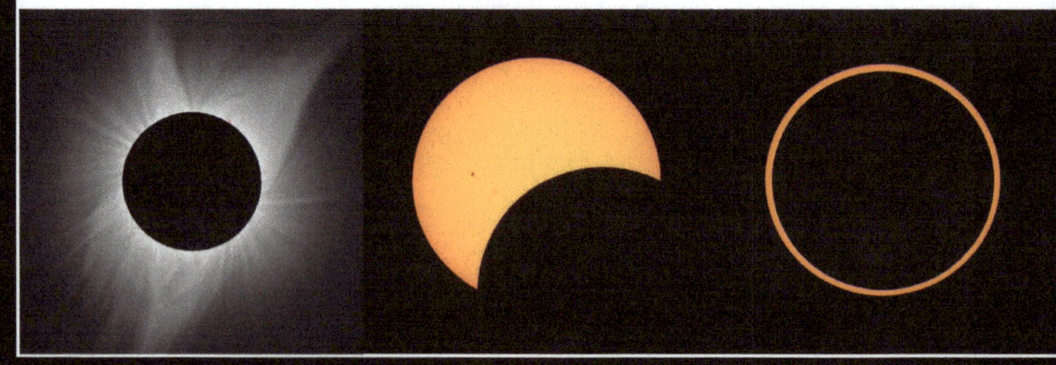

ttps://syzygies.com/hybrid-solar-eclipse/

In addition, our team composition had also changed. We were missing Paul Kamstra and Randy Talbot from our 2017 shoot, who were unable to attend. We were also without Kevin Kurz from 2017 and 2019. We were fortunate to add Katherine Neslund to the team.

Following our established approach, we spent over two years preparing for the eclipse. We studied the geography along the eclipse path and the geometry of the eclipse. When the time came, we flew from the United States to Sydney, Australia, followed by another flight to Perth, Australia. From Perth, we had a 14-hour drive to Exmouth in northwest Australia to get to the only portion of the continent located in the central path of the eclipse and thus the optimal location of our potential shooting sites.

As a result of our studies, and our penchant for adding new equipment, we added two medium format cameras and their lenses, as well as a Canon 600mm EF lens and Canon R5 body. The new cameras had significantly faster write speeds as did the newest generation of storage media. While we are always nervous on the way to an eclipse, we were as prepared as we could be for our third adventure. Once we arrived at our chosen location, Brittany, Katherine, and I started setting up the cameras for the wonderful seaside shoot. It was a beautiful, albeit windy, day.

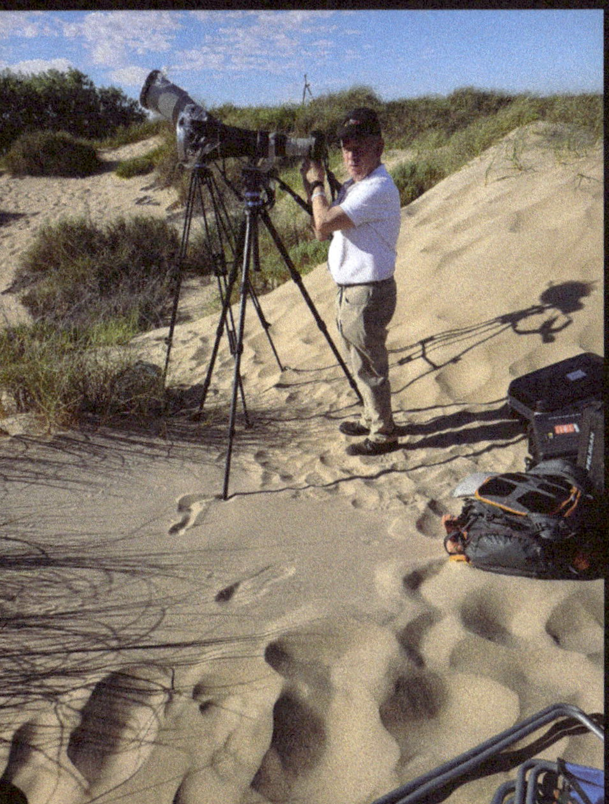

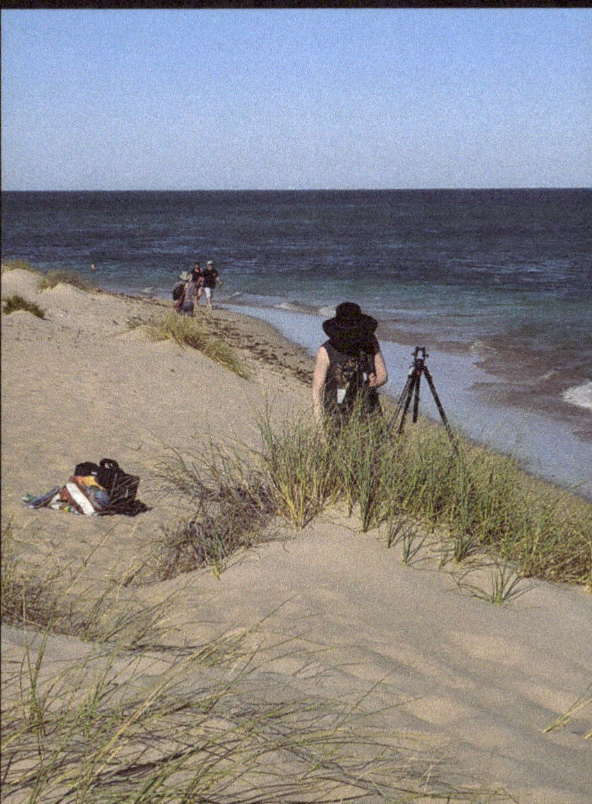

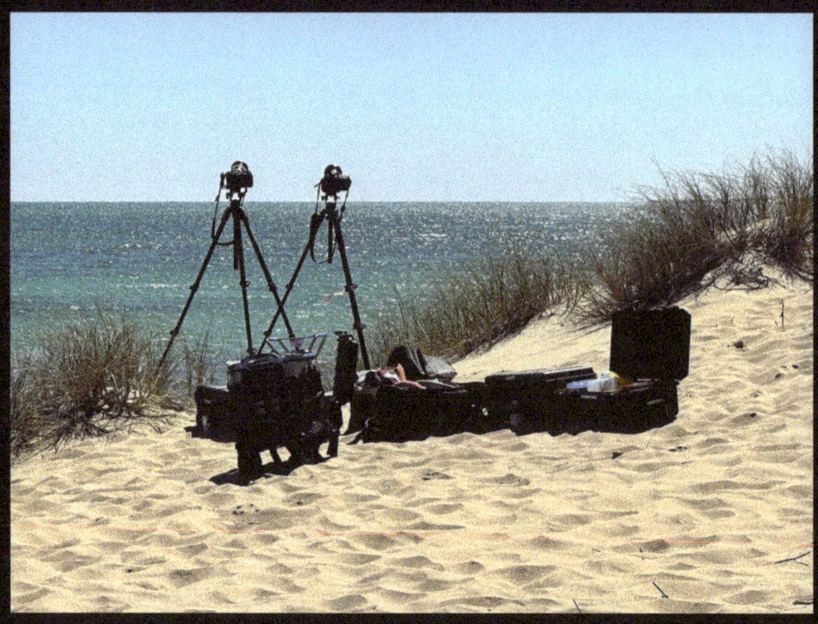

We started taking photos at approximately 9:58:14 on the morning of April 20th. Below is one of the last images of the Sun we took before the start of the partial eclipse. Unlike the Chilean eclipse, you can see sunspots on the left center of the Sun.

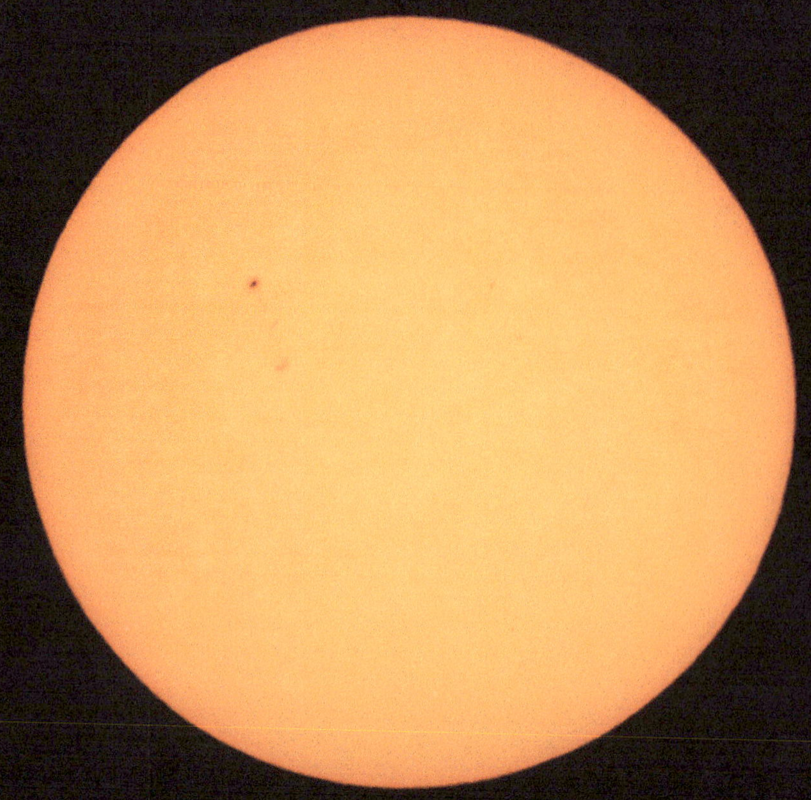

The partial eclipse began with first contact (C1) at 10:03 a.m., and by 10:07 a.m. the Moon's profile had become prominent.

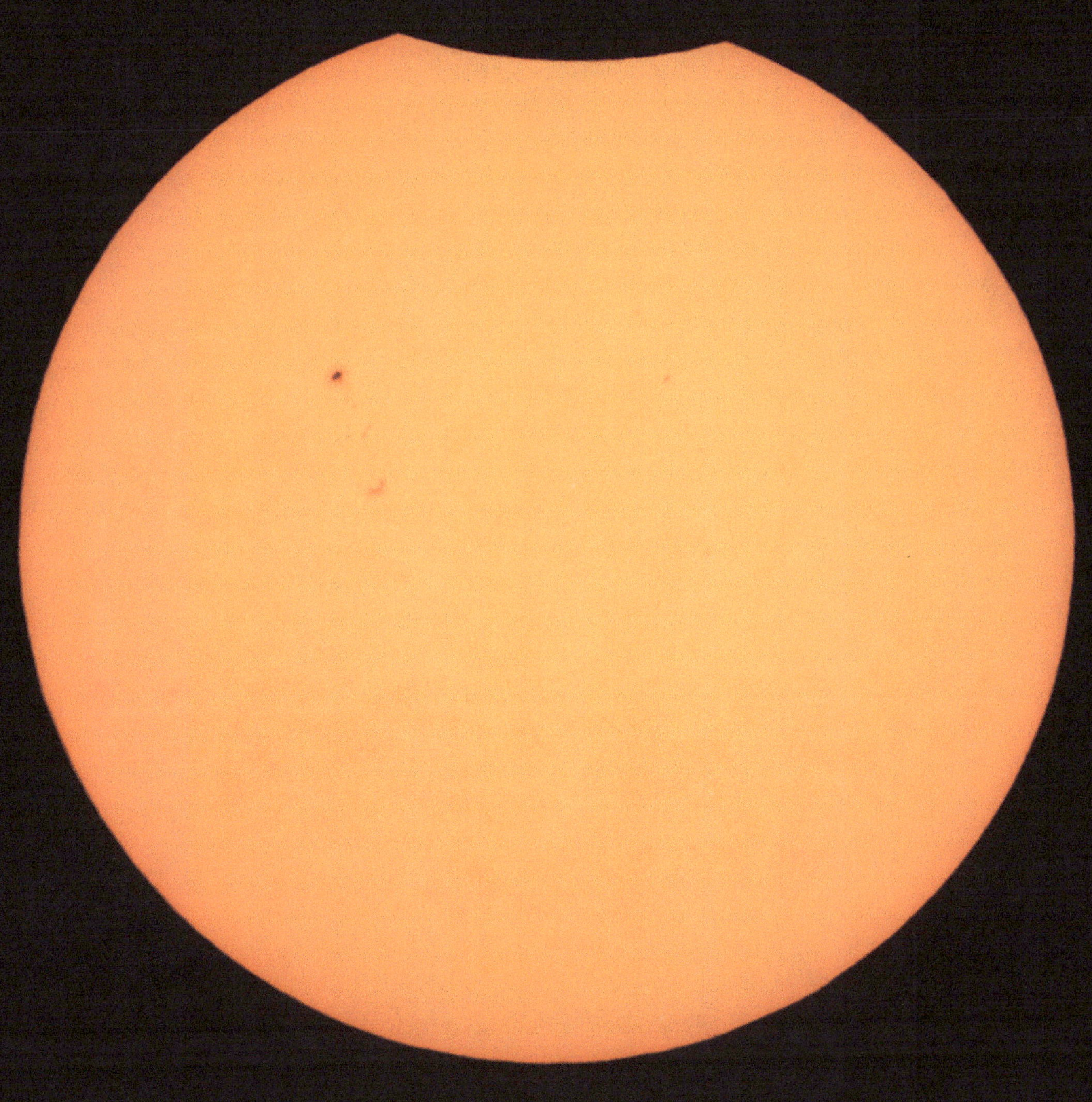

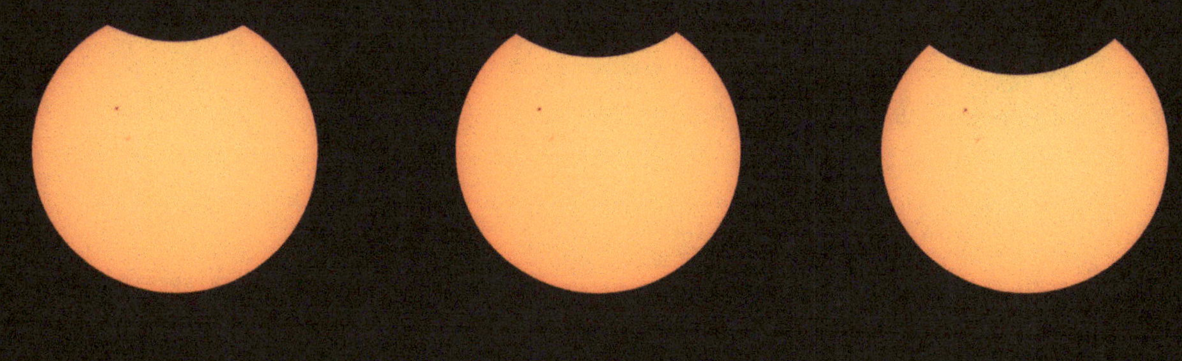

10:13:21 10:17:51 10:22:56

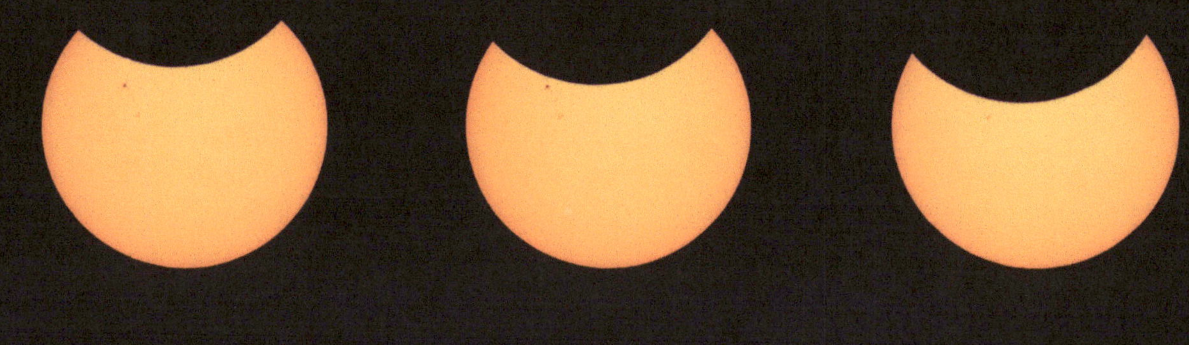

10:27:51 10:33:06 10:38:14

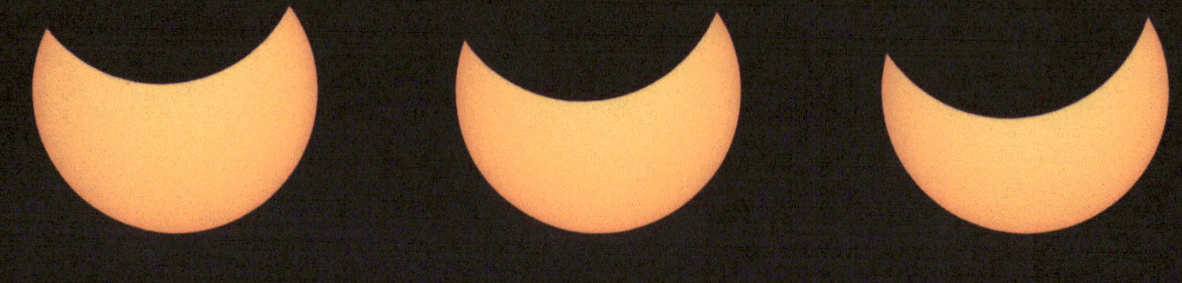

10:43:04 10:48:09 10:53:07

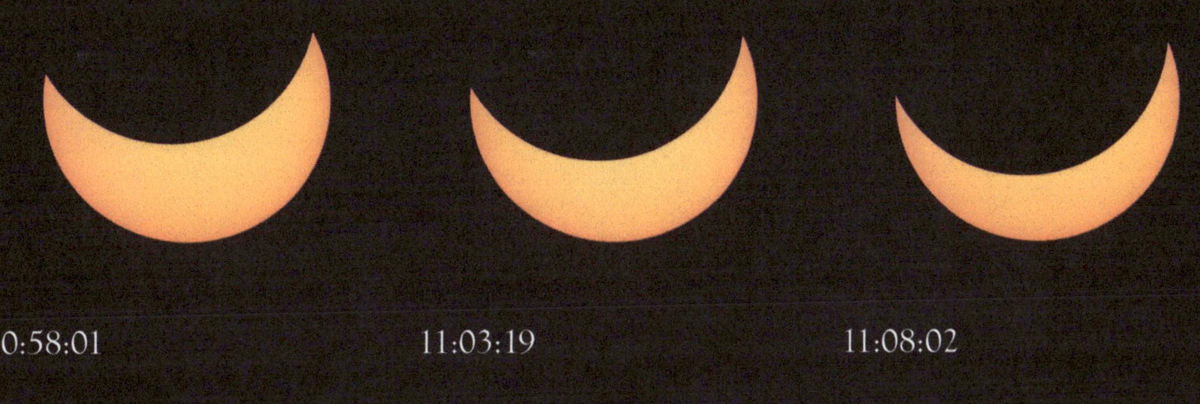

10:58:01 11:03:19 11:08:02

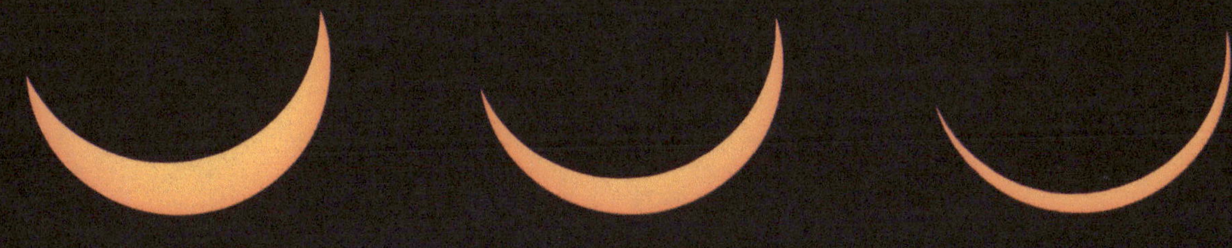

11:13:04 11:18:02 11:23:07

In the last seconds of the initial partial phase of the eclipse, we obtained some of the most wonderful images of the diamond ring, Baily's beads, and the features of the chromosphere. The next 3 images which were taken over 16 seconds show how quickly the diamond ring turns into Baily's beads.

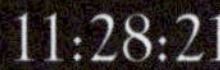

11:28:21

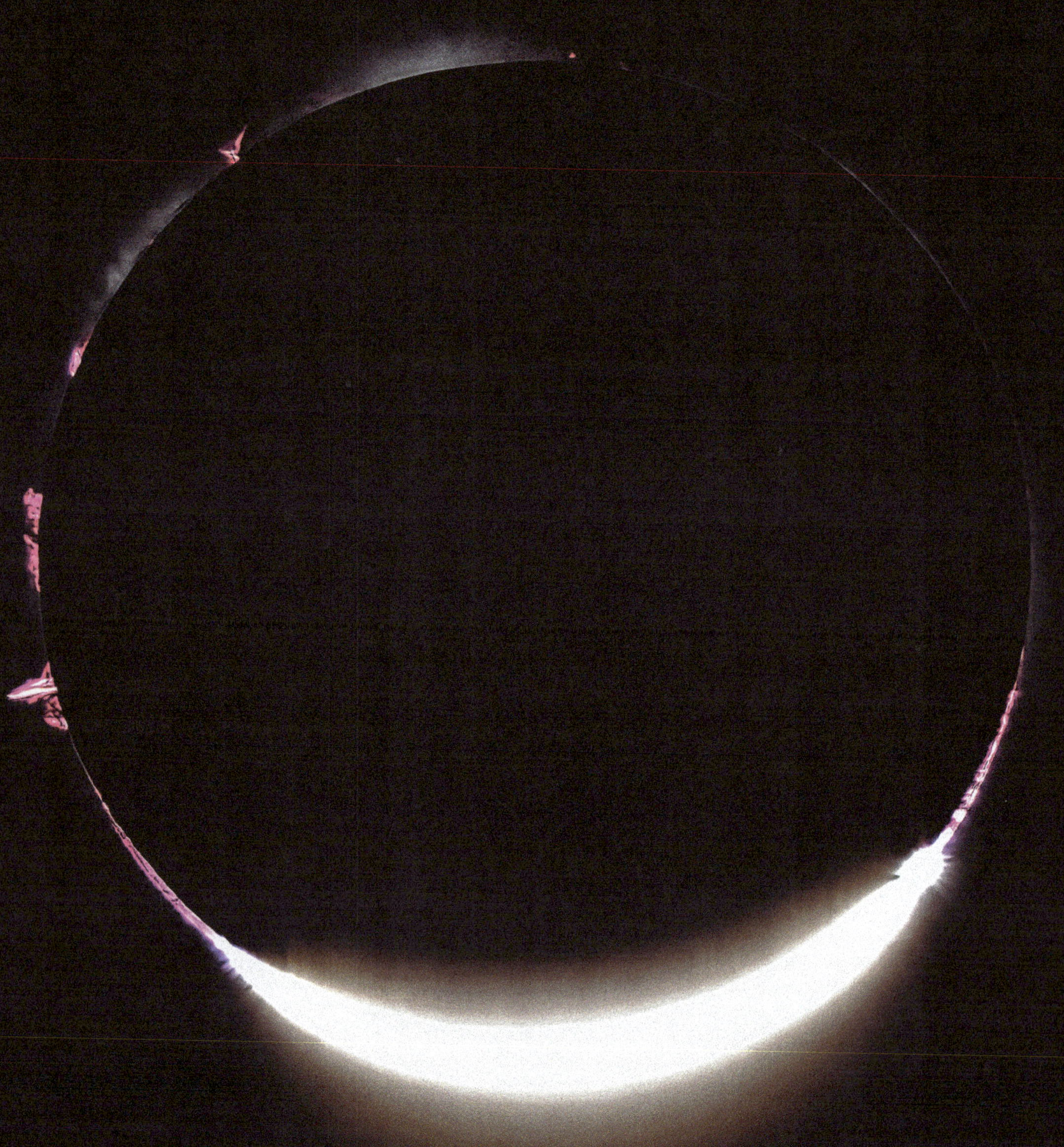

Note on the top left edge of the Sun there is an arching solar flare that leaves the Sun and then returns to the surface of the Sun.

11:28:33

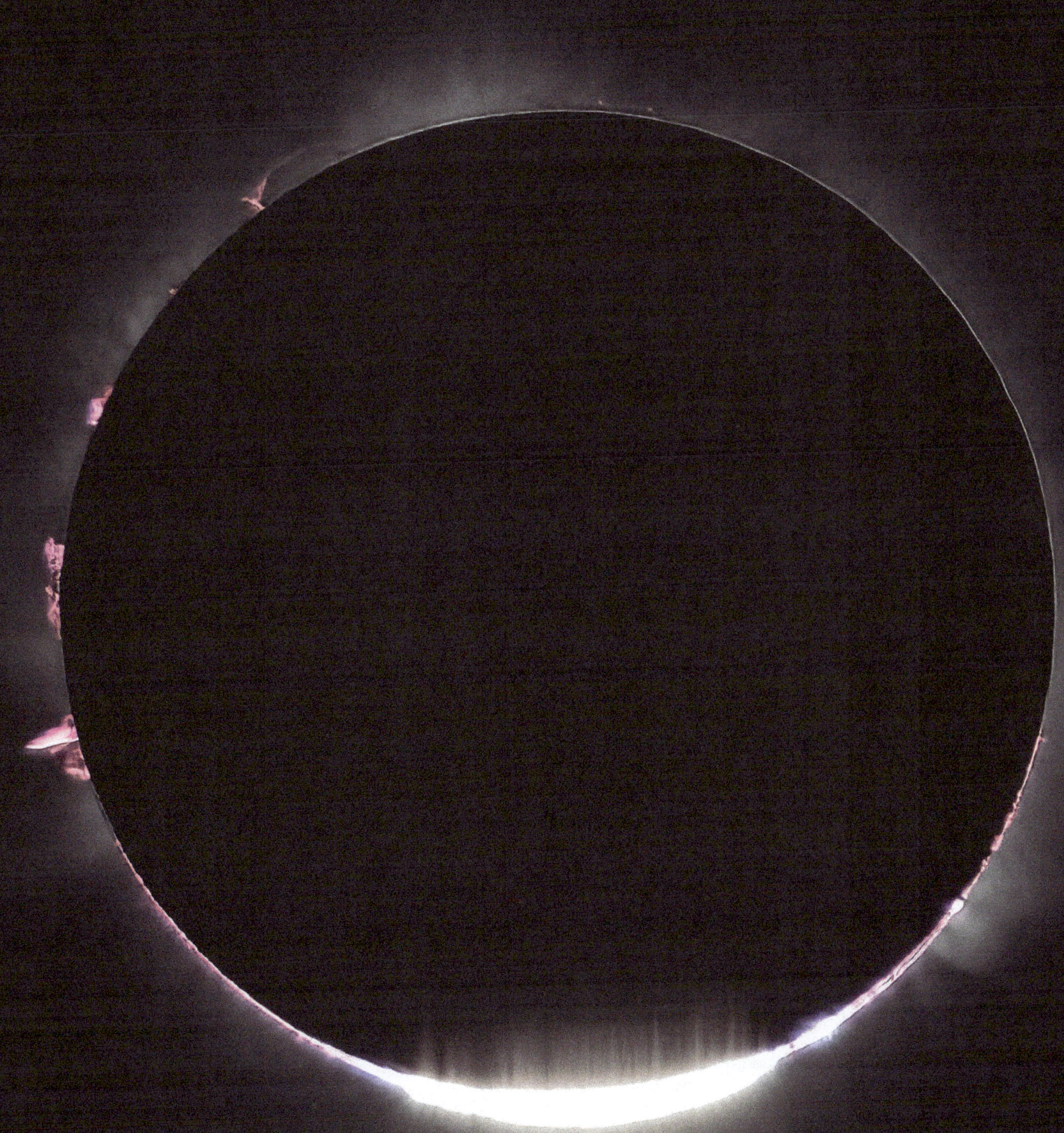

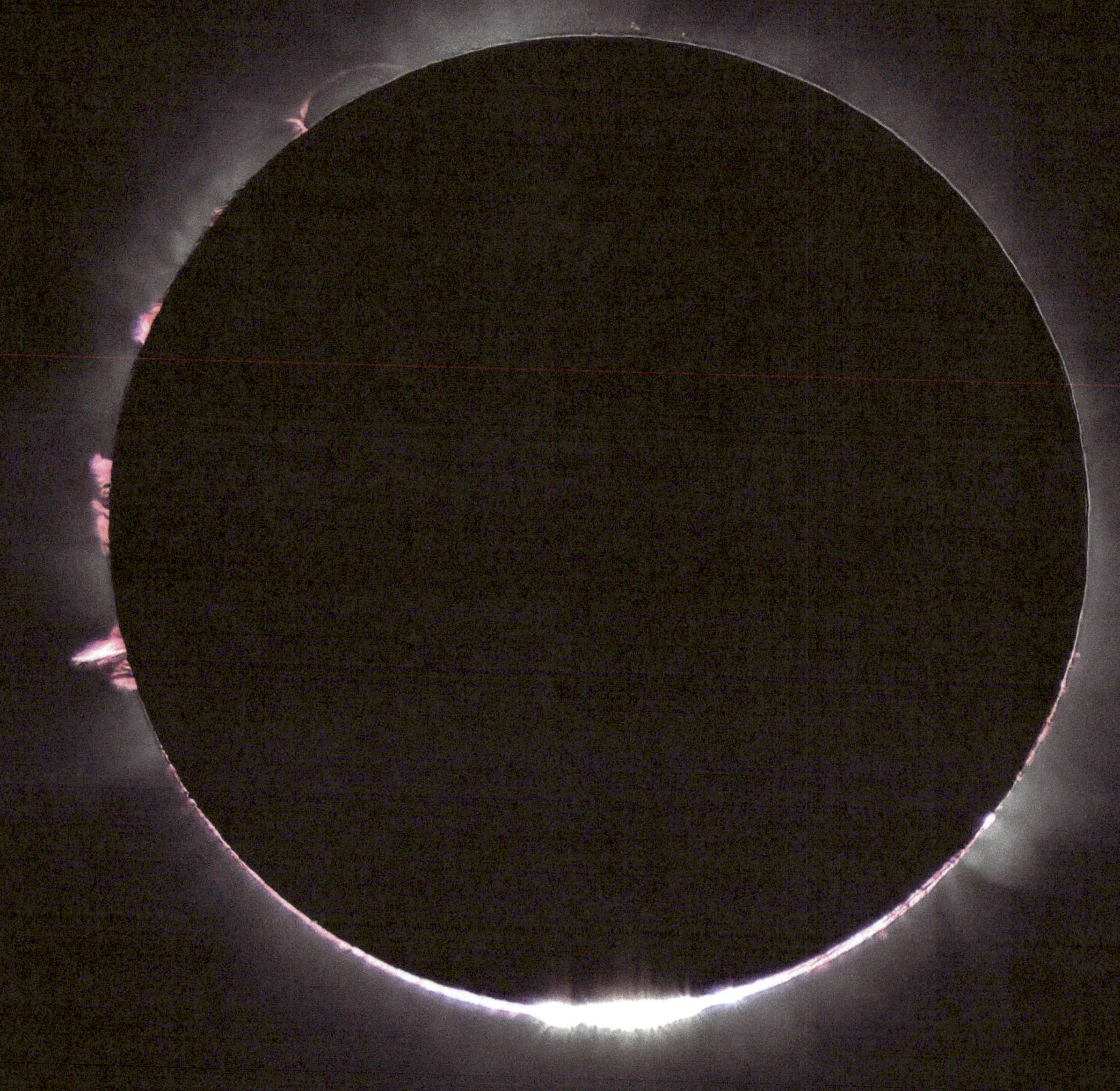

11:28:37

Second contact (C2) occurred after the above image of Baily's beads. At that point, the 58-second totality commenced revealing a spectacular corona made especially dramatic by the level of solar activity. I believes it is one of the most spectacular images he has ever seen and that it deserves its own page.

2023 Brittany's Flower

The corona on the previous page is our composite of the five shot bracket shown below.

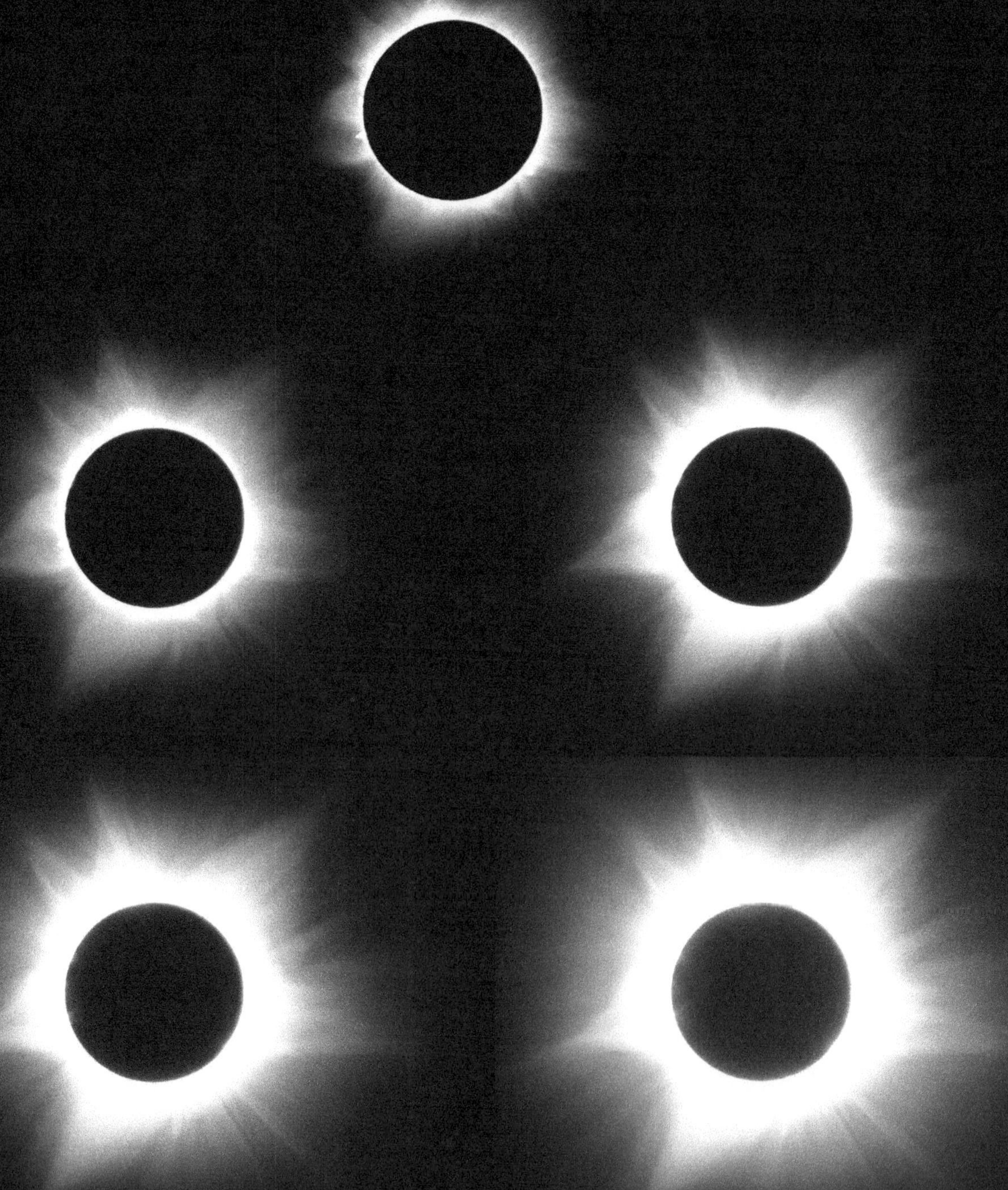

Like our Earth, the Sun has an atmosphere. The corona is the outermost part of the Sun's atmosphere and can only be observed (without specialized equipment) during total eclipses. Because the corona of each eclipse is unique, we like to have one camera dedicated to capturing this feature. In Australia, we believe we hit the jackpot with the preceding composite image of the corona.

As the preceding pictures have shown, totality was accented by the prominences of the chromosphere as well as solar flares.

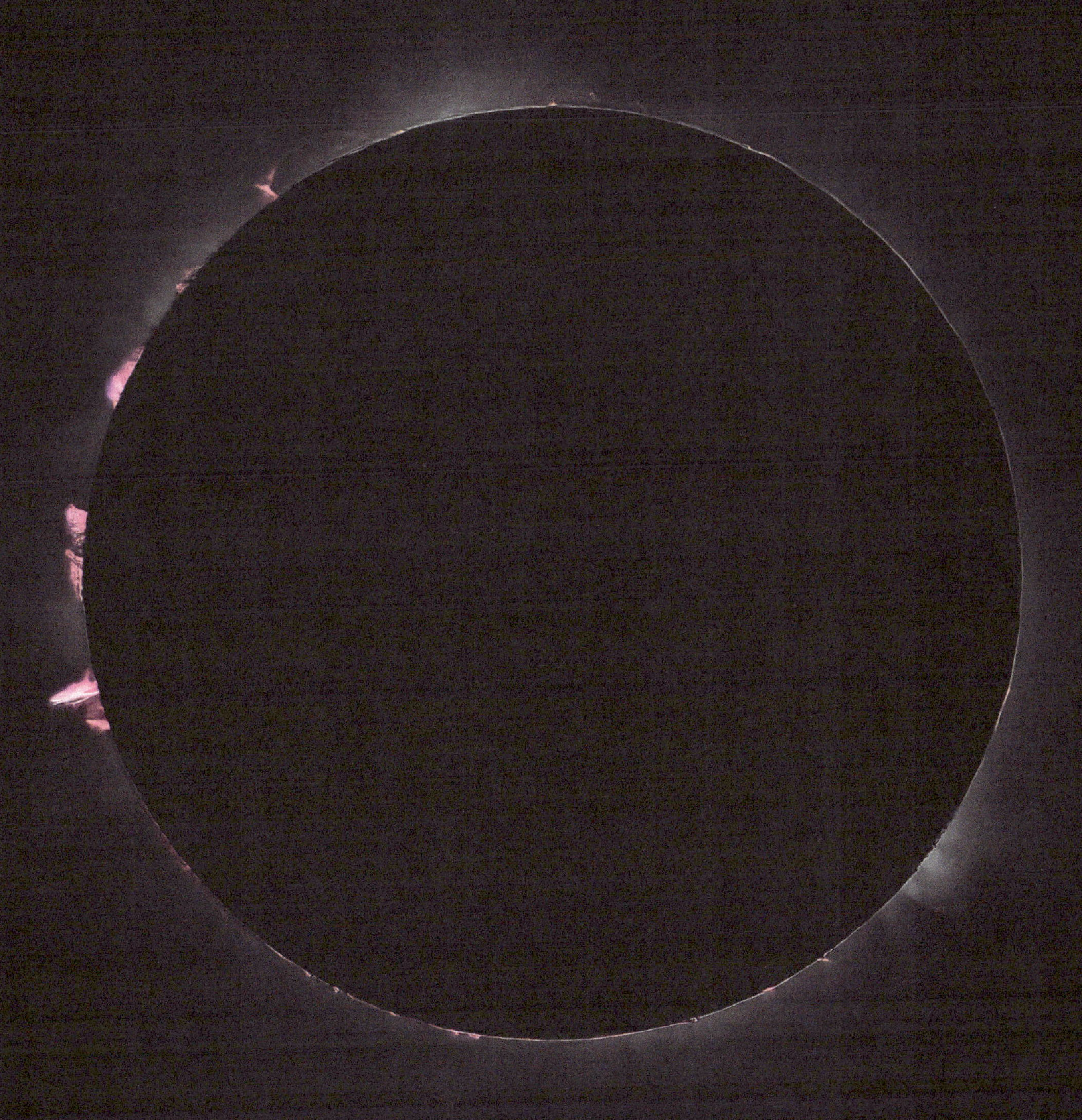

The image below shows the moments of totality and provides an excellent example of the striking color gradation of the sky during totality, from the bright sky at sea level to the royal blue above.

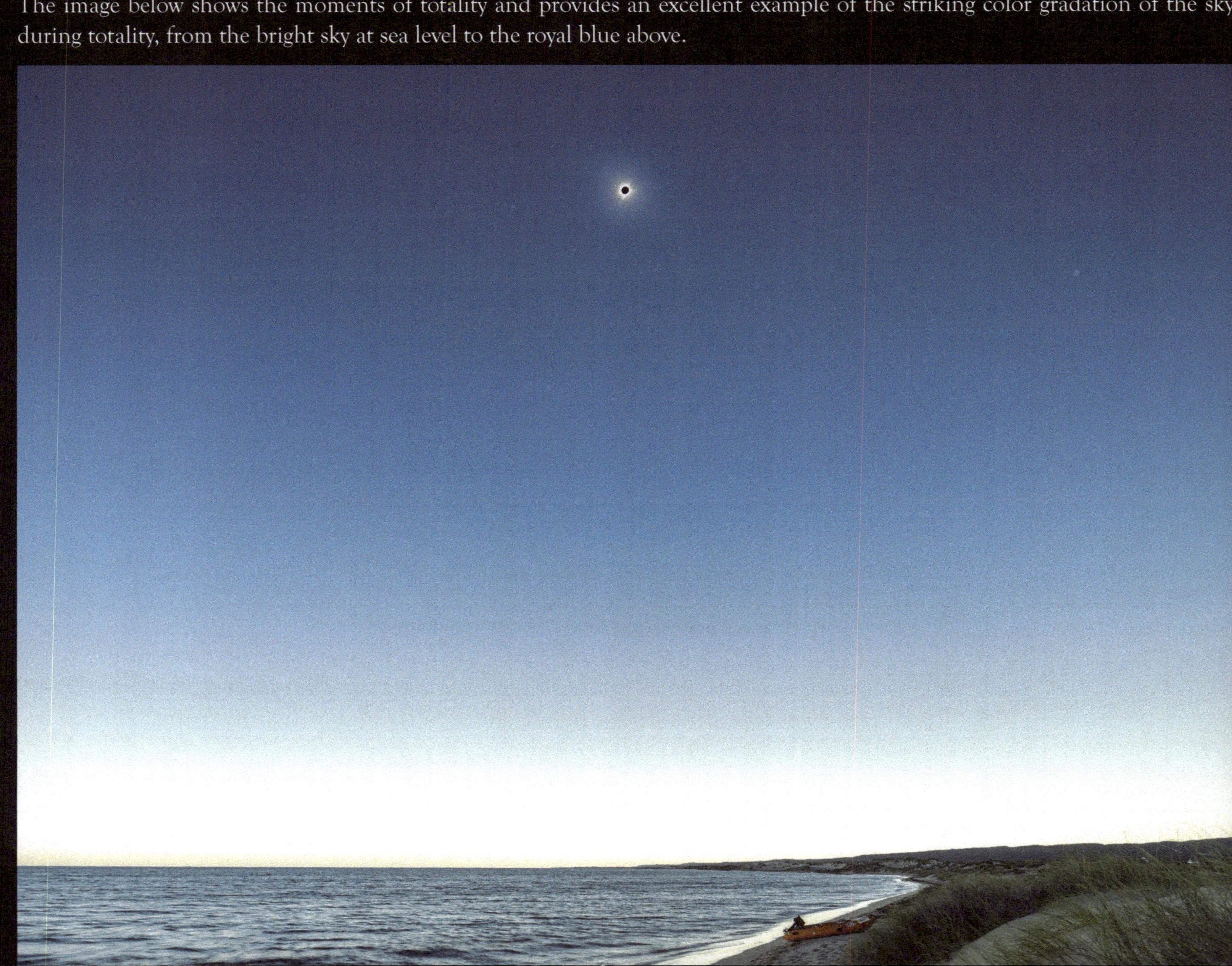

At third contact (C3), the Sun began to reappear on the reverse side of the Moon, first as Baily's beads and then as the diamond ring effect.

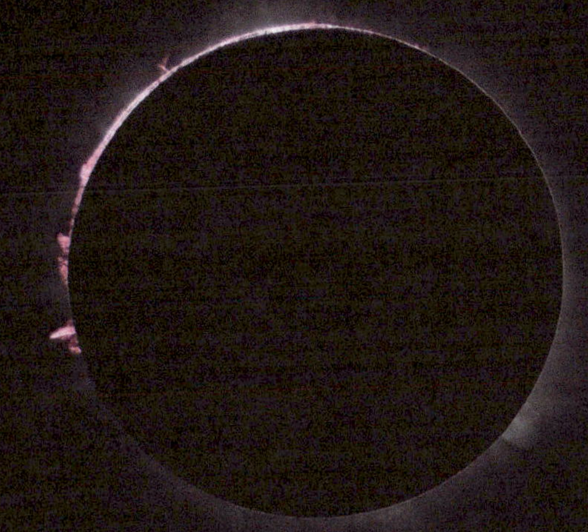

11:29:34

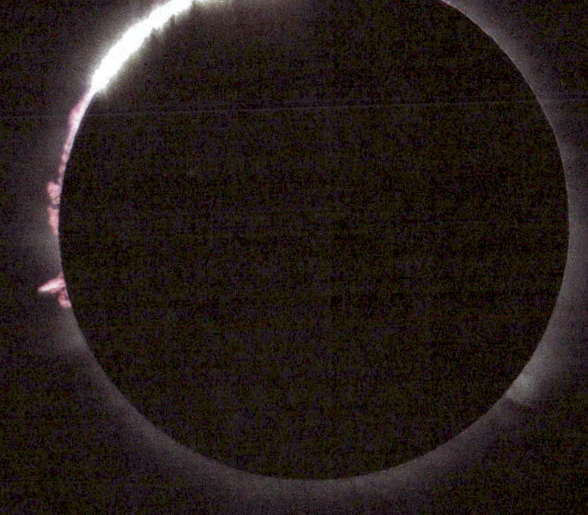

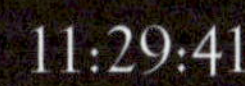

11:29:41

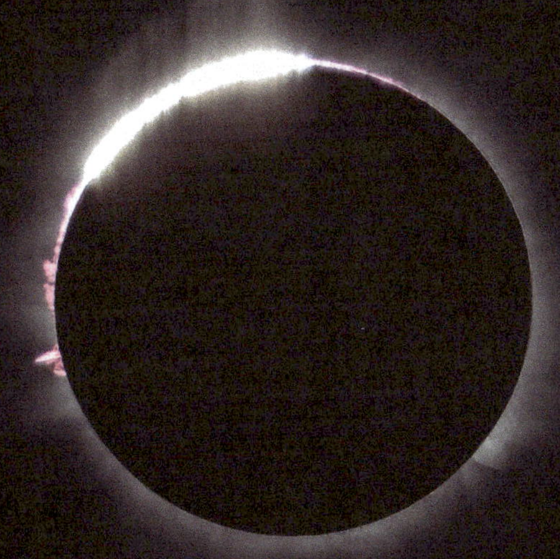

11:29:42

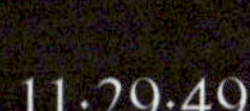

11:29:49

We replaced our solar filters on our cameras and resumed shooting our five-minute intervals of the second portion of the partial eclipse.

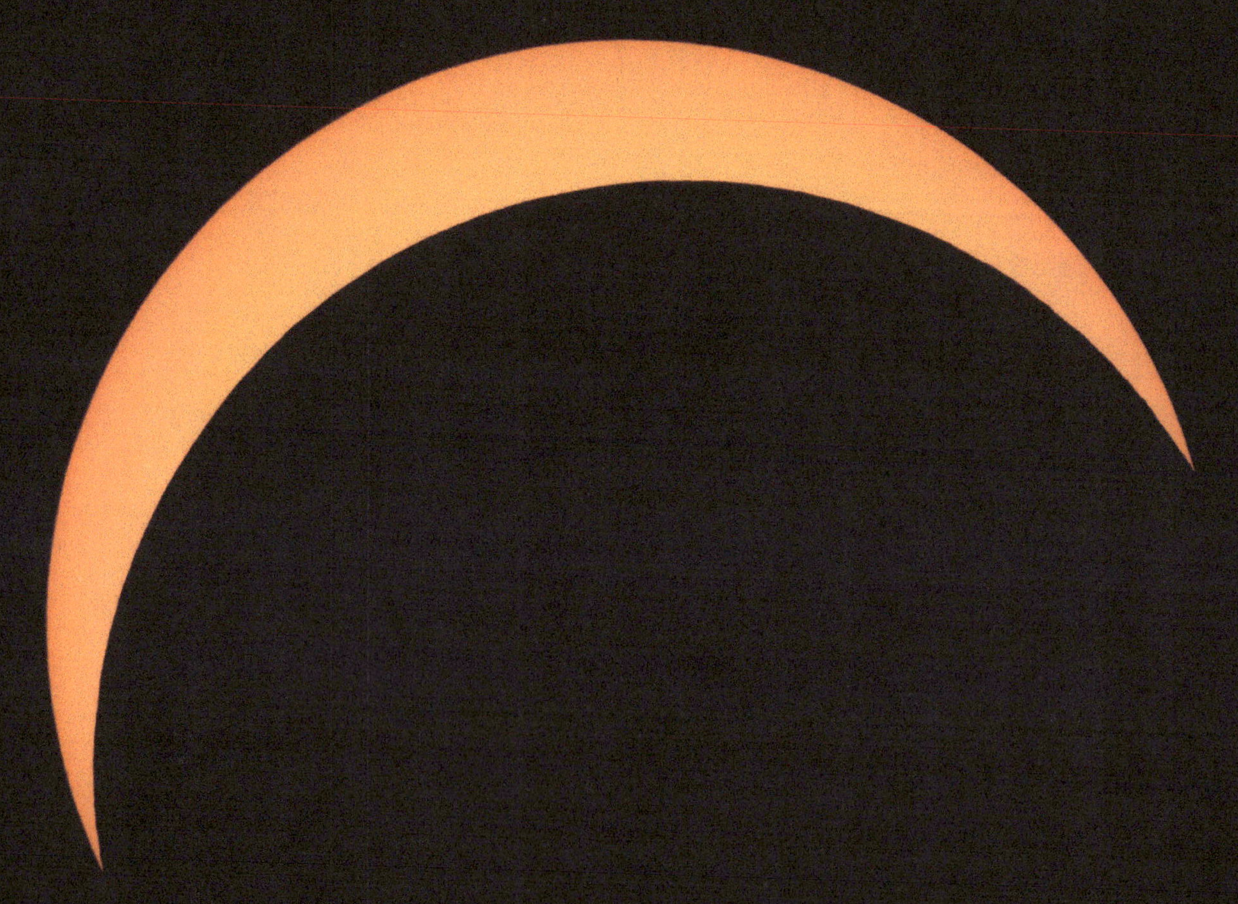

11:41:02

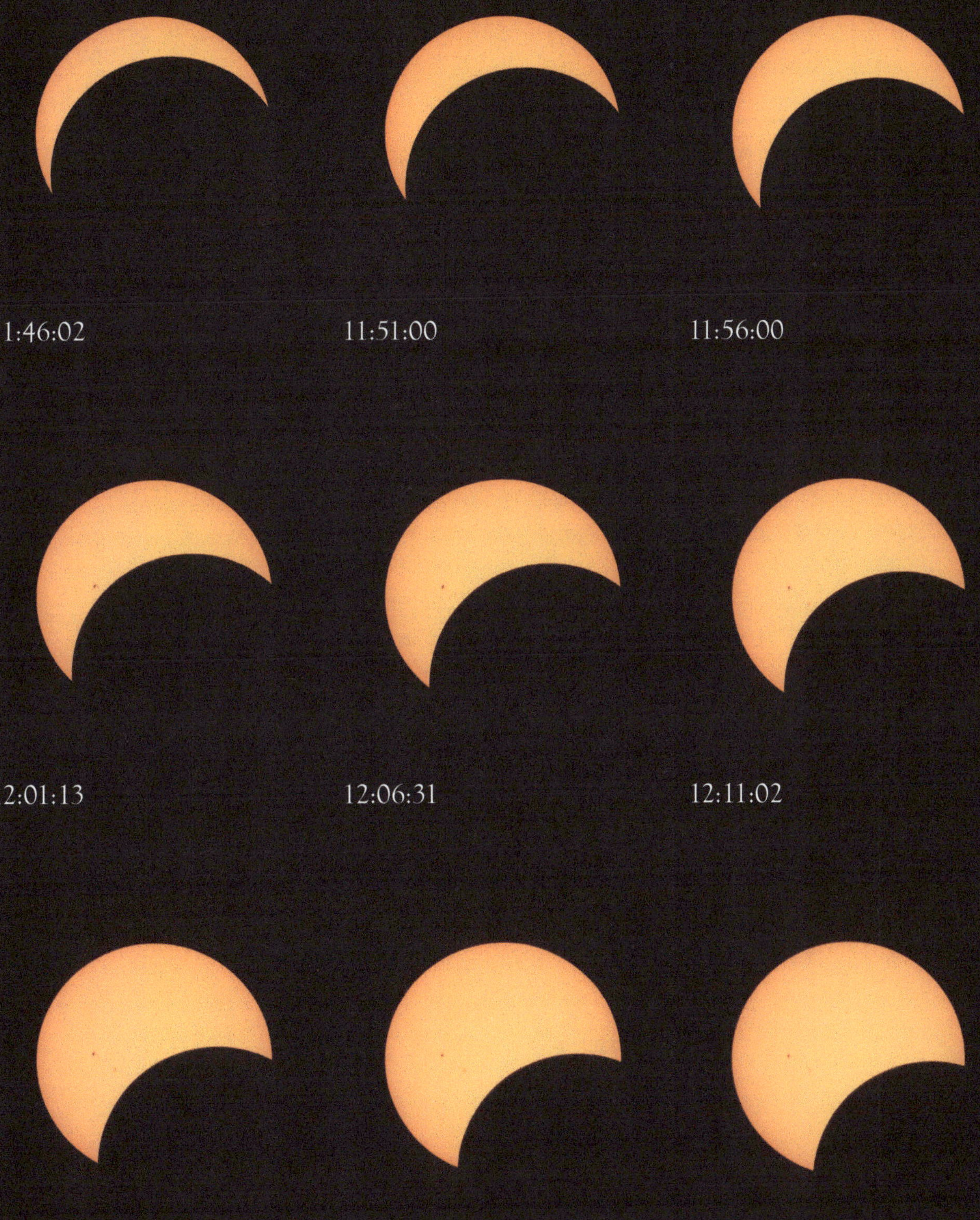

12:16:16 12:21:06 12:26:01

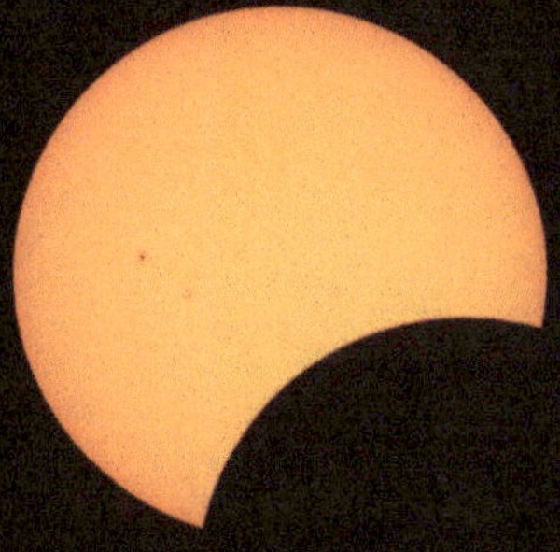

12:31:05 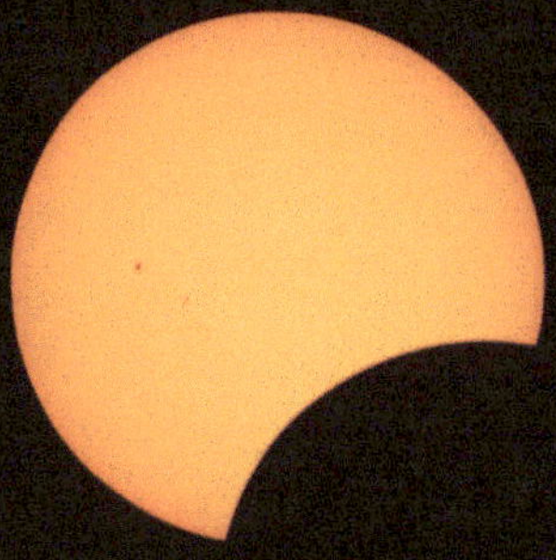 12:35:56 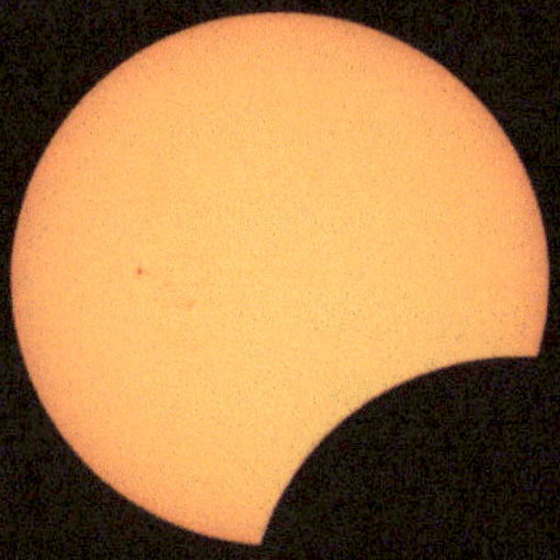 12:41:01

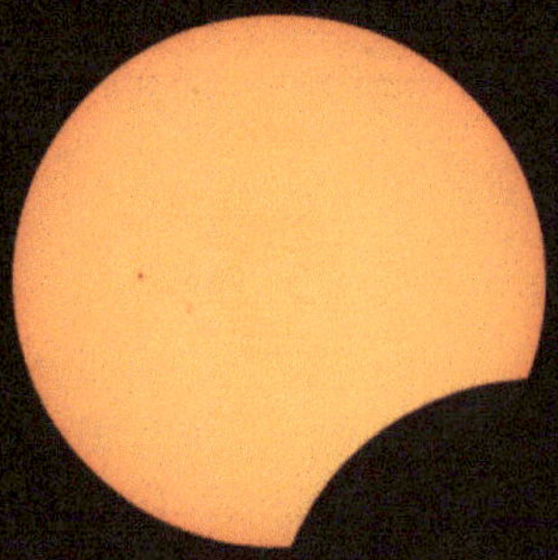

12:46:12 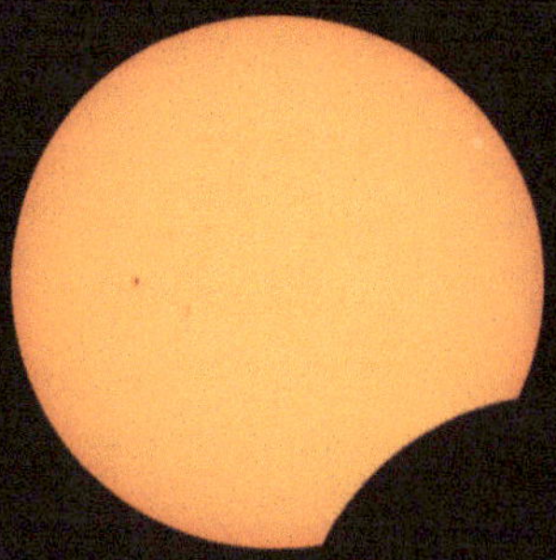 12:51:04 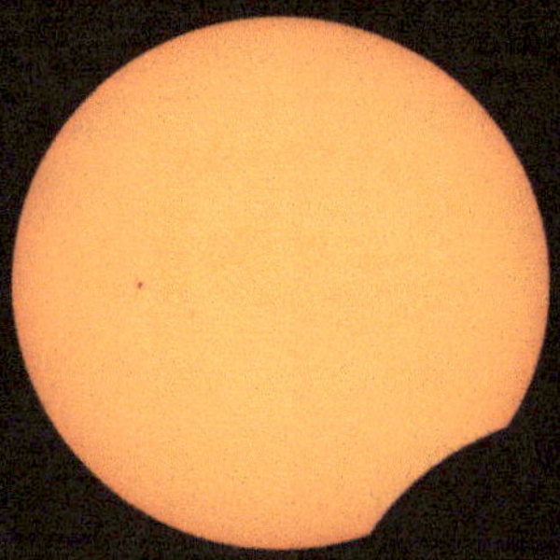 12:56:08

The eclipse ended with fourth contact (C4) at 1:01 p.m. with bright clear skies over the crystal blue waters of the Indian Ocean.

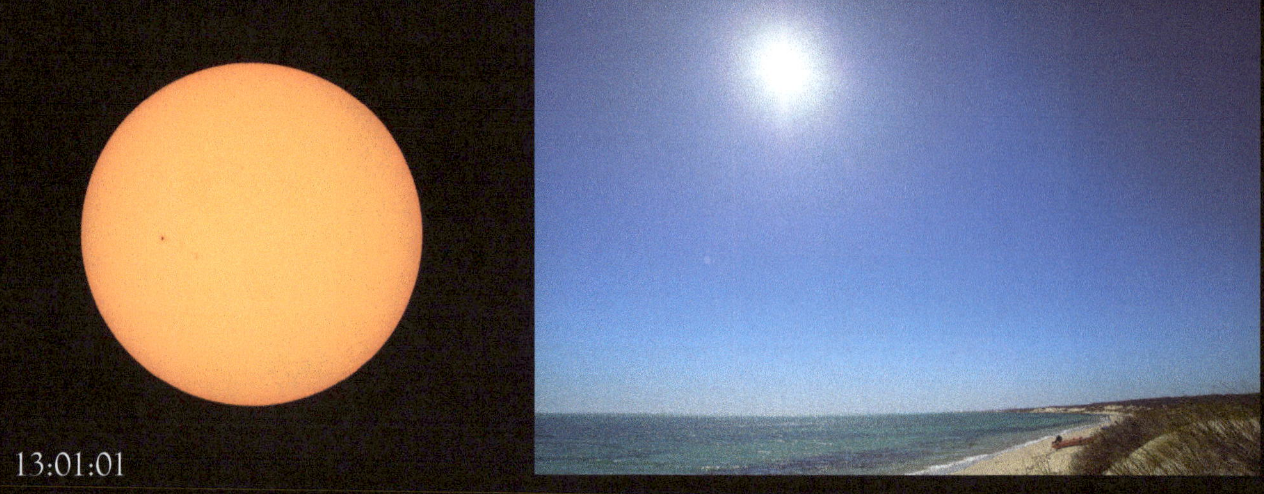

13:01:01

The following page features our time lapse composite of the 2023 Australian Hybrid Eclipse created with a Canon EOS 5DS R and Zeiss Distagon T* 15mm f/2.8 ZE lens.

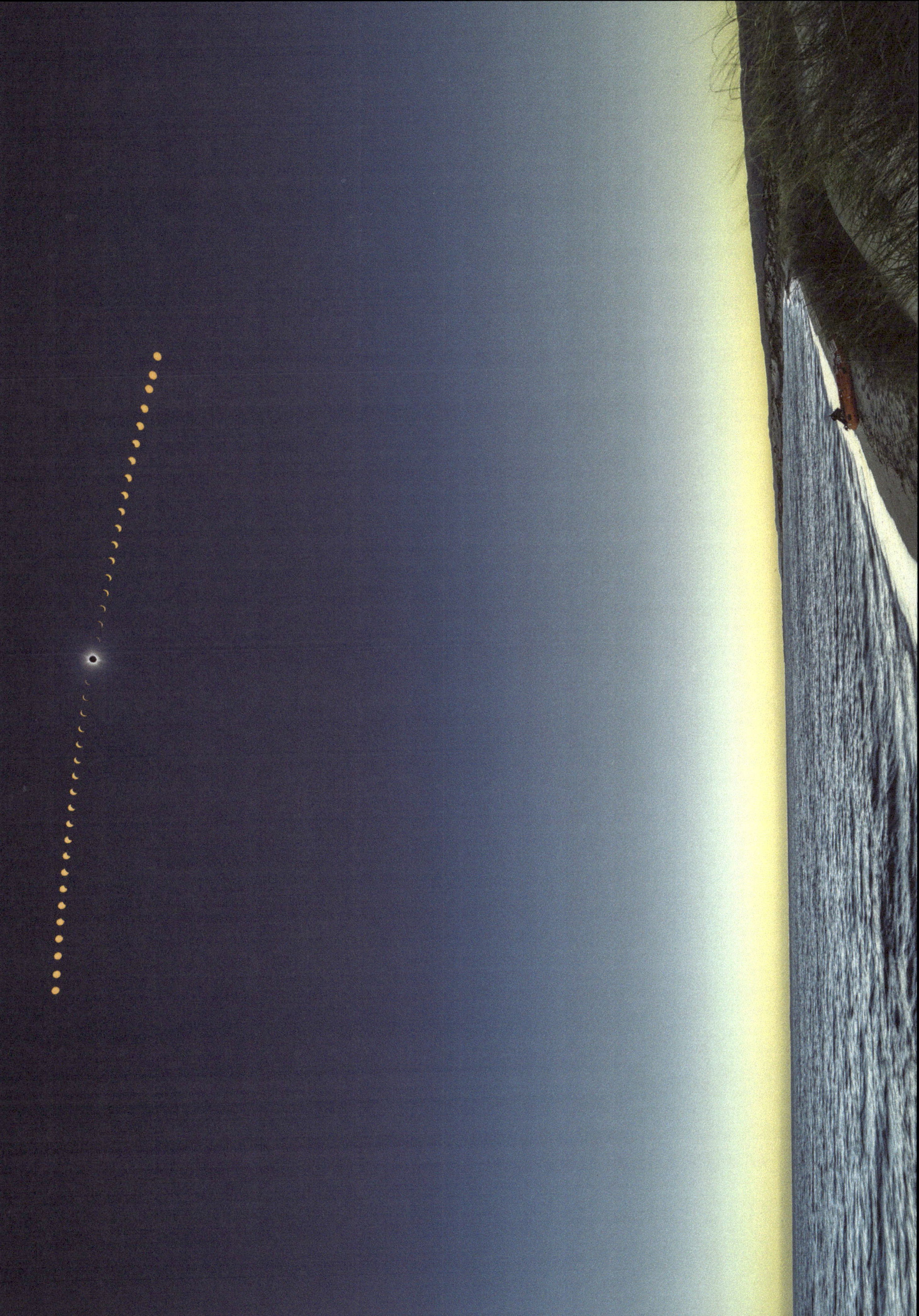

PART IV

2023 The U.S. New Mexico Annular Eclipse

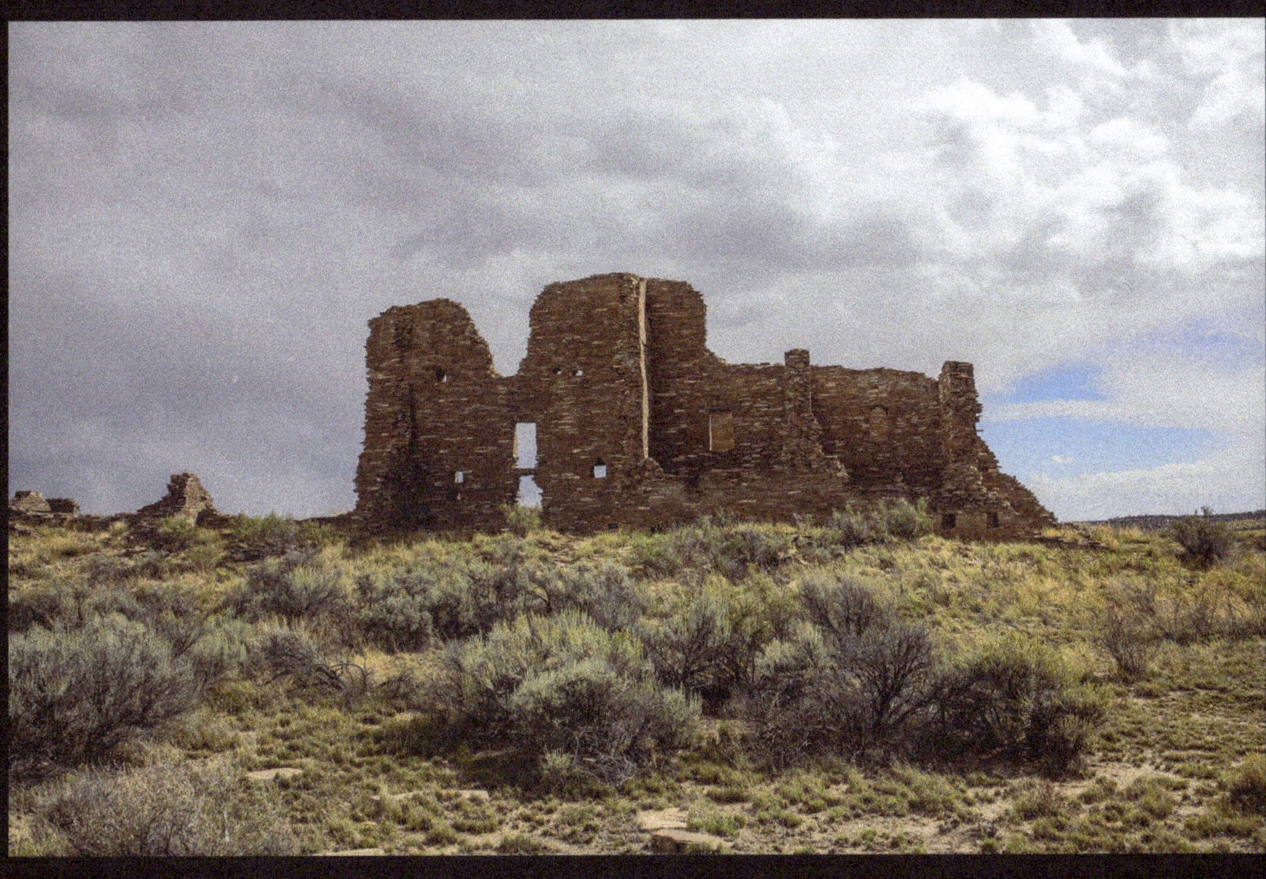

Great American Eclipse Shoot Site

Pueblo Pintado National Park.

Pueblo Pintado, New Mexico

October 14, 2023

We had the incredible opportunity to capture the 2023 Annular Eclipse in New Mexico at Pueblo Pintado, the ruins of an Ancestral Puebloan public building dating back to around 900 AD.

Located near the renowned Chaco Culture National Historical Park, this site holds significant historical and cultural importance. Chaco Culture, designated as both a national historical park and a UNESCO World Heritage Site, is often referred to as "The Center of an Ancient World" by the National Park Service. Visitors are encouraged to explore the monumental structures and stunning landscape of Chaco, which served as a thriving regional center for the ancestral Pueblo people from 850 to 1250 AD.

During our visit to Chaco, the Park Rangers informed us about the limited access to the park during the eclipse, allowing only around 150 cars. They recommended Pueblo Pintado National Park, a lesser-known gem spanning just one acre, where very few visitors get to

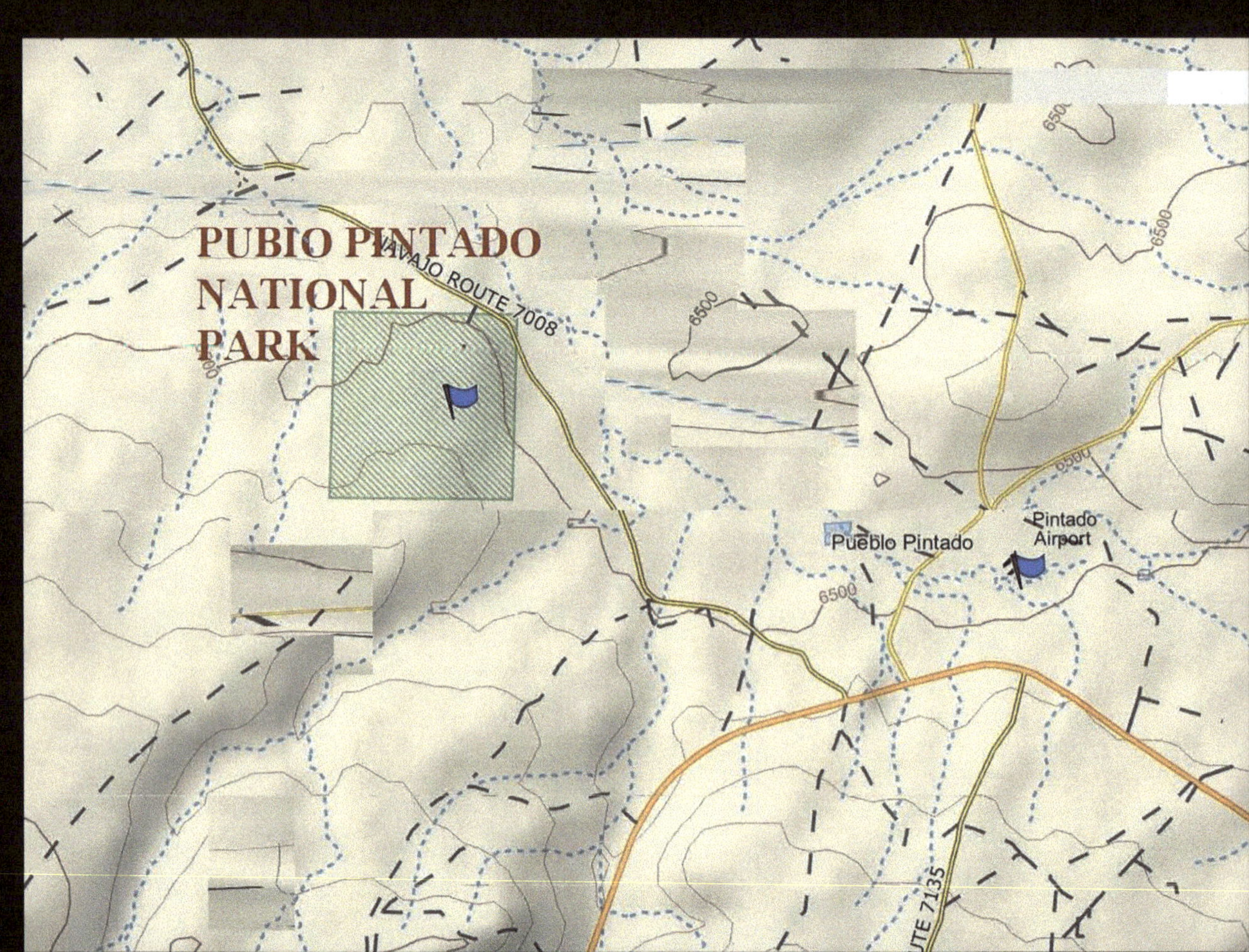

venture. We are grateful to the Rangers for their professionalism and valuable advice, as we were the sole photographers present at Pueblo Pintado for the duration of the eclipse.

The images captured during the Annular Eclipse offer a glimpse into this extraordinary celestial event. While a typical eclipse has a totality, an annular eclipse is unique as the moon is farther from Earth and closer to the sun, creating a mesmerizing "ring of fire" effect during totality. This fleeting moment lasts only a second, making it a challenge to capture. The collection includes images leading up to the ring of fire, the moment of totality, and the aftermath, as well as a wide-angle view of the eclipse in its entirety.

We look forward to sharing a more extensive selection of images in our upcoming book, showcasing the awe-inspiring beauty of the Annular Eclipse at Pueblo Pintado.

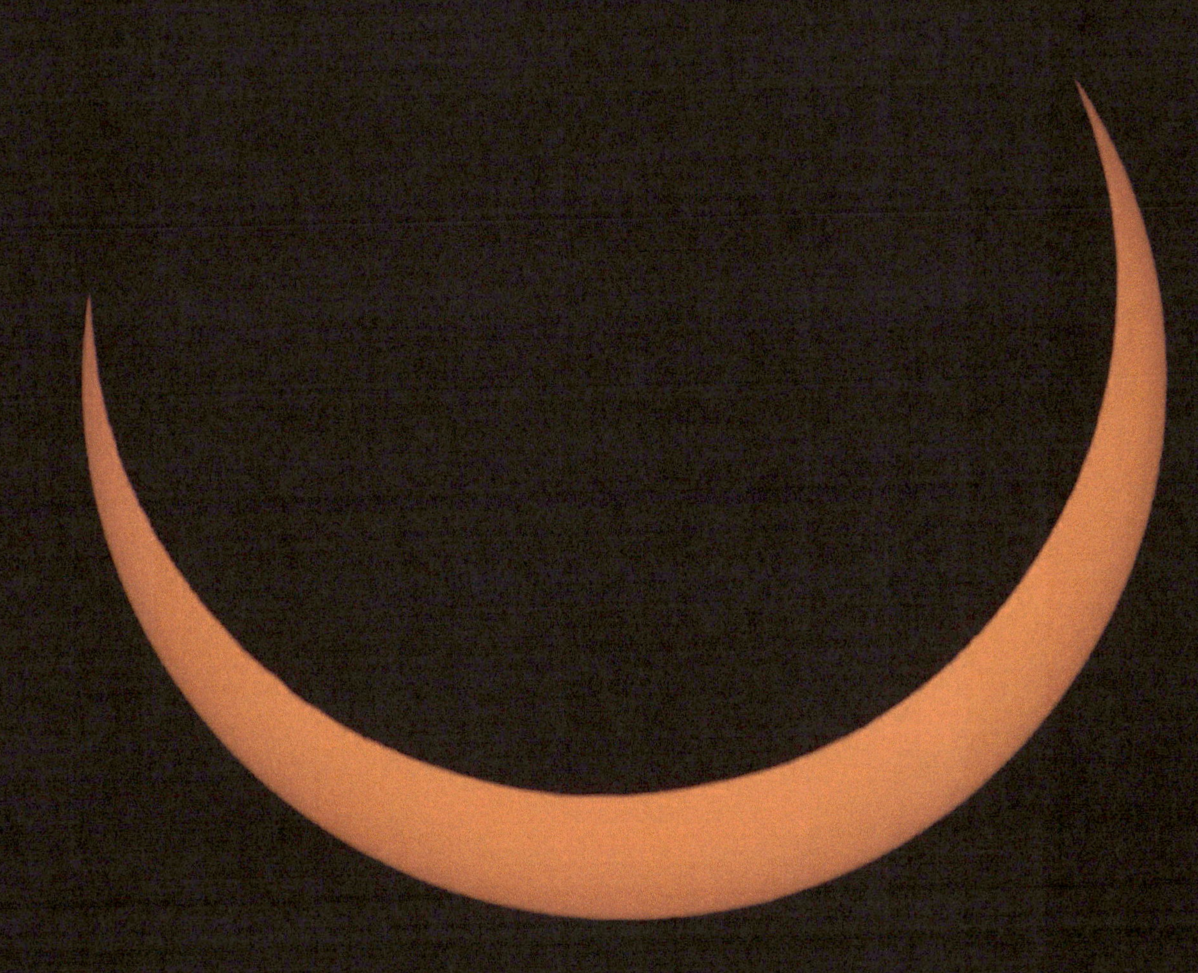

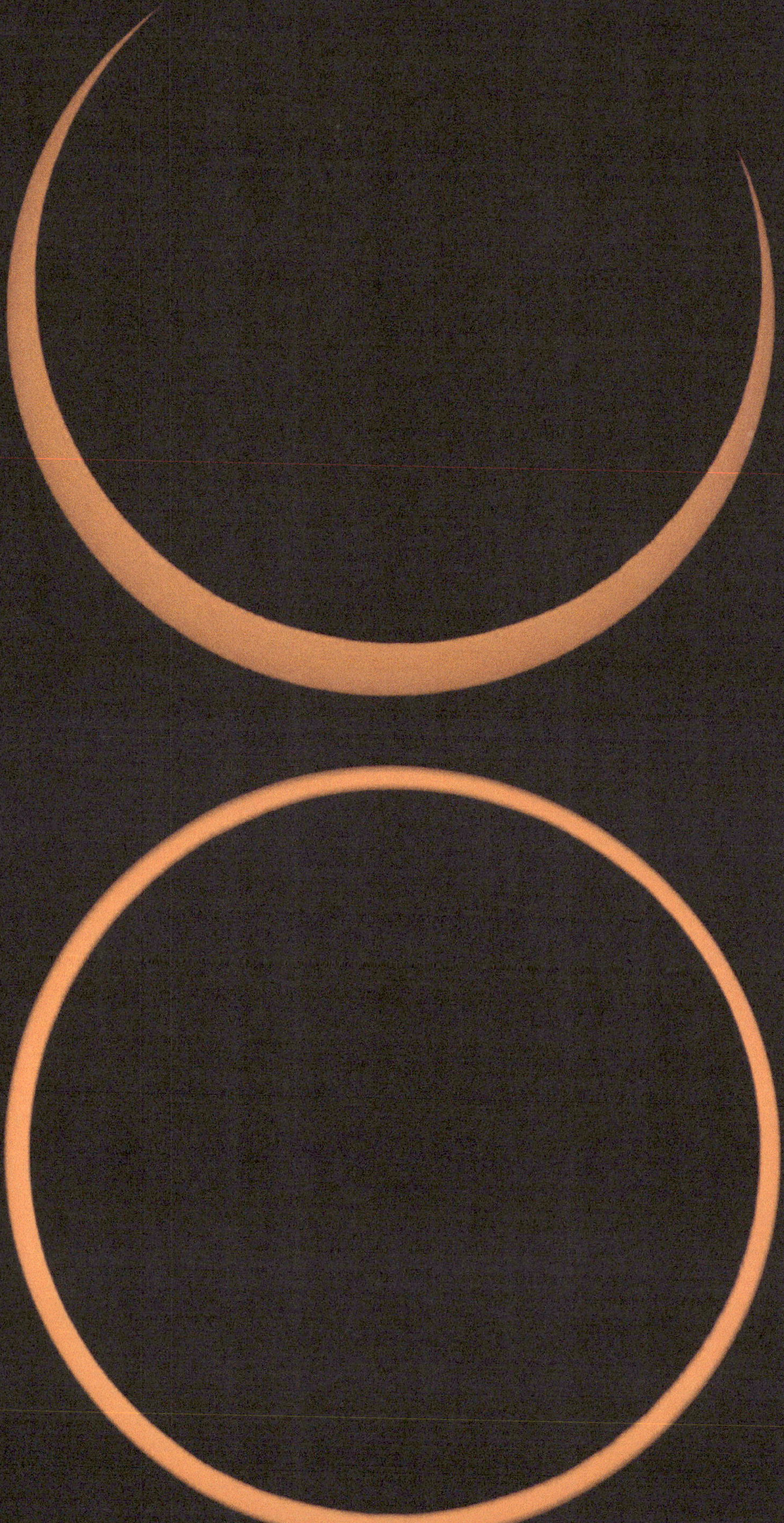

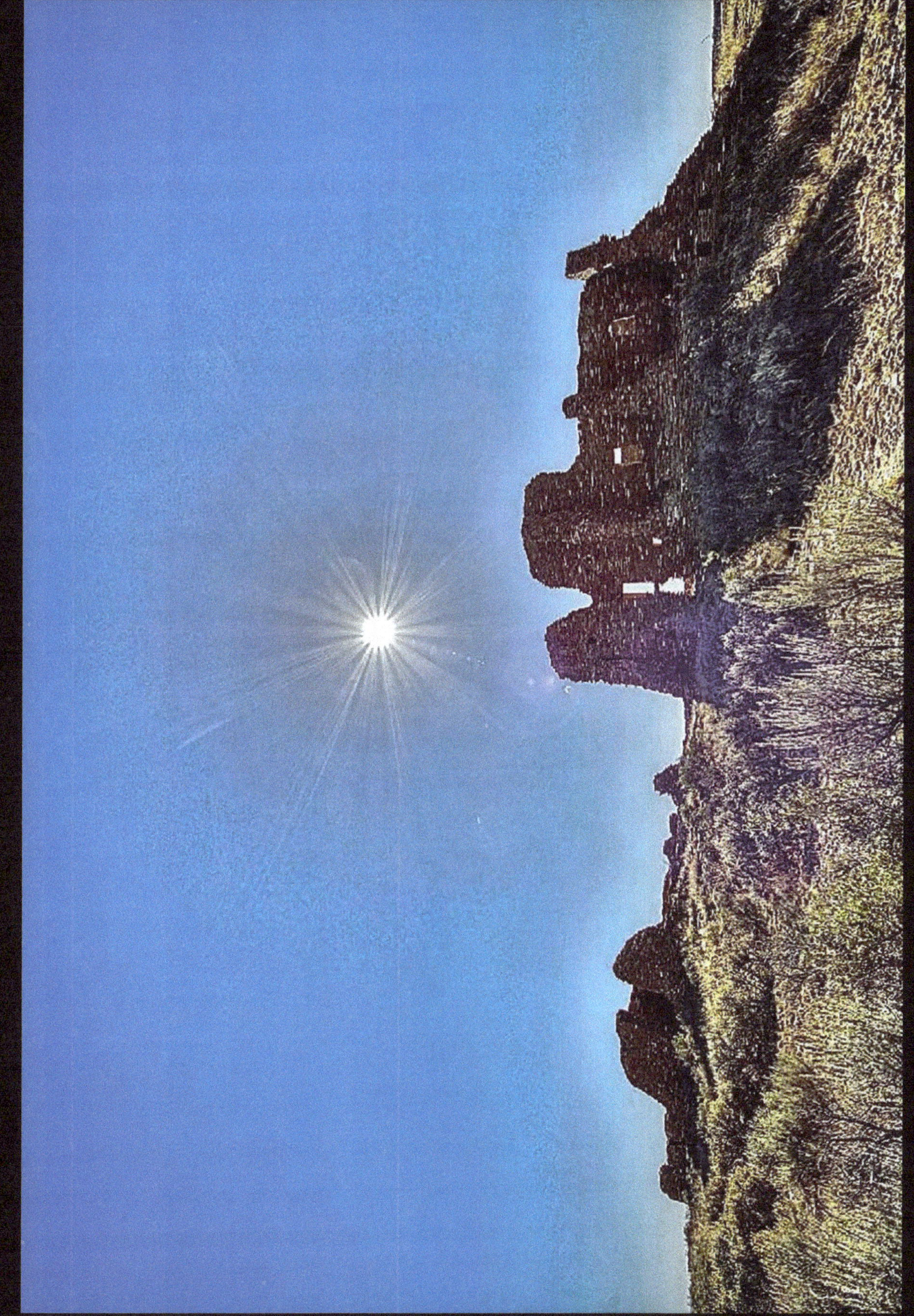

Totality of the 2023 U.S. New Mexico Annular Eclipse

Future Eclipses

DATE	Eclipse Type	Eclipse Magnitude	Central Duration	Geographic Area
2024 Oct 02	Annular	0.933	07m25s	Annular: S Chile, S Argentina
2026, Feb 17	Annular	0.9237	02m5s	S Argentina & Chile, S Africa, Antarctica
2026 Aug 12	Total	1.039	02m18s	Arctic, Greenland, Iceland, Spain
2027 Feb 06	Annular	0.928	07m51s	Annular: Chile, Argentina, Atlantic
2027 Aug 02	Total	1.079	06m23s	Morocco, Spain, Algeria, Libya, Egypt, Saudi Arabia, Yemen, Somalia
2028 Jan 26	Annular	0.921	10m27s	Annular: Ecuador, Peru, Brazil, Suriname, Spain, Portugal
2028 Jul 22	Total	1.056	05m10s	Total: Australia, N. Z.
2030 Jun 01	Annular	0.944	05m21s	Annular: Algeria, Tunisia, Greece, Turkey, Russia, N. China, Japan
2030 Nov 25	Total	1.047	03m44s	S Africa, S Indian Oc., E. Indies, Australia

PART V

Shooting an Eclipse

SAFETY

DO NOT SKIP THIS PART

- ***Shooting or looking at an eclipse (at any point other than totality during a total solar eclipse) can cause significant damage to your eyes and your cameras. It is critical that you use NASA-approved protection for your eyes and solar-grade filters for your cameras (except during totality). Annular eclipses, even at full annularity, must also be viewed with protective solar-specific eyewear. NASA published a section of its website on eclipse eye safety that outlined basic safety measures and approved eclipse eyewear manufacturers. Also, please review our "Filters and Safety" section at the end of this book. Here is the link to the NASA website: https://www.nasa.gov/content/eye-safety-during-a-total-solar-eclipse.***

PLANNING AN ECLIPSE SHOOT

There are two fundamental questions that you need to consider before planning to photograph an eclipse. Your answers will determine how to approach your shoot.

1. Do you want to include only close-up, detailed features of the eclipse in your pictures? For example, close-up pictures of the corona, Baily's beads, prominences, and totality.

   Or

2. Do you want to photograph the eclipse framed in the context of the landscape and other surroundings?

For the most part, these two questions will help determine your location and equipment choices. The answers will also help you to identify the specific lens and camera combination(s) you will need.

If you are going to take close-up pictures of just the eclipse without the surrounding landscape, you will be able to take your pictures anywhere along the path of totality. However, shooting an eclipse can still be a complex project due to issues like weather and sky conditions. Below are websites that provide climate data, such as rainfall and cloud cover averages, by time of year and geographic location. Research your location options along the path of totality pertinent to the time of the upcoming eclipse. You can also find websites specifically devoted to data collection and predictions for the regions in the path of future eclipses. As of today's writing, some sites we use and recommend are:

- weatherbase.com
- worldclimate.com
- eclipsophile.com
- timeanddate.com

In our shoot of the August 21, 2017 eclipse, we planned to photograph everything. We wanted to capture images of the corona, Baily's beads, the diamond rings, prominences, a time lapse of the entire eclipse process, and the landscape. As a result, we used nine cameras, six of which were equipped with solar filters, and a variety of lenses manned by six photographers. We recognize that we may have gone a little overboard, but we thought it was a once-in-a-lifetime opportunity.

As committed umbraphiles[1], we continue to build on our research and experience. For example, we went to Chile in 2019 and Australia 2023 for those total eclipses as well as New Mexico for the October 2023 annular eclipse. We have already started the planning process to shoot the eclipses in North America in April 2024, in Patagonia in October 2024, in Spain in 2026, and most importantly in Egypt 2027. Hopefully we will see you there!

SHOOTING AN ECLIPSE

It is imperative to understand that an eclipse is an event in motion. Eclipses occur because of the alignment of celestial bodies in motion and thus are not stationary events that occur at a constant coordinate in the sky. How it will appear to you, as the observer, is that the Sun will catch up to the Moon, slip behind it, reemerge, and continue its way.

[1]A person who chases eclipses is known as a umbraphile. One who loves eclipses, often traveling to see them.

CHART 1

Geometric Mechanics of an Eclipse

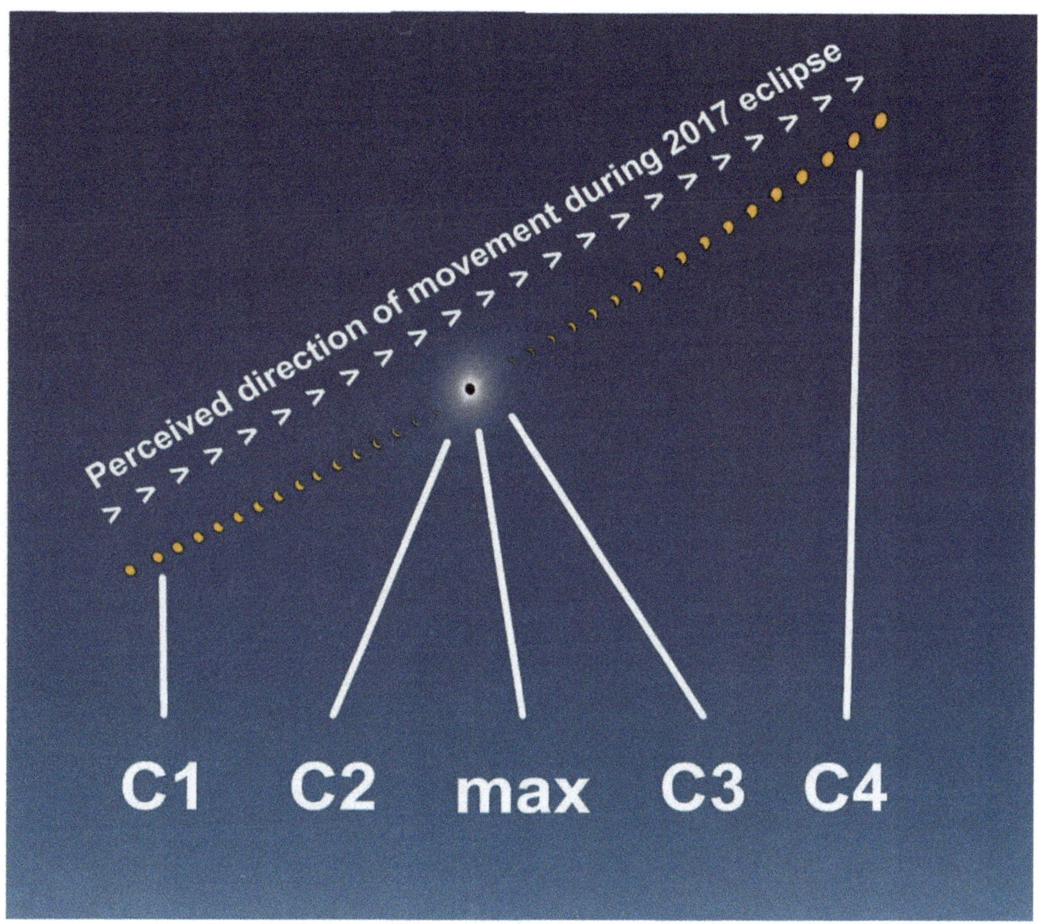

Because of the earth's rotation, the Sun will move both vertically and horizontally in the sky throughout the eclipse event, as it does any other day, from east to west. (The technical term for this is diurnal motion.) Whether that is left to right or right to left is dependent on the hemisphere from which it is viewed. The angle of the Sun above the horizon is called the altitude (ALT), and the position of the Sun relative to geographical north is called the azimuth (AZI). Both are measured in degrees and vary by time of day and the geographical location of the observer. The duration of totality will also vary by geographical location. Note that the closer you are to the center line of totality, the longer the duration of totality will be. You will need all this information for your planning process.

INITIAL CONSIDERATIONS

The following chart shows the horizontal field of view in degrees of two objects that are in space. According to **Chart 2**, the maximum horizontal field of view for you will need for your lens will probably be no more than approximately 0.52 degrees if you are just shooting a close-up of the eclipse itself.

CHART 2 Field of View of the Moon and the Sun

Astronomical Body	Approximate Average Distance in Miles	Horizontal Field of View in Degrees
Moon (Radius)	1,059 Miles	0.265°
Moon (Diameter)	2,159 Miles	0.517°
Moon (Distance)	239,900 Miles	
Sun (Radius)	432,288 Miles	0.266°
Sun (Diameter)	856,575 Miles	0.572°
Sun (Distance)	92,960,00 Miles	

There are a couple of websites that will provide you with the time, altitude, and azimuth for each of the following events for any location you select on the interactive map:

1. Start of the partial eclipse (C1 or First Contact)
2. Start of the total eclipse (C2 or Second Contact)
3. Maximum Totality
4. End of the total eclipse (C3 or Third Contact
5. End of the partial eclipse (C4 or Fourth Contact)

The websites we are using as of the time of writing this book are:

- https://www.timeanddate.com/eclipse/
- https://nso.edu/for-public/eclipse-science/

We previously used NASA's interactive eclipse maps, but they are unfortunately no longer available.

Chart 3 below shows the type of information that appears when you drop a marker at any point on the interactive maps along the path of totality.

CHART 3

Lat.: 43.4589° N:
Long. 110.7317° W

Total Solar Eclipse
Duration of Totality: 2m13.9s
Magnitude: 1.01
Obscuration: 100.00%

Clear Marker

Event.	Date.	Time (UT).	Alt	Azi
Start of partial eclipse (C1):	2017/08/21	16:16:45.7	38.6°	113.1°
Start of total eclipse (C2):	2017/08/21	17:35:00.0	50.4°	134.4°
Maximum eclipse:	2017/08/21	17:36:06.8	50.5°	134.8°
End of total eclipse (C3):	2017/08/21	17:37:13.8	50.7°	135.2°
End of partial eclipse (C4)	**2017/08/21**	**19:00:34.3**	**57.9°**	**168.3°**

Knowing how wide and how tall a picture your camera and specific lens will capture is critical to the eclipse photography planning process, especially if your goal is to create a time-lapse image of the entire eclipse from First to Fourth contact.

Chart 4 shows positions of the Sun (orange) relative to the Moon (blue) during the various phases of the eclipse, as well as images that you may be able to capture. Again, the websites listed above provide the total range of movement and trajectory of the Sun during the eclipse. Understanding what will and will not fit into your frame is crucial in the eclipse photograph planning process. (Note that the size of the Moon relative to the Sun is exaggerated for the purposes of this illustration.)

CHART 4

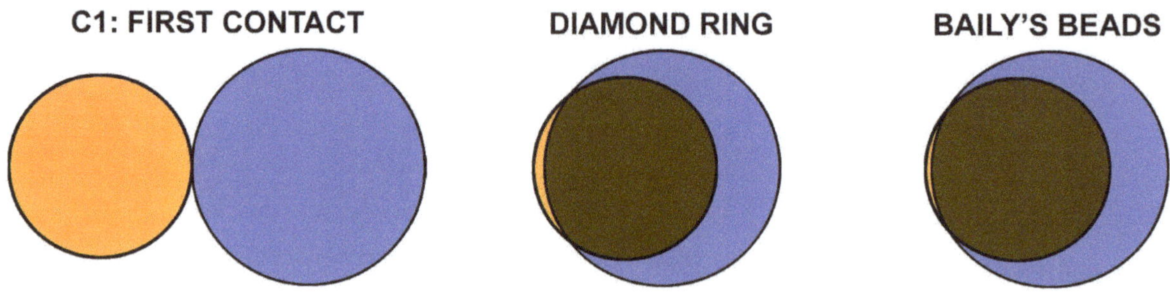

TOTALITY

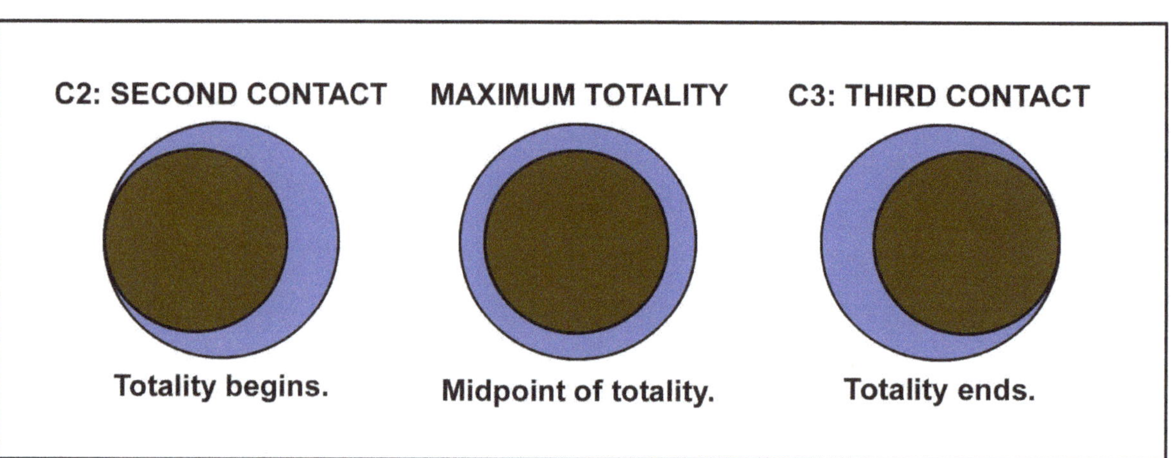

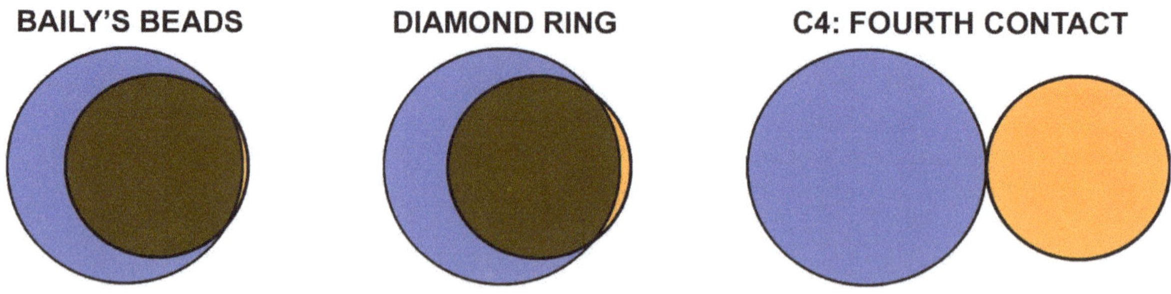

Sun shown in orange. Moon shown in blue. Relative size exaggerated for illustrative purposes.

CLOSE-UP SHOTS OF THE ECLIPSE WITHOUT ANY FOREGROUND

For the 2017 eclipse photographs that were shot without any foreground, we used a 500mm lens with a 2x extender (effectively 1000mm) and a 70-200mm lens with a 2x extender (effectively 140–400mm). This included our close-up shots of the partial eclipse phases, diamond rings, Baily's beads, and features of totality (corona, chromosphere, prominences, etc.).

As **Chart 3** shows (repeated from page 3), the August 21, 2017, eclipse had a vertical span of 19.4° and a horizontal span of 55°. As a result, we needed a lens with a field of view of no less than 19.4° by 55° just to account for the Sun's movement across the sky during the almost three hours from C1 to C4. To capture the foreground we wanted, we also needed to take the maximum altitude of the eclipse relative to the horizon into consideration (57.9°).

Chart 5 (located on the next page) depicts the horizontal movement (horizontal span) of the eclipse, the vertical movement (vertical span) of the eclipse, and the foreground we included in our time-lapse composite image of the eclipse. We also included the uneclipsed Sun five minutes before C1 and five minutes after C4 in the final composite illustrated in Chart 5.

When choosing your lens for a time-lapse progression, always give yourself some wiggle room and extra background instead of a tight frame.

CHART 5

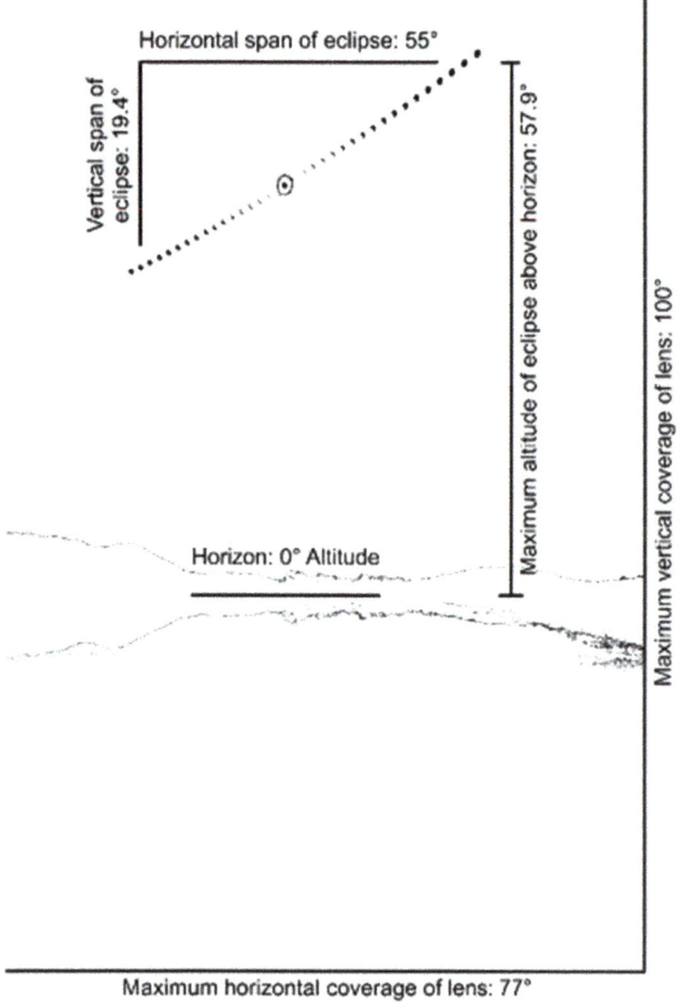

CHART 3

(Repeated from page 85)

Lat.: 43.4589° N
Long.: 110.7317° W

Clear Marker

Total Solar Eclipse
Duration of Totality: 2m13.9s
Magnitude: 1.01
Obscuration: 100.00%

Altitude Azimuth

Event	Date	Time (UT)	Alt	Azi
Start of partial eclipse (C1) :	2017/08/21	16:16:45.7	38.6°	113.1°
Start of total eclipse (C2) :	2017/08/21	17:35:00.0	50.4°	134.4°
Maximum eclipse :	2017/08/21	17:36:06.8	50.5°	134.8°
End of total eclipse (C3) :	2017/08/21	17:37:13.8	50.7°	135.2°
End of partial eclipse (C4) :	2017/08/21	19:00:34.3	57.9°	168.3°

The first image on the next page shows the lines representing the azimuths for C1 (the start of the partial eclipse), maximum totality, and C4 (the end of the partial eclipse). The images below the map reflect the pictures you can obtain at each of these instances.

IMAGES 1-4

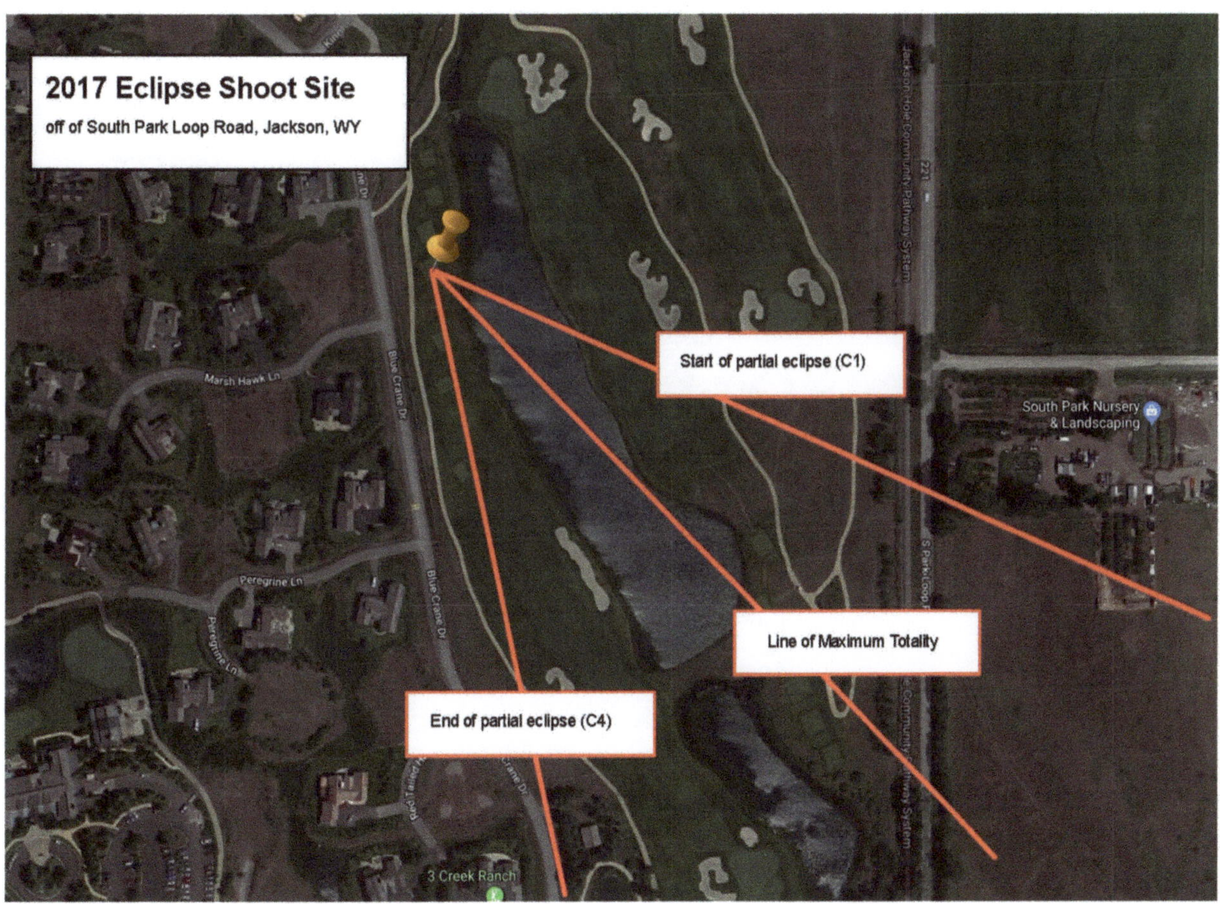

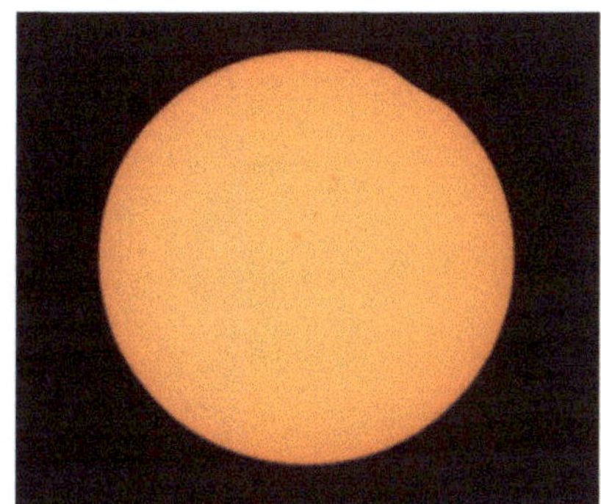
C1: Start of Partial Eclipse

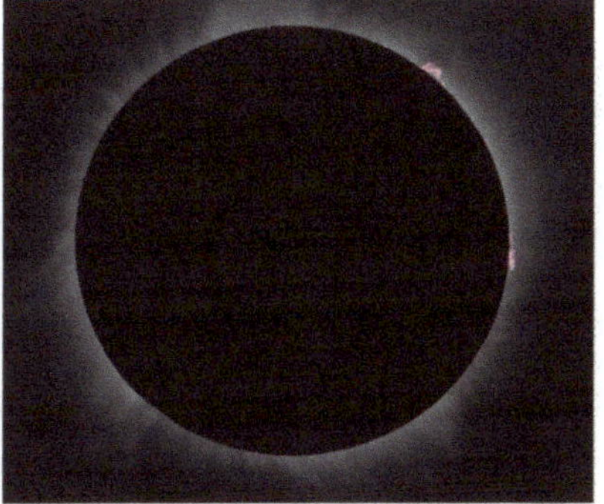
Maximum Totality

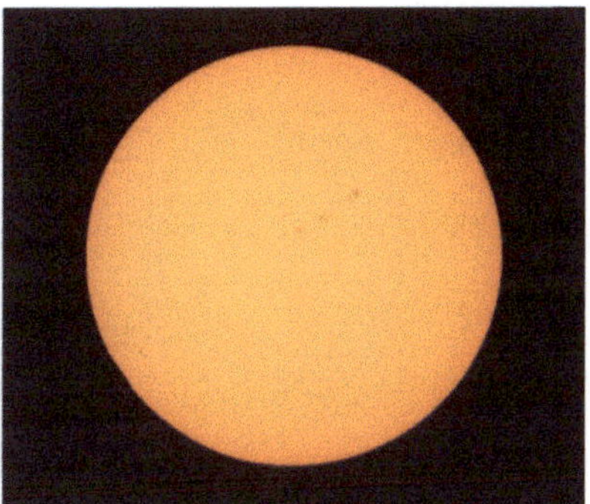
C4: End of Partial Eclipse

Chart 6 below shows, in degrees, the field of view of several common lenses. These are based on effective focal lengths specifically full-frame 35mm cameras. The information in this chart does not apply to cropped sensors.

CHART 6[2] FIELD OF VIEW IN DEGREES FULL FRAME 35MM CAMERA

Effective Focal Length	Long Edge in Degrees	Short Edge in Degrees	Diagonal in Degrees
8mm Fisheye	180°	180°	180°
15mm Fisheye	142°	94°	180°
10mm	121°	99°	129°
11mm	116°	93°	125°
12mm	111°	88°	121°
14mm	104°	81°	114°
15mm	100°	77°	111°
16mm	97°	74°	107°
17mm	93°	70°	103°
20mm	84°	62°	94°
24mm	74°	53°	84°
28mm	65°	46°	75°
35mm	54°	38°	63°
50mm	40°	27°	47°
70mm	29°	19°	34°
85mm	24°	16°	28°
100mm	20°	14°	24°
105mm	20°	13°	23°
135mm	15°	10°	18°
200mm	10.3°	6.9°	12.3°
300mm	6.9°	4.6°	8.2°
400mm	5.2°	3.4°	6.2°
500mm	4.1°	2.7°	4.9°
600mm	3.4°	2.3°	4.1°
800mm	2.6°	1.7°	3.1°
1000mm	2.1°	1.4°	
1200mm	1.88°	1.26°	2.05°
2000mm	1.0°	0.7°	

[2]Please note that EPS lenses are designed for crop-frame sensors and do not require that the crop factor described below be taken into consideration.

CROP SENSORS

Once you know the field of view for the image you plan to shoot, you need to determine how your camera's crop factor will impact the actual field that your camera will achieve[3]. Please remember that a crop sensor has the effect of reducing the field of view of a lens. Therefore, you will always need a wider lens when you are using a crop sensor versus a full frame sensor.

Assume that after deciding your picture site you need a field of view of approximately 100° by 77° degrees[4]. According to **Chart 6**, if you were using a full frame sensor you would use a 15mm lens. If you have a crop sensor, you need to determine which lens will provide you that field of view.

Next, you will need to determine which full-frame lens will provide the field of view you want. Here are the steps:

1. Determine the effective focal length you need for your picture. In our example that is approximately 100° by 77° degrees.
2. Determine which lens provides you that field of view on a full frame sensor. In our example, that is 15mm lens. See highlighted section of **Chart 6**.
3. You then need to know your camera's sensor's cropping factor. In our example below, the camera has an APS-H sensor with a crop factor of 1.3 using a standard lens.
4. Compute the effective field of view of the lens with your camera's cropping factor. (Full-frame cameras do not have a cropping factor.)

The formula is:

Lens that Achieves the Necessary FOV on a Full Frame Sensor in mm		Crop Factor		Needed Lens Focal Length in mm
15	÷	1.3	=	11.5

[3]Points of View has an angle of view and a depth of field calculator that you might find useful. You can find it at: https://www.pointsinfocus.com/tools/depth-of-field-and-equivalent-lens-calculator/#{%22c%22: [{%22f%22:13,%22av%22:%228%22,%22fl%22:50,%22d%22:3048,%22cm%22:%220%22}],%22m%22:0}

[4]See **Chart 5** for a visual example of the proposed shot.

As a result of this analysis the lens you need is a standard 10mm or 11mm lens to achieve the necessary field of view that is equivalent to the field of view of a 15mm lens on a full-frame camera.

It is critical that you check with your camera and lens manufacturer to determine *if* the field of view for your lens and camera combination varies from **Chart 6**. When you compare the field of view of your camera and lens configuration with the trajectory of the eclipse at your shooting location, you will be able to select the best combination for your needs.

PLANNING AN ECLIPSE SHOOT WITH A FOREGROUND

If you want to capture foreground in an eclipse picture, then there is a lot more work involved in planning than one might first think. Fortunately, while the analysis involves several steps, the process is simple. To plan the shoot, use the following steps:

1. **Identify the Eclipse's Path.** Currently, the best way to identify the eclipse path is by using The National Solar Observatory's website, https://nso.edu/maps/eclipse. Time and Date also has a good mapping program. From there, you can select the upcoming eclipse you would like to research. For example, Time and Date's website map for the April 8, 2024, eclipse over North America, can be found at:

   https://www.timeanddate.com/eclipse/solar/2024-april-8
   https://www.timeanddate.com/eclipse/map/2024-april-8

The National Solar Observatory's map of the entire eclipse path and all the information you will need will be on the same page, and can be found at: https://nso.edu/for-public/eclipse-map-2024/.

With Date and Time's map you must look at different pages to get all the information. First you will need to select "Detailed eclipse path map" and then drop a pin on the interactive map. Information such as the following from the October 2023 annular eclipse will be displayed:

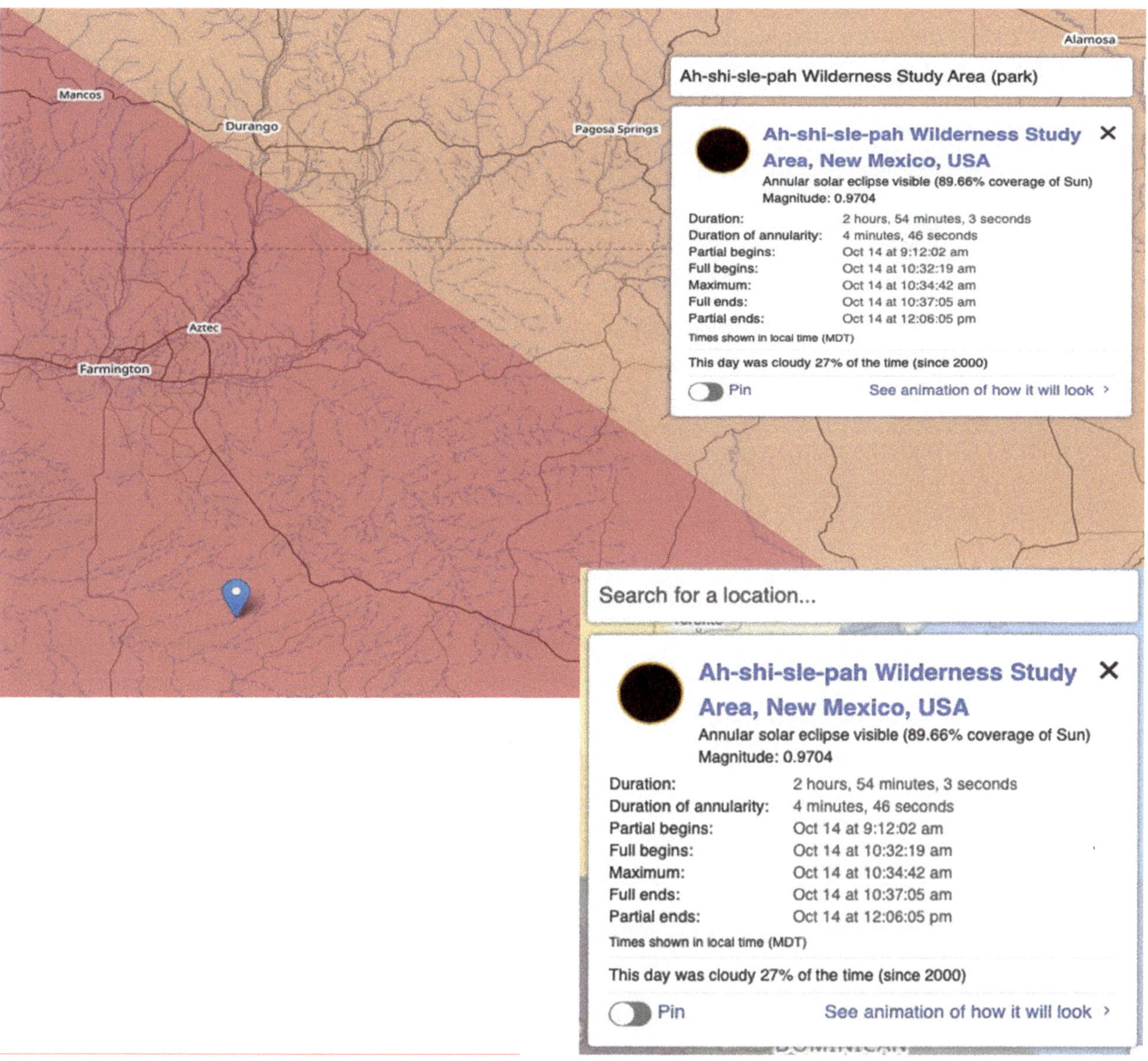

From here, you will need to pull up the following information pertinent to the location you selected:

The animation shows what the eclipse approximately looks like. Stages and times of the eclipse are outlined below.

Time	Phase	Event	Direction	Altitude
9:12:02 am Sat, Oct 14		Partial Eclipse begins The Moon touches the Sun's edge.	117°	21.0°
10:32:19 am Sat, Oct 14		Full Eclipse begins The Annular phase starts	134°	34.0°
10:34:42 am Sat, Oct 14		Maximum Eclipse Moon is closest to the center of the Sun.	135°	34.4°
10:37:05 am Sat, Oct 14		Full Eclipse ends The Annular phase ends.	136°	34.7°
12:06:05 pm Sat, Oct 14		Partial Eclipse ends The Moon leaves the Sun's edge.	162°	44.0°

2. **There is an Eclipse Service that I personally use.** NSO is the national center for ground-based solar physics in the United States (www.nso.edu) and is operated by the Association of Universities for Research in Astronomy (AURA) under a cooperative agreement with the National Science Foundation Division of Astronomical Sciences. The following is an image of their map of the 2024 eclipse:

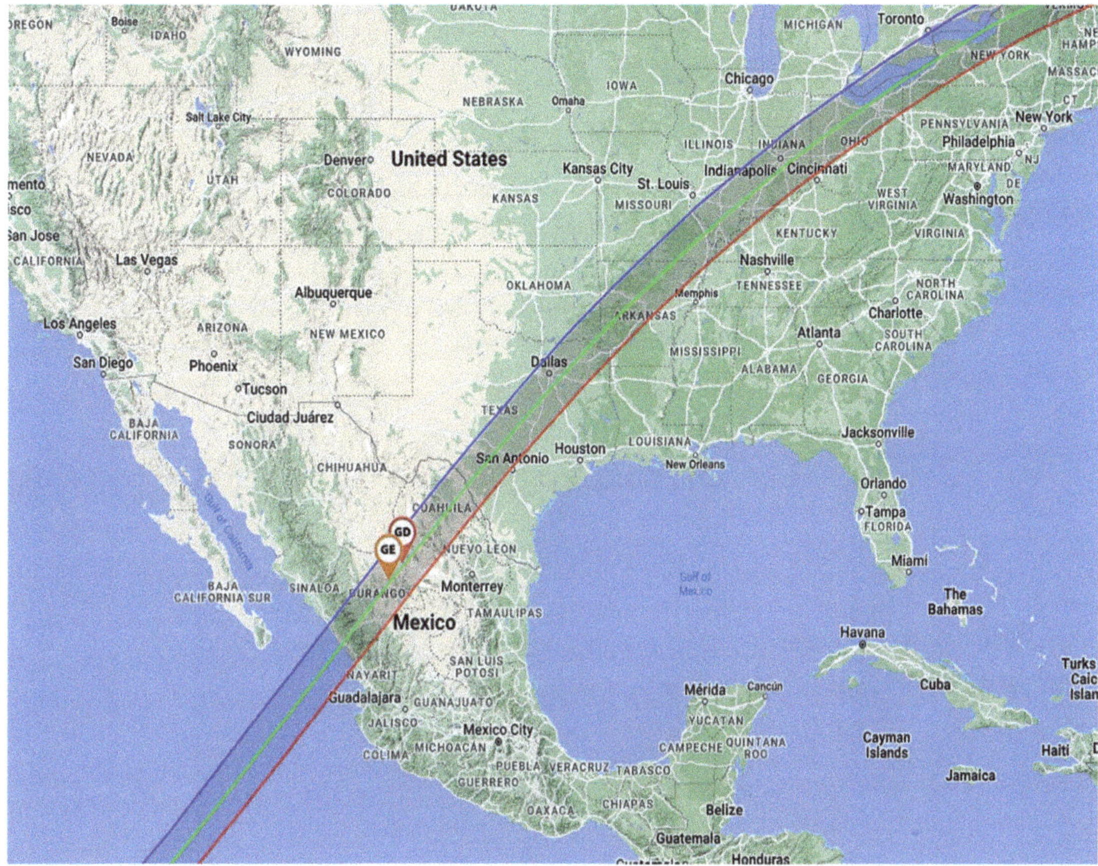

Once you have a location that you want to explore, just click on the location and the information will be placed on the face of the map. See below: https://nso.edu/for-public/eclipse-map-2024/

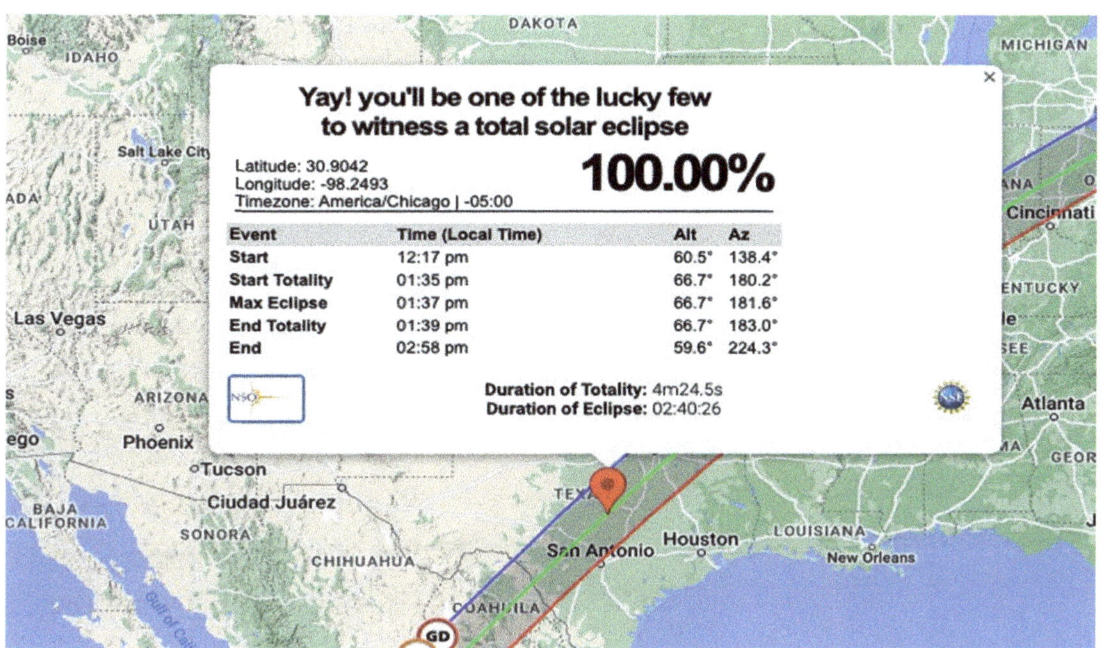

3. **Identifying the Eclipse's Elevation and Trajectory.** The following screen shot of the NASA Website we used for the 2017 eclipse (**Chart 3** and **Chart 7**) provides two essential data points for shooting an eclipse:

   a. The path of the eclipse, including the band of totality, and
   b. A chart showing the time, altitude, and azimuth of the eclipse from any marker that you place on the map.

   NOTE: On the NASA map you *MUST* be somewhere between the blue lines to see totality. On the Time and Date website you must be within the red band. On the NSO website, you need to be between the blue and red lines. The closer you are to the center of this band, the greater the duration of totality.

Chart 7 which is identical to NSO's interactive map shows the 2017 path of totality. The blue lines indicate the borders of totality, while the red line shows the center of the path of totality. **Chart 3** and **Chart 7** (below) show you the type of information that you receive when you drop a marker on a specific location. This feature provides an abundance of information including:

1. Start of the partial eclipse (C1 or First Contact),
2. Start of the total eclipse (C2 or Second Contact),
3. Maximum totality,
4. End of the total eclipse (C3 or Third Contact), and
5. End of the partial eclipse (C4 or Fourth Contact).

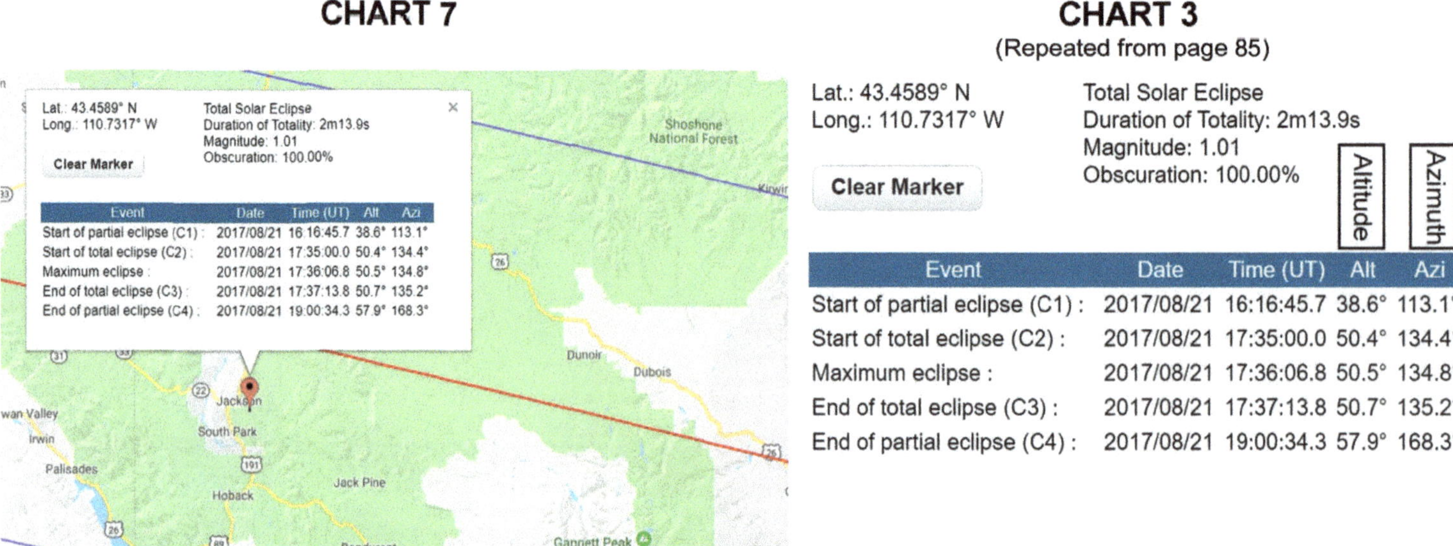

Lat.: 43.4589° N
Long.: 110.7317° W

Total Solar Eclipse
Duration of Totality: 2m13.9s
Magnitude: 1.01
Obscuration: 100.00%

Clear Marker

Event	Date	Time (UT)	Alt	Azi
Start of partial eclipse (C1) :	2017/08/21	16:16:45.7	38.6°	113.1°
Start of total eclipse (C2) :	2017/08/21	17:35:00.0	50.4°	134.4°
Maximum eclipse :	2017/08/21	17:36:06.8	50.5°	134.8°
End of total eclipse (C3) :	2017/08/21	17:37:13.8	50.7°	135.2°
End of partial eclipse (C4) :	2017/08/21	19:00:34.3	57.9°	168.3°

Chart 3 and **Chart 7** show the altitude (ALT) (the vertical angle in degrees) and the azimuth (AZI) (the horizontal angle in degrees at each phase) of the eclipse. These charts also provide these angles in degrees for each of the four main instances of contact and maximum totality. These angles are all computed from where you drop the marker of your proposed shooting location. How exactly the information is displayed will vary by website. We are providing the resources we have used and are using as of the writing of this book. Should you encounter any difficulty in using our resources, perform a search for "interactive eclipse map" of the eclipse you want to research.

Composing with a foreground. Shooting an eclipse with foreground can be challenging. Picking the elements and understanding how they will interact with the path of the eclipse is a critical part of the shooting process. For example, you should know the foreground's geometry to appropriately plan your pictures. Luckily, this geometry is simple and will be explained shortly. Knowing how to read and measure elevation is also a critical part of this process. Most maps show the elevation of an object measured from sea level. Because of this, it is important to know the elevation of your shooting location. You must measure the elevation difference between the shooting site's elevation and the foreground object's elevation to compute the elevation angle in degrees. Google Earth is a great tool for finding this information.

1. **Finding Your Shooting Location**. Once you have identified the path of totality, you need to plan where you want to shoot the eclipse shoot. We reviewed countless potential sites and visited approximately ten locations when preparing for the 2017 eclipse. Where you shoot is only limited by your imagination (and the path of totality). Since we wanted to include the surrounding landscape in our composition, it was necessary for us to scout possible locations in advance and understand the correlation between the foreground object's elevation in degrees and the eclipse's trajectory.
2. **The Object's Elevation[5].** You will need to determine the highest or lowest point of any object in feet from your shooting site. This can be either a positive or negative number for each object, depending upon its relationship to the horizon. Furthermore, you can have objects with a positive number and another object with a negative number in the same image. It is then necessary to compute the absolute difference for each of the objects' elevation from the shooting site.

[5]Any object that is below the horizon will create a negative number. However, that number must be changed to a positive number to determine the total elevation that you need to account for. Please see **Chart 5** for a visual understanding of this matter.

3. **The Object's Distance.** You also need to determine the distance from the shooting site to each object you plan to include in your picture. Once you have determined the relative elevation change and distance, you will be able to compute the elevation change in degrees[6].
4. **Elevation in Degrees.** Correct calculation of the change in relative elevation, in degrees, from the shooting site is critical because it will be the same unit of measurement used to track an eclipse. Once you have this information, you should compare that number with the ALT and AZI values of the eclipse. Please be mindful of anything that would obscure a portion of the eclipse in your pictures (such as buildings, trees, mountains, ect.) as the Sun travels along its arc through the sky. If you want to include any of the ground below the horizon, add that in as well.

There are an unlimited number of places along the path of totality where you can grab a wonderful shot. Because we are very partial to mirror images, we like to include some form of water in our shots. Use your imagination and visualize the setting that is most interesting to you. You will discover your preferences as you go.

Once you have picked a location and identified the necessary field of view (in degrees), horizontally and vertically, to attain you desired composition, the next step is to choose the corresponding lens that has an equal or greater field of view that you need (see **Chart 6**). Please remember to also review the section on Crop Sensors if that is applicable.

SHOOTING AN ECLIPSE WITH A FOREGROUND

When we decided to shoot the 2017 eclipse, getting a good foreground was very important to us. We also wanted, if possible, for the foreground to include a mirror image. One of my first good photographs was a mirror image of Mount Moran at the Oxbow Bend in the Grand Teton National Park. We wanted this theme, a mirror image, to be the hallmark lapse composite image of the eclipse with landscape as a foreground.

To get a mirror image of the landscape, we needed to use a very wide-angle lens. We chose to use a Zeiss 15mm with a field of view of 77° by 100° (portrait orientation). The Sun's 55° of horizontal movement would fit easily into the 77° of horizontal coverage provided by the 15mm Zeiss. The lens's 100° of vertical coverage would easily include the Sun at its maximum altitude of 57.9°, the space above it, the horizon, and the reflections we wanted that were below the horizon. All of these were possible for our full-frame camera mounted with a Zeiss 15mm lens.

---

[6]Please see the "OH NO, THE MATH" section which shows you how to compute the Elevation Angle

OH NO, THE MATH!
COMPUTING THE PHOTOGRAPHIC ANGLES

Following are the three steps you'll take to ensure that your image will capture all of the elements you want in your composition:

1. Compute the eclipse's total horizontal angle of movement (AZI) in degrees.
2. Identify the eclipse's maximum vertical position (ALT) in degrees.
3. Compute the elevation angle in degrees (either positive or negative) of objects in the foreground.

To compute the elevation angle in degrees, you will need to determine the relative change in altitude between the shooting site and the foreground object or feature. For instance, if you are taking a picture at an elevation of 1,000 feet, and the elevation of the object is 10,000 feet, the relative change in elevation is 9,000 feet. The relative change in altitude between you and any foreground features is what matters.

Computing the eclipse's total horizontal angle of movement (AZI) in degrees. From the information provided by an interactive eclipse map for your photo location, you will know the azimuth (horizontal position relative to north) range of where the eclipse will occur in the sky from beginning to end.

The first example I will show you is indicated in green on the compass (**Chart 8** below). To calculate the horizontal angle of movement, you need to do the following: First, go to **Chart 3** and identify the starting azimuth (C1) which is 113°. You will then identify the ending azimuth (C4) which is 168°. To find the total horizontal angle in degrees, compute the difference in degrees from C1 to C4, which, in this example, is 55°. This means the camera and lens combination you choose must have a horizontal field of view of at least 55.0° plus any horizontal margin you want for a background or "wiggle room."

CHART 8
(Repeated from page 85)
Lat.: 43.4589° N
Long.: 110.7317° W

CHART 3
Obscuration: 100.00%
Total Solar Eclipse
Duration of Totality: 2m13.9s
Magnitude: 1.01

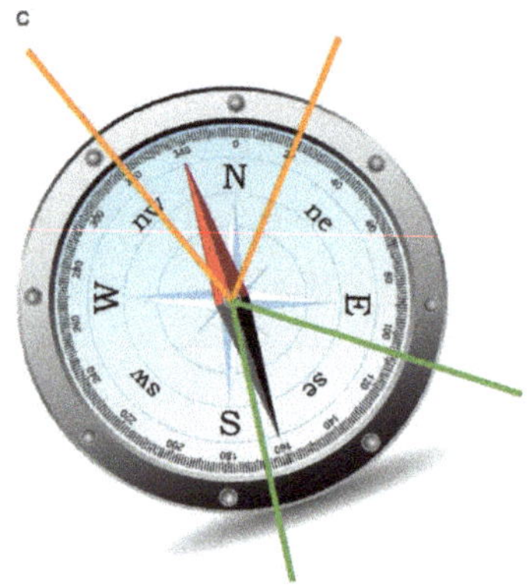

Clear Marker | Altitude | Azimuth

Event (UT)	Date	Time	Alt	Azj
Start of partial eclipse (C1):	2017/08/21	16:16:45.7	38.6°	113.1°
Start of total eclipse (C2):	2017/08/21	17:35:00.0	50.4°	134.4°
Maximum eclipse:	2017/08/21	17:36:06.8	50.5°	134.8°
End of total eclipse (C3):	2017/08/21	17:37:13.8	50.7°	135.2°
End of partial eclipse (C4):	2017/08/21	19:00:34.3	57.9°	168.3°

C1 = 113°

Sometimes, an eclipse may cross geographic north, indicated by 0° or 360°. The second example, indicated in orange on **Chart 8** above, shows how that is calculated. First, identify the difference between C1 (320°) and due north (use 360° when moving west to east), which is 40°. Then compute the difference between due north (use 0° when moving east to west) and C4 (20°), which is 20°. Then add these two results together for a total of 60°. You now know that the total horizontal angle of movement in the second (orange) example is 60°.

Computing the eclipse's total vertical angle of movement (ALT) in degrees. Just like the azimuth positions, the information provided by an interactive eclipse map for your location (illustrated in **Chart 3**) includes the altitude positions of the eclipse from start to finish. To plan for the vertical components of your shot, you will need to compute the vertical angle of the eclipse and then compute the elevation angle of objects you want to include in your foreground.

1. **Computing the Vertical Angle.** Identifying the vertical angle (ALT) is relatively simple. Just look for the highest number in the ALT column of **Chart 3**. This will give you the maximum vertical angle in degrees of the Sun's position. On **Chart 3** above, this number is 57.9°. In addition to the 57.9° you may need to add two additional amounts:

    a. The vertical angle you computed that you need to include any desired foreground below the horizon, and
    b. Any additional space that you want for a background above the Sun.

2. **Computing the relative elevation angle in degrees of objects in the foreground.** I strongly recommend that you use an online calculator to compute the relative angle of elevation of any object in the proposed picture. My favorites are (click on the blue portion of the link):

   https://calculator-online.net/angle-of-elevation-calculator/
   https://www.easycalculation.com/trigonometry/angle-elevation-calculator.php

   To compute the angle of elevation, you will need to know two things:

   a. The distance of the object from the photo site, and
   b. The relative elevation difference of the object or feature from the photo site. On most maps the indicated elevation of any site is the elevation above sea level.

   For example,

1. You are taking a picture from an indicated elevation height of 1,000 feet (1,000 feet above sea level), and the elevation of the object you are considering shows an indicated elevation height of 10,000 feet (10,000 feet above sea level), then the relative change in elevation is 9,000 feet
2. Once you have computed this angle, you are ready to preplan your shots using any of the wonderful online calculators. If you choose to compute the elevation angle yourself, you can use the following Excel formula:

ANGLE IN DEGREES = ATAN(E3) * 180/PI ()

CHART 9

	A	B	C	D	E	F	G	H	I
1	EXAMPLE 1								
2	HEIGHT		DISTANCE		ATAN(E3)		USE FORMULA IN		ELEVATION IN
3	2,400	÷	15,870	=	0.1512		"= ATAN(E3) *180/PI ()"		8.60°
4	EXAMPLE 2								
5	HEIGHT		DISTANCE		ATAN (E8)		USE FORMULA IN		ELEVATION IN
6	1,200	÷	3,000	=	0.4		"= ATAN(E8) *180/PI ()"		28.1°

Having determined the elevation angle, including the de-elevation of anything that is below the horizon that you want in the foreground of your picture (such as a reflection in water or a river valley below your position), you will be able to adequately preplan your photographs. Be sure to take into consideration any object that may obstruct either your view of the eclipse or any more distant object that you intend to include in your composition (**Chart 10**).

CHART 10

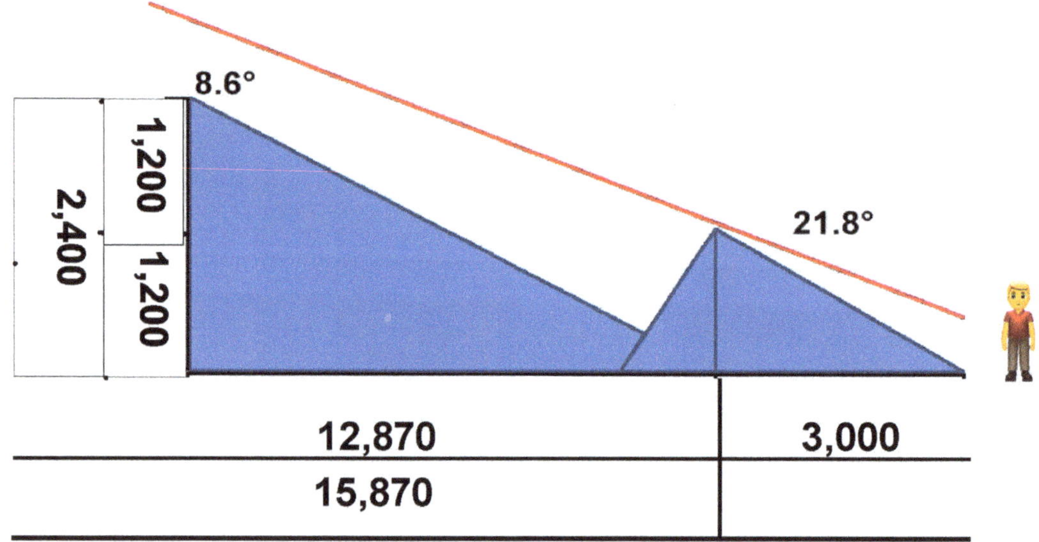

As you can see from this example, you cannot stand at the bottom of the lower peak and obtain a picture of the summit of the higher hill. When you review maps as part of your planning process, you should determine the relative elevation angle of each object that may interfere with the image you are trying to obtain.

SELECTING YOUR LENS

Once you have computed your desired field of view horizontally and vertically, you will have all the information you need to select the lens or lenses that would best work for your shoot. In this case the maximum vertical angle (ALT) in degrees is 57.9°, and the horizontal (AZI) is 55.0°. Don't forget to add additional degrees in order to include your desired foreground as well as some additional space to allow for any error in estimating your camera positioning. Also, be sure to account for some additional buffer space to frame your subject matter. The next step will be to take these two numbers and compare them to the lenses in Chart 6. In our case, we chose a 15mm lens which is 100° × 77°. This choice of lens offered us the extra room we needed to properly frame the photo.

Sometimes there will not be a lens that is wide enough to take the picture you want. In this case, we suggest you use two identical cameras and lenses and plan for a panorama that you can stitch together in post-production. If you have a minimum of 40° of overlap, you should be able to merge the two photos automatically with available post-production software. We believe that we will be facing this issue for our composite image when we shoot the 2027 eclipse in Egypt.

Bear in mind that in addition to the identical cameras and lenses, you will also need to use identical settings on the cameras. Even identical cameras and lenses will have their own unique properties in how they reproduce color. You can try to set up custom color profiles for each, however, this is complicated and may not yield the results you want. We recommend just setting all the cameras to the same white balance preset (daylight) and then manually matching them later in postproduction.

The following theoretical example is using two 15mm lenses and DSLR cameras mounted on tripods side by side to photograph an eclipse with a wide range of horizontal movement (102.9°) at a high altitude. You can see the angles and the overlap of the two images:

CHART 11

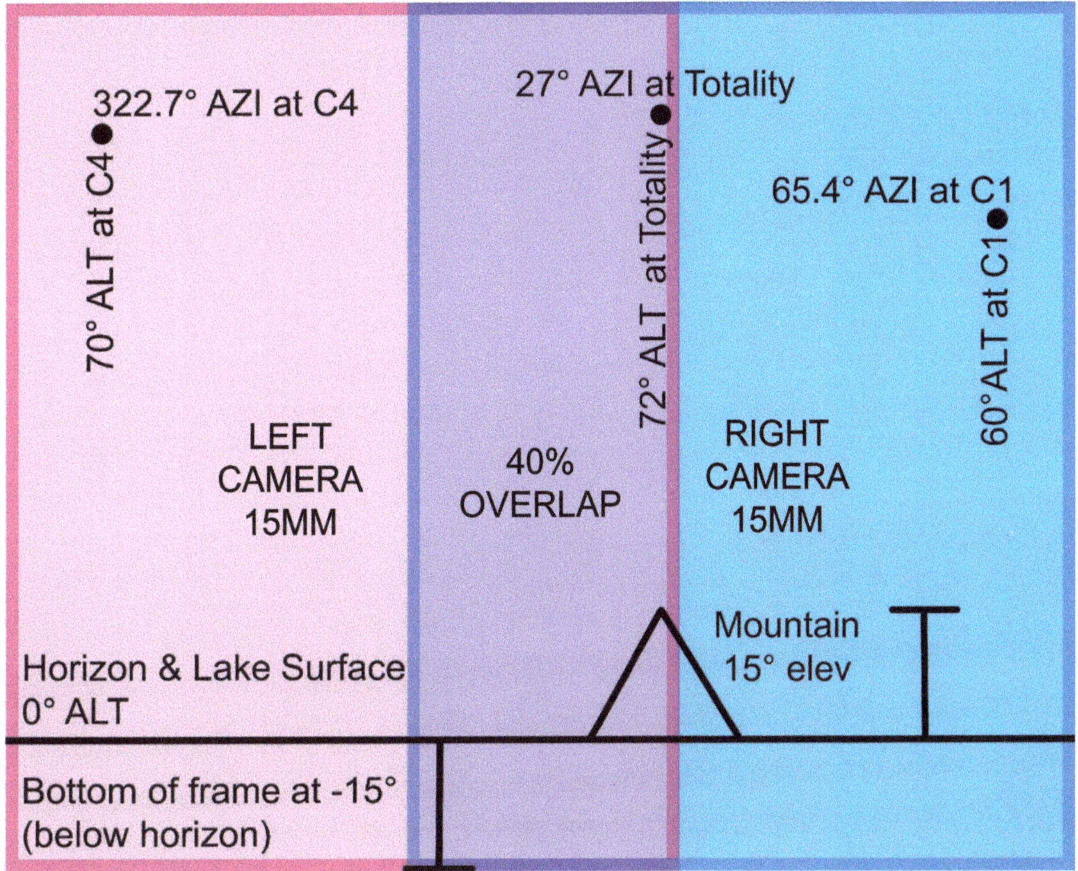

TECHNICAL STUFF

METADATA. One of the reasons we added the metadata section to the book was so that you could see the camera, lens, filter, and settings we used for each picture. During all partial phases of the eclipse (C1 to C2 and C3 to C4), except for Baily's beads and the diamond rings, we used a solar filter on each of the lenses.

MANUAL FOCUSING. One of the basic principles of eclipse photography is focusing your images manually. The principal reason for this is that the objects you are focusing on, in this case the Sun and Moon, are distant and therefore are very small. Most autofocus systems are unable to focus precisely on them. Additionally, autofocus systems rely on contrast, and the surface of the Sun itself does not have enough contrast for an autofocus system to function optimally. Using the autofocus setting will generally result in soft, out of focus images as the camera searches for a focal point. Finally, you can't just set the lens on infinity. You will still need to micro focus. If you set your focus at the beginning, you shouldn't have to make any other changes.[7]

RAW. If your camera has the option to shoot raw files, shoot raw. Period. When you shoot raw, you are capturing not so much an image as a packet of information. Think of it like ingredients for a recipe. You get your ingredients, you go home, and you make your cake. You have the option to tweak your recipe here and there and choose which aspects of the cake you'd like to highlight. Is it the best frosting or is the actual cake the star of the show? Simply put, with raw format, you get to take the information your camera gathers and decide how you want to present that information in final image form.

Raw is often considered a "safety net" for the times when photographers make mistakes, allowing details to be salvaged where they would be lost in other file formats. Additionally, it gives you, the creator, full control over every aspect of your images. JPEG is a compressed image format, leaving the decision-making about things like highlight and shadow detail, color, and contrast up to the camera. When you are shooting in jpeg, you are throwing away most of the available visual information, losing a huge amount of detail at the pixel level and minimizing your options for stylistic decisions later. And in the case of user error, instead of ingredients to work with, you'll just be stuck with a crumbly cake where your best option is to try to salvage it with way too much frosting. TRUST US AND JUST STICK WITH RAW.

[7]You may want to use live view and zoom in for sharpness of a distant point. Sunspots provide an excellent focal point for manual focusing.

WHITE BALANCE. While astronomically speaking, our Sun is "yellow," its light defines what we here on Earth describe as "white." In imaging fields, standard daylight white balance is designated around 5500K. Most cameras will give you the option to choose your white balance, and when shooting an eclipse, you will want to set your camera(s) to daylight white balance. You can select the preprogramed option in your camera (usually a Sun icon on a dial or in the digital menu), which is our recommendation, or you can manually set your white balance to somewhere in the 5400–5600K range. If you choose the latter route, do some research and field testing to determine what Kelvin temperature best reproduces neutral daylight on your equipment (make sure you are viewing test photos on a monitor that has been properly calibrated using a system such as those offered by X-rite and Datacolor). Again, keep in mind that each camera and lens will have its own nuances in how it reproduces color, so if you're super picky like us, do the leg work to figure out the settings that will yield satisfactory results for you. The reason we chose to keep it simple and use the camera's internal daylight setting is because those white balance settings have been programed for that make and model. In our opinion, that will likely be the best starting point. You can always tweak white balance in post-production if you start from a consistent setting.

So why not just stick with auto white balance (AWB)? Good question. Typically, when you're shooting a range of subject matter in a variety of lighting conditions, at various times of day, with and without flash, AWB is a good place to live and let the camera's software do the color balancing act for you. Here's an easy way to think about it: AWB's job is to assess the image data and find a happy medium where the overall average of color within the image comes out to a neutral medium without any overbearing color cast. For example, if you shoot pale sisters in red dresses, the camera is going to see all that red and choose a color balance in the cyan range to balance it out. As a result, the girls' skin tone will gain a cyan cast. The camera did its job, but it doesn't know not to counteract the red because you've told it to color balance automatically based on what it sees in the frame, regardless of subject material.

Now, let's talk about why this is important for eclipse photography. We know the Sun is white. YOU know the Sun is white. But if you set your camera to AWB, it will adjust each picture based on what's in the frame and what light is available. It doesn't know you're shooting the Sun, so don't give your camera the option to do your thinking for you. If you set your camera to daylight balance, every photo you take will have a consistent white balance. The amount and color of light will change as the eclipse progresses. Capturing both the subtle and dramatic changes in light color and quality is an important part of the documentation process. The only way to do this is to tell your camera to stick with the Sun as the definition of white and not make its own judgement calls about what white should be. It doesn't matter if you're shooting with a telephoto or wide-angle lens. It doesn't matter if you're shooting with a filter that renders the Sun white or orange. Keep your color balance set to a consistent value. Then, if you do need to tweak your color balance in post-production, make the same exact change to every image instead of leaving it up to the headache of image-by-image guesswork.

BRACKETING. Bracketing is a process of taking the same shot more than once using different settings to incrementally let in light from the primary exposure. We used the same settings on each camera during the partial eclipse phases. When you review the metadata on the pictures, you may have questions about why we chose the various settings since the image settings in the book varied from the base setting[8].

We shot a five-stop bracket series throughout the partial phases of the eclipse. Automatic Exposure Bracketing (AEB) changes the shutter speed or aperture (you choose which) automatically allowing you to capture five consecutive exposures at five different stops without having to adjust the settings manually. We took two pictures with incrementally shorter exposures and two pictures with incrementally longer exposures from the base setting. This process resulted in bracketed exposure groups.

The following series reveals the results of our five-stop bracket approach during the partial eclipse while shooting with a solar filter. Bracketing is an amazing tool that is relatively easy to master. The Canon Knowledge Base[9] provides detailed instructions on how to set this up a Canon digital camera.

CHART 12

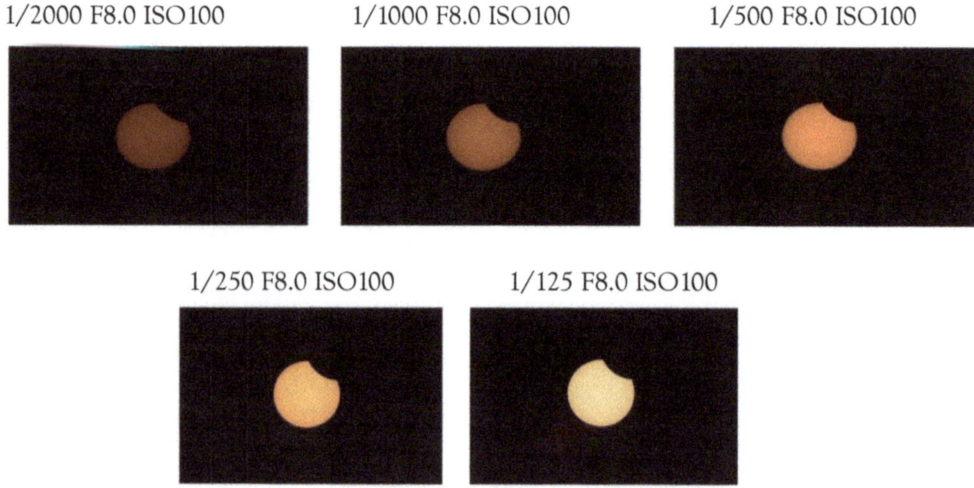

[8]The base shutter speed setting for the brackets we used was 1/500th of a second.

[9]https://support.usa.canon.com/kb/index?page=content&id=ART166279&actp=LIST.

We used several different Canon cameras that were all programed to shoot a five-shot/five-stop bracket at five-minute intervals from C1 until seven minutes before totality began (C2). Seven minutes after the end of totality (C3) we resumed shooting the five-shot/five-stop bracket at five-minute intervals until the conclusion of the eclipse (C4). We found this 5-5- 5 approach to be exactly what we needed.

To simplify the firing and timing process, we used Hahnel Captur digital remotes that fired four of the DSLR's simultaneously. As a result, we had a significant number of images of the partial eclipse phases that were all taken simultaneously with incrementally different exposures.

SAFETY, FILTERS, AND TIMING

If you want to shoot the entire eclipse from start to finish, you are going to need a neutral density solar filter. It is imperative that you have solar filters in place before you begin photographing the Sun or the partial eclipse. This is critical to prevent damage to your equipment and your eyes. Most solar filters for photography will still say not to look directly at the Sun through your camera, but you can use the live view function (if this function is available on your camera) on a DLSR *or* use a mirrorless camera to safely focus and compose your images.

You should decide the time intervals you will be using to take your photos to capture a consistent progression of the partial eclipse. According to *Totality: Eclipses of the Sun, 11th Edition*, the Sun moves its own diameter every two and half minutes. In our last eclipse we shot a bracketed series of the partial eclipse every five minutes.

You should remove your filter a few minutes before totality begins. You will need to adjust your camera settings to capture the diamond ring and Baily's beads that precede C2, the start of totality. You can also program a second set of bracket groups for this portion of the eclipse. Be very careful not to violate the safety rules about looking at any portion of the partial eclipse (including the diamond ring and Baily's beads) without following NASA's safety rules and using NASA- approved eye protection. Continue shooting unfiltered through the conclusion of totality and the second appearance of Baily's beads and the diamond ring.

If you want to photograph the second half of the eclipse until its conclusion (C3 to C4), replace the filter on your lens immediately following the second diamond ring. Before resuming photography, you should wait the same amount of time after the second diamond ring as you did between your last filtered shot and the first diamond ring. For us this was seven minutes. This will keep your spacing consistent if you intend to do a time-lapse composite image. After this time has elapsed, proceed with shooting at your regularly timed intervals until C4 (end of partial phases).

FILTERS AND SAFETY

If you plan to shoot any part of the partial (or an annular) eclipse, you MUST use a solar-grade neutral density (ND) filter. We recommend using neutral density filters with at least 16 2/3 stops. ND filters are the category of filters that block light to allow for things like:

1. Slow shutter speeds (blur waterfalls into ephemeral veils, turn a turbulent shoreline to glass, etc.) or
2. Wider apertures in bright light conditions.

Neutral density filters come in various "stop" values or in a variety of graduated options.

SOLID NEUTRAL DENSITY FILTERS

The most common types of solid (not-graduated) neutral density filters you will find on the market range from a partial stop to 10 stops (ND 3.0). This is where it gets tricky.

During the summer before the 2017 eclipse, solar filters were nearly impossible to find. As a result, some photographers turned to 8 stop (ND 2.7) or 10 stop (ND 3.0) filters thinking they were "close enough." A lot of sellers were also advertising these filters as "solar" filters. This was inaccurate. This mistake can, and will, lead to burned retinas and damaged sensors. Your eyes and your camera are far too valuable for "close enough," which really isn't very close at all.

FILTER MATH

The **minimum** neutral density value you need to photograph the Sun is ND 5.0 or 16 2/3 stops (ND 5.0). An ND 5.0 filter lets in only 00.001% of ambient light, blocking 99.999% of sunlight, while an ND 3.0 (10 stops) lets in 00.1% of the ambient light and blocks 99.900% of sunlight. You may wonder why such a small difference (just 6 2/3 stops) isn't "close enough."

The following table shows that a ND 3.0 filter lets in 10,113% more light than a ND 5.0 filter does. If you want to compute the values yourself, here is the formula:

Neutral Density Light Formula[10]

Light Reduction = 1 / 2 (the number of stops)

CHART 13 Neutral Density Filter Light Blocking Comparison

	ND Filter Type Characteristics	ND Filter Type Characteristics	Additional Light Let in by ND 3.0 Filter than an ND 5.0 Filter
Neutral Density Filter Number	ND 5.0	ND 3.0	
Percentage of Light Permitted Through the ND Filter	0.0010%	0.0980%	10,113%
Number of Stops	16.67	10	

Going from an aperture of f/2.8 to f/4, you are cutting in half the amount of light entering your camera. Neutral density filters work the same way. For each higher stop a neutral density filter is rated, its light-blocking ability is doubled. That means the difference between a 10 stop (ND 3.0) filter and a 16 2/3 stop (ND 5.0) filter, (which we believe is bare minimum to take solar pictures safely) is almost two to the seventh power. That means a 10 stop (ND 3.0) filter lets in approximately one hundred times the light than a 16 2/3 stop (ND 5.0) filter. That is a major problem and can cause significant damage to your camera and your eyes.

A 16 2/3 stop (ND 5.0) filter is the minimum rating for safe solar photography. Therefore, if you plan to photograph the partial phases, procure a neutral density filter of minimum 16 2/3 stops (ND 5.0 or higher) or refrain from shooting the partial phases all together. (By the way, if the filter looks like anything other than a piece of opaque black glass, it's not a

[10]https://www.cambridgeincolour.com/tutorials/neutral-density-filters.htm (See Section on Neutral Density Filters ("Technical Note: recall that each "stop" of light- reduction corresponds with a halving of light. A given filter strength therefore passes only 1/2 of the strength of the initial incoming light, where "strength" is the filter strength in stops. For example, a 3-stop ND filter therefore only passes 1/8th the incoming light (since 1/23 = 1/(2*2*2) = 1/8)."))

solar filter.) Stacking multiple lower-grade ND filters to achieve a solar-grade light-blocking equivalent is not an option[11].

Never use a rear-mount filter for solar photography[12]. Don't Use the Rear Filter Tray. Most of the large Canon L-series super-telephoto lenses have a rear mounted slip-in filter tray. NEVER use a solar filter in this tray. This filter mounting system is designed for terrestrial photography using traditional photography filters. It is not designed to house a filter to be directed celestially into the Sun. At these magnifications, you will destroy the filter- like taking a magnifying glass to a leaf and put your lens, sensor, and your eyes in danger. The intense light and heat could fry aperture and image stabilization mechanisms, damage the autofocus sensor and, if the mirror is locked up ruin your sensor. Buy the correct front-mounted solar filter. They're relatively inexpensive and completely safe.

To be effective for the purposes of solar photography, neutral density filters must be mounted on the front of the lens, at the point where light enters the lens. This may seem like a no-brainer, but there are lenses on the market (such as the 500mm Canon) that accept rear-mount filters. We believe that you should not use them in solar photography regardless of their reported light-blocking potential. Unfiltered sunlight entering the lens at full strength will then be focused and intensified as it travels through the lens elements. This may cause damage to the internal components of your lens.

There are a myriad of styles and manufacturers of front-mount neutral density photographic filters. Some are round and screw directly to your lens. Some are square and slide into a holder mounted to the front of your lens. Some filters are "low-profile" and designed to eliminate or greatly minimize vignetting. For wide-angle lenses, we recommend a "low-profile," threaded, round solar filter. Note: please verify that any filter you purchase has a very good threading system. If you aren't using a wide-angle lens and you have already made the investment into a square filter kit; it might be most economical for you to grab a compatible square solar filter from the manufacturer of your choice. Just know that the mounting apparatus may cause vignetting.

After much painstaking research, we chose to go with Formatt-HiTech's Firecrest Neutral Density 5.4 Solar Eclipse Filter (18 stops) for all our lenses capable of accepting front-mounted

---

[11]https://photo.stackexchange.com/questions/91988/would-stacking-thinner-nd-filters-perform-as-well-as-one-greater-nd-filter0

[12]Canon DLC Home August 3, 2017 - Photo Knowledge Base - Corporate - Being Safe Using Solar Filters.

filters. There were a variety of factors that went into this decision, but our considerations were quality, availability, profile, reputation, and value. You can spend days reading up on neutral density filter manufacturers, test results, and preferences (even ease of cleaning) from blogging, tech-minded photographers all over the internet (and we did). At the end of the day, you must make your best educated decision based on your own experiences or brand loyalty and priorities in what you want and need from your filter. As long as it's at least a 16 2/3 stop (ND 5.0) filter, choose whatever works best for you and your photography inventory.

If your lens doesn't accept front-mounted filters, or if you can't find a source for filters to fit the large diameter of the lens you intend to use, you still have options. After concluding our research, we determined that our best option was to use solar telescopic filters for the lenses that do not accept front-mounted accessories. We then chose filters from Thousand Oaks Optical who manufacturers telescopes and telescope accessories. These filters come in a huge range of sizes, and you can acquire them from many retailers. Our preferred retailer for telescope accessories is Cloud Break Optics in Seattle. In the summer of 2017, they rescued us after the manufacturer failed to deliver our filters. Thank you, Matt Dahl, for saving us at the last minute!

Telescope filters are designed to fit snugly over the front lens element. How we made this work for our large telephoto lenses was to measure the diameter of the lens hood (if you don't have a hood, just measure the front of your lens) and purchase the filter model closest in size (rounded up, of course). We mounted our filter for the Canon 500mm lens by using water pipe insulation wedged between the filter and the hood. It worked.

You can use adhesive foam strips (you will likely need more than is included with your filter) to custom-fit the inside diameter of the filter mount to your equipment. Just make sure to create a light seal to eliminate the possibility of stray light sneaking in. We chose to place our filter over the lens hood so that we would have some options in how we secured the filter to the camera while still being able to remove it quickly and easily before totality and then replace it afterwards.

NOTE: When choosing a telescope filter for solar photography, select the "full aperture" category. We also prefer glass instead of polymer if available. It's worth reading about the various kinds of filter materials available and the advantages and disadvantages of each. Most importantly, *always* inspect your filters before each use, and *never* use one that is scratched or damaged. You must also inspect your solar grade eye protection before each use! We cannot stress enough the importance of thorough inspection prior to each use.

We had one set of filters that were 16 2/3 stops and one set that were 18 stops. Because we wanted to keep our aperture and shutter speed settings consistent while achieving the same exposure, we compensated by one stop in the ISO. Cameras with the Thousand Oaks Optical telescope filters were set to ISO 100, and cameras with the 18-stop Formatt- HiTech filters were set to ISO 200. Note that some solar telescope filters have even greater light-blocking properties. If the base settings we have provided are too dark, adjust your camera settings accordingly.

Most solar filters will display the Sun with an orange hue. The Formatt-HiTech filters neutralize this effect with coatings, but we kind of liked the Sun's orange coloration rendered by the Thousand Oaks Optical filters. We made everything consistent in post-production with simple coloration layers over darker exposures from the same bracket groups to insure similar tonality. Understanding your tools (including everything from cameras & accessories to post-production software) and envisioning your final product in advance is crucial to successful eclipse photography.

Just remember to research recommended settings for each phase of the eclipse. Plan your settings in advance and go shoot.

CHART 14 lists all the lenses and filter combinations we have used:

CHART 14

Canon 5DS R	15mm Zeiss	Formatt-HiTech	Hahnel Captur Transceiver
Canon 5DS R	500mm Canon with 2x extender	Thousand Oaks Optical	Hahnel Captur Transceiver
Canon 5D Mark III	24mm Sigma	Formatt-HiTech	Hahnel Captur Transceiver
Canon 5D Mark IV	70-200mm Canon with 2x extender	Formatt-HiTech	Hahnel Captur Transceiver
Canon R5	600mm Canon with a 2x extender	Thousand Oaks Optical	Hahnel Captur Transceiver
Canon 5D Mark IV	500mm Canon with 2x extender	Thousand Oaks Optical	none
FujiFilm GFX 100s	Fujifilm Gf 23mm	Formatt-HiTech	none
FujiFilm GFX 100s	Fujifilm Gf 30mm	Formatt-HiTech	

BASE CAMERA SETTINGS DURING PARTIAL ECLIPSE PHASES FOR ND 5.0 to ND 5.4 FILTERS

F-STOP	F8
SHUTTER SPEED	1/500
ISO	100-200

EQUIPMENT LIST FOR 2017

- Cameras & Lenses

Zeiss Distagon T* 15mm f/2.8 (on Canon EOS 5DS R)	Canon EF500mm f/4L IS USM +1.4x III (on Paul's Canon EOS 5D Mk IV)
Canon EF 500mm f/4L IS II USM with Canon Extender EF 2x III (on Canon EOS 5DS R)	Canon EF100-400mm f/4.5-5.6L IS II USM (on Paul's Canon EOS 6D Mk II)
Sigma 24mm f/1.4 DG HSM ART (on Canon EOS 5D MarkIII)	EF24-105mm F/4L IS II USM (on Canon EOS 7D Markil)
Canon EF 70-200mm f/2.8L IS II USM with Canon Extender EF 2 III (on Canon EOS 5D MarkIV)	Canon EF 600mm f/4L IS II USM with Canon Extender EF 2x III (on Canon EOS R5)

Our Newest Lenses

Canon	RF 1200mm f/8L IS USM	Thousand Oaks Optical Filter	Canon 1.4 and 2.0 Extender
Fuji	Fujifilm Gf 23mm and 30mm	Formatt-HiTech	none

Extenders

Canon	Extender EF 2x Ill
Canon	Extender EF 1.4x Ill
Canon	Extender RF 2x
Canon	Extender RF 1.4x
Fuji	Extender GF 1,4x TC WR

Filters

- Formatt-HiTech Firecrest Neutral Density 5.4 Solar Eclipse Filter (multiple)
- White Light Solar Filter (SolarLite) S-8375 (multiple)

Transceivers

- Hahnel Captur Transceiver (multiple)

Tripods

- head and legs for each camera

Batteries

- Make sure that you have extra camera batteries with chargers.
- Great tip from Brittany: put a rubber band around batteries that are charged. Remove this rubber band once you use the battery.

Other Equipment

Flashlights + red cellophane gels attached with rubber bands (6)	Bags for rocks to weigh down tripods if windy
Pads and Paper	Cam Ranger
Lens cleaning supplies (one kit per camera set-up)	Colored stickers and ribbons to code each camera set-up
Waterproof bags	Duct tape
Mylar blankets to protect cameras from overheating	Swiss army knife or another pocketknife
NASA-approved eclipse viewing glasses from American Paper Optics / BH Photo Video	Towels (in case equipment gets wet or you must wadc to Get to your location)
Mini Gaff tape roll (one per set-up)	Sturdy footwear
Clothes pins (6 per camera) to secure mylar blankets if necessary	Sunscreen
Memory cards	Layered clothing, jacket
Felt for telescope filters	Laminated eclipse procedure instructions for each camera
Rocket air blaster	Cable releases for all cameras
Small tool kit	Stop watches
Battery and cords for cellphone charging	

RESOURCES

1. The most valuable resource you have at your disposal are interactive eclipse maps, such as provided by timeanddate.com and NSO.edu. These will give you all the information you need when choosing your location and planning your shots. Remember that you may have to dig a little bit to find all the information you want, such as the altitude and azimuth measurements.
2. It would also be wise to check eclipse weather sites to confirm your research about the best possible weather predictions. We recommend checking weather conditions and predictions along the eclipse's path. As of today's writing, we believe that the best weather site is: http://eclipsophile.com.
3. For more information about solar eclipses and eclipse photography, be sure to pick up a copy of the latest edition of *Totality: Eclipses of the Sun* by Mark Littmann, Fred Espenak, and Ken Willcox. Fred Espenak's website www.mreclipse.com is also a wealth of information. We used both resources for determining all our camera settings, gaining a better understanding of eclipses, and knowing what to expect when the time came. There is also great information about editing your eclipse photos.

PART VI

Metadata

Eclipse	Photo	File Name	Camera	Lens	Filter	ISO	F-stop	Shutter Speed	Time Stamp
COVER									
2023 Australia	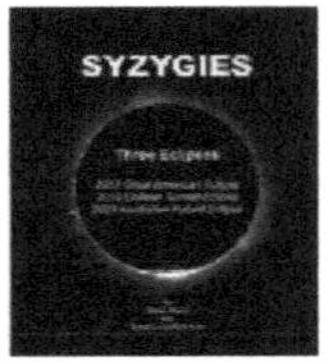	20230420_ SD0154_ 0306	Canon EOS 5DS R	Canon EF600mm f/4L IS II USM with Canon Extender EF 2X III	none	400	f/8.0	1/8000	11:28:21 AM on 4/20/23
INTRODUCTION									
2017 USA	B Roll Images on look search for shoot location								
2017 USA	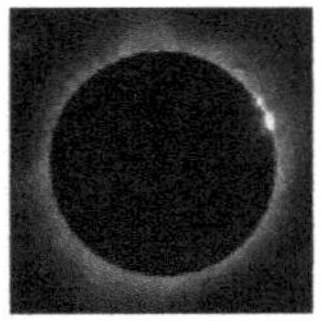	_C1_6375. JPG.	Canon EOS 5DS R	Canon EF500mm f/4L IS II USM with Canon Extender EF 2X III	none	100	f/8.0	1/500	11:36:58 AM

PART I										
2017 USA		COMPOSITE of 26 images	Canon EOS 5D Mark III	Sigma 24mm f/1.4 DG HSM Art Lens for Canon EF	Formatt-Hitech Firecrest ND 5.4 / 18-stop during partial phases only None during totality	200	f/8.0	Partials: 1/500 Totality: 1/250 1/60 1/45 1/30 1/15 1/8 1/4 1/2 1" 2"	10:10:54 AM to 1:00:00 PM
2017 USA	B Roll Images of Team preparing for the eclipse shoot								
2017 USA		20170821_ CF0077_ 0004	Canon EOS 5DS R	Canon EF500mm f/4L IS II USM with Canon Extender EF 2X III	Thousand Oaks Optical Solar filter	100	f8/0	1/250	10:15:17 AM
2017 USA		20170821 _CF0077 _0014	Canon EOS 5DS R	Canon EF500mm f/4L IS II USM with Canon Extender EF 2X III	Thousand Oaks Optical Solar filter	100	f/8.0	1/250	10:17:22 AM

...Continued

Eclipse	Photo	File Name	Camera	Lens	Filter	ISO	F-stop	Shutter Speed	Time Stamp
2017 USA	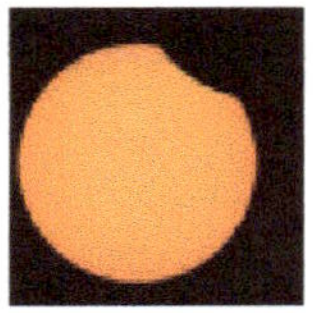	20170821 _CF0077 _0039	Canon EOS 5DS R	Canon EF500mm f/4L IS II USM with Canon Extender EF 2X III	Thousand Oaks Optical Solar filter	100	f/8.0	1/250	10:22:29 AM
2017 USA	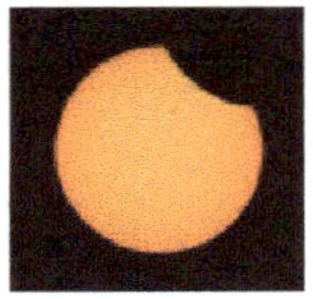	20170821 _CF0077 _0044	Canon EOS 5DS R	Canon EF500mm f/4L IS II USM with Canon Extender EF 2X III	Thousand Oaks Optical Solar filter	100	f/8.0	1/250	10:27:13 AM
2017 USA	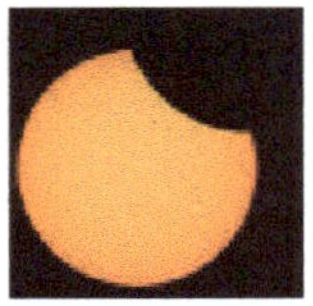	20170821 _CF0077 _0059	Canon EOS 5DS R	Canon EF500mm f/4L IS II USM with Canon Extender EF 2X III	Thousand Oaks Optical Solar filter	100	f/8.0	1/250	10:32:19 AM
2017 USA	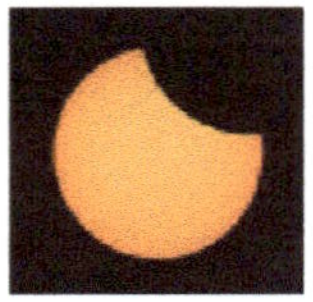	20170821 _CF0077 _0069	Canon EOS 5DS R	Canon EF500mm f/4L IS II USM with Canon Extender EF 2X III	Thousand Oaks Optical Solar filter	100	f/8.0	1/250	10:37:24 AM
2017 USA	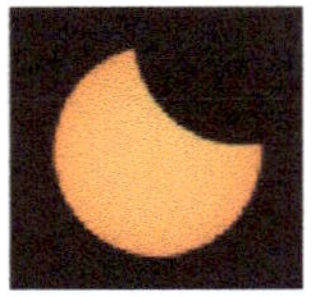	20170821 _CF0077 _0079	Canon EOS 5DS R	Canon EF500mm f/4L IS II USM with Canon Extender EF 2X III	Thousand Oaks Optical Solar filter	100	f/8.0	1/250	10:42:19 AM
2017 USA	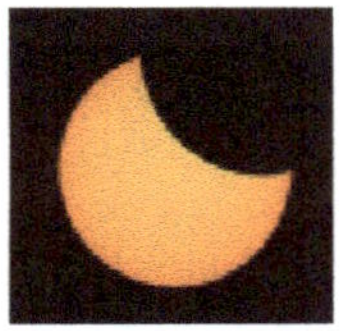	20170821 _CF0077 _0084	Canon EOS 5DS R	Canon EF500mm f/4L IS II USM with Canon Extender EF 2X III	Thousand Oaks Optical Solar filter	100	f/8.0	1/250	10:47:12 AM

2017 USA		20170821_CF0077_0094	Canon EOS 5DS R	Canon EF500mm f/4L IS II USM with Canon Extender EF 2X III	Thousand Oaks Optical Solar filter	100	f/8.0	1/250	10:52:40 AM
2017 USA		20170821_CF0077_0109	Canon EOS 5DS R	Canon EF500mm f/4L IS II USM with Canon Extender EF 2X III	Thousand Oaks Optical Solar filter	100	f/8.0	1/250	10:57:17 AM
2017 USA		20170821_CF0077_0119	Canon EOS 5DS R	Canon EF500mm f/4L IS II USM with Canon Extender EF 2X III	Thousand Oaks Optical Solar filter	100	f/8.0	1/250	11:02:16 AM
2017 USA		20170821_CF0077_0129	Canon EOS 5DS R	Canon EF500mm f/4L IS II USM with Canon Extender EF 2X III	Thousand Oaks Optical Solar filter	100	f/8.0	1/250	11:07:17 AM
2017 USA		20170821_CF0077_0139	Canon EOS 5DS R	Canon EF500mm f/4L IS II USM with Canon Extender EF 2X III	Thousand Oaks Optical Solar filter	100	f/8.0	1/250	11:12:19 AM
2017 USA		20170821_CF0077_0144	Canon EOS 5DS R	Canon EF500mm f/4L IS II USM with Canon Extender EF 2X III	Thousand Oaks Optical Solar filter	100	f/8.0	1/250	11:17:12 AM

...Continued

Eclipse	Photo	File Name	Camera	Lens	Filter	ISO	F-stop	Shutter Speed	Time Stamp
2017 USA	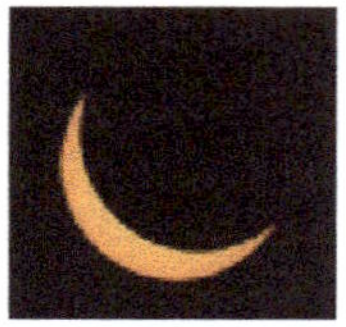	20170821 _CF0077 _0164	Canon EOS 5DS R	Canon EF500mm f/4L IS II USM with Canon Extender EF 2X III	Thousand Oaks Optical Solar filter	100	f/8.0	1/250	11:22:18 AM
2017 USA	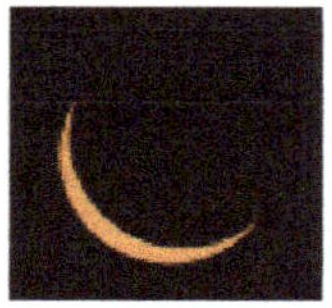	20170821 _CF0077 _0174	Canon EOS 5DS R	Canon EF500mm f/4L IS II USM with Canon Extender EF 2X III	Thousand Oaks Optical Solar filter	100	f/8.0	1/250	11:27:19 AM
2017 USA	B Roll images of Team preparing for totality								
2017 USA	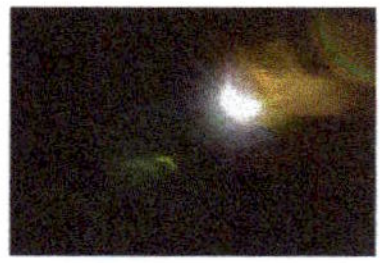	20170821 _CF0074 _0194	Canon EOS 5D Mark IV	Canon EF70-200mm f/2.8L IS II USM +2x III	none	200	f/8.0	1/2000	11:30:37 AM
2017 USA	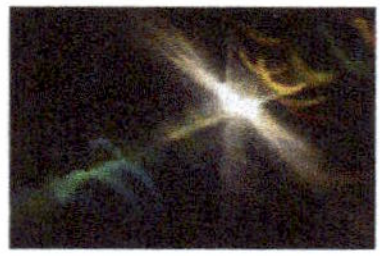	20170821 _CF0074 _0198	Canon EOS 5D Mark IV	Canon EF70-200mm f/2.8L IS II USM +2x III	none	200	f/8.0	1/125	11:30:41 AM
2017 USA	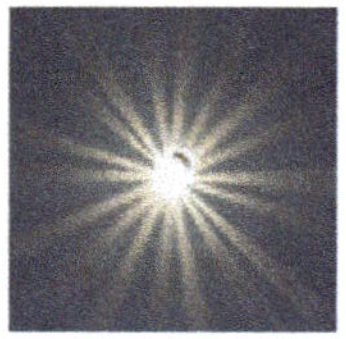	20170821 _CF0076 _0132	Canon EOS 5D Mark III	Sigma 24mm f/1.4 DG HSM Art Lens for Canon EF	none	200	f/8.0	1/15	11:34:28 AM

2017 USA		20170821 _CF0076 _0133	Canon EOS 5D Mark III	Sigma 24mm f/1.4 DG HSM Art Lens for Canon EF	none	200	f/8.0	1/250	11:34:30 AM
2017 USA		20170821 _CF0076 _0137	Canon EOS 5D Mark III	Sigma 24mm f/1.4 DG HSM Art Lens for Canon EF	none	200	f/8.0	1/15	11:34:35 AM
2017 USA		20170821 _CF0076 _0138	Canon EOS 5D Mark III	Sigma 24mm f/1.4 DG HSM Art Lens for Canon EF	none	200	f/8.0	1/250	11:34:37 AM
2017 USA		20170821 _CF0076 _0142	Canon EOS 5D Mark III	Sigma 24mm f/1.4 DG HSM Art Lens for Canon EF	none	200	f/8.0	1/15	11:34:41 AM
2017 USA		20170821 _CF0076 _0143	Canon EOS 5D Mark III	Sigma 24mm f/1.4 DG HSM Art Lens for Canon EF	none	200	f/8.0	1/250	11:34:42 AM
2017 USA		20170821 _CF0077 _0194	Canon EOS 5DS R	Canon EF500mm f/4L IS II USM with Canon Extender EF 2X III	none	100	f/8.0	1/1000	11:34:34 AM

...*Continued*

Eclipse	Photo	File Name	Camera	Lens	Filter	ISO	F-stop	Shutter Speed	Time Stamp
2017 USA		20170821 _CF0076 _0132	Canon EOS 5D Mark III	Sigma 24mm f/1.4 DG HSM Art Lens for Canon EF	none	200	f/8.0	1/15	11:34:28 AM
2017 USA		20170821 _CF0076 _0132	Canon EOS 5D Mark III	Sigma 24mm f/1.4 DG HSM Art Lens for Canon EF	none	200	f/8.0	1/15	11:34:28 AM
2017 USA		20170821 _CF0076 _0137	Canon EOS 5D Mark III	Sigma 24mm f/1.4 DG HSM Art Lens for Canon EF	none	200	f/8.0	1/15	11:34:35 AM
2017 USA		20170821 _CF0076 _0142	Canon EOS 5D Mark III	Sigma 24mm f/1.4 DG HSM Art Lens for Canon EF	none	200	f/8.0	1/15	11:34:41 AM
2017 USA		20170821 _CF0076 _0147	Canon EOS 5D Mark III	Sigma 24mm f/1.4 DG HSM Art Lens for Canon EF	none	200	f/8.0	1/15	11:34:46 AM

2017 USA	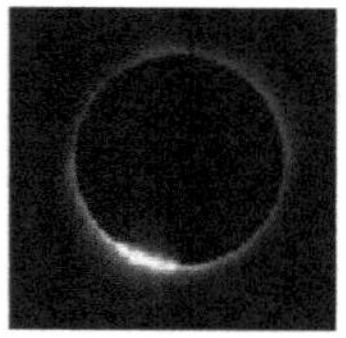	20170821_CF0077_0199	Canon EOS 5DS R	Canon EF500mm f/4L IS II USM with Canon Extender EF 2X III	none	100	f/8.0	1/1000	11:34:40 AM
2017 USA	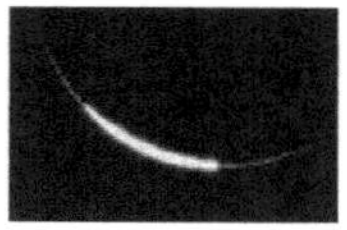	20170821_CF0077_0196	Canon EOS 5DS R	Canon EF500mm f/4L IS II USM with Canon Extender EF 2X III	none	100	f/8.0	1/8000	11:34:37 AM
2017 USA	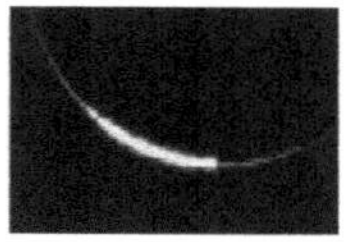	20170821_CF0077_0197	Canon EOS 5DS R	Canon EF500mm f/4L IS II USM with Canon Extender EF 2X III	none	100	f/8.0	1/4000	11:34:38 AM
2017 USA	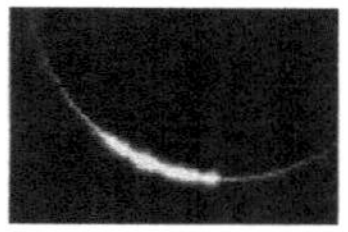	20170821_CF0077_0198	Canon EOS 5DS R	Canon EF500mm f/4L IS II USM with Canon Extender EF 2X III	none	100	f/8.0	1/2000	11:34:39 AM
2017 USA	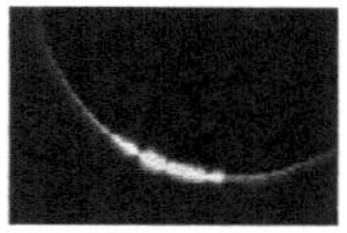	20170821_CF0077_0199	Canon EOS 5DS R	Canon EF500mm f/4L IS II USM with Canon Extender EF 2X III	none	100	f/8.0	1/1000	11:34:40 AM
2017 USA	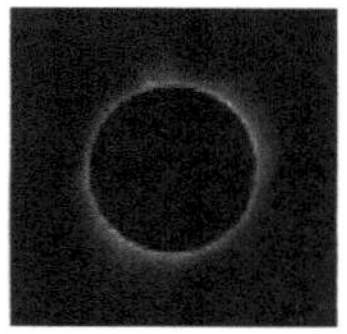	20170821_CF0077_0245	Canon EOS 5DS R	Canon EF500mm f/4L IS II USM with Canon Extender EF 2X III	none	100	f/8.0	1/500	11:35:58 AM
2017 USA	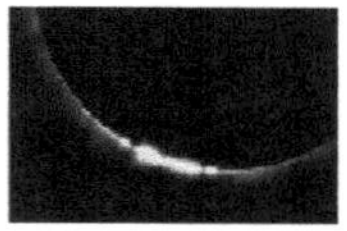	20170821_CF0077_0200	Canon EOS 5DS R	Canon EF500mm f/4L IS II USM with Canon Extender EF 2X III	none	100	f/8.0	1/500	11:34:41 AM

...Continued

Eclipse	Photo	File Name	Camera	Lens	Filter	ISO	F-stop	Shutter Speed	Time Stamp
2017 USA		20170821 _CF0077 _0201	Canon EOS 5DS R	Canon EF500mm f/4L IS II USM with Canon Extender EF 2X III	none	100	f/8.0	1/8000	11:34:42 AM
2017 USA		20170821 _CF0077 _0202	Canon EOS 5DS R	Canon EF500mm f/4L IS II USM with Canon Extender EF 2X III	none	100	f/8.0	1/4000	11:34:43 AM
2017 USA		20170821 _CF0077 _0203	Canon EOS 5DS R	Canon EF500mm f/4L IS II USM with Canon Extender EF 2X III	none	100	f/8.0	1/2000	11:34:44 AM
2017 USA		COMPOSITE 20170821 _CF0074 _0243- 0204	Canon EOS 5D Mark IV	Canon EF70-200mm f/2.8L IS II USM +2x III	none	100	f/8.0	1/15 1/250	11:34:51 AM to 11:35:51 AM

2017 USA		COMPOSITE of 43 images	Canon EOS 5DS R	Zeiss Distagon T* 15mm f/2.8 ZE	Formatt-Hitech Firecrest ND 5.4 / 18-stop during partial phases only None during totality	200	f/8.0	Partials: 1/500 Totality: 1/90 1/60 1/45 1/30 1/20 1/6 1/4 1/2 1" 2" 4"	10:10:54 AM to 1:05:00 PM
2017 USA		COMPOSITE	Canon EOS 5D Mark III	Sigma 24mm f/1.4 DG HSM Art Lens for Canon EF	none	200	f/8.0	1/250 1/60 1/45 1/30 1/15 1/8 1/4 1/2 1" 2"	multiple values

...Continued

Eclipse	Photo	File Name	Camera	Lens	Filter	ISO	F-stop	Shutter Speed	Time Stamp
2017 USA		PANO_20170821_113614	Google Pixel	N/A	none	N/A	N/A	N/A	11:37:16 AM
2017 USA		20170821_CF0077_0275	Canon EOS 5DS R	Canon EF500mm f/4L IS II USM with Canon Extender EF 2X III	none	100	f/8.0	1/500	11:36:48 AM
2017 USA		20170821_CF0077_0270	Canon EOS 5DS R	Canon EF500mm f/4L IS II USM with Canon Extender EF 2X III	none	100	f/8.0	1/500	11:36:39 AM
2017 USA		20170821_CF0077_0275	Canon EOS 5DS R	Canon EF500mm f/4L IS II USM with Canon Extender EF 2X III	none	100	f/8.0	1/500	11:36:48 AM
2017 USA		20170821_CF0077_0278	Canon EOS 5DS R	Canon EF500mm f/4L IS II USM with Canon Extender EF 2X III	none	100	f/8.0	1/2000	11:36:56 AM
2017 USA		20170821_CF0077_0280	Canon EOS 5DS R	Canon EF500mm f/4L IS II USM with Canon Extender EF 2X III	none	100	f/8.0	1/500	11:36:58 AM

2017 USA		20170821 _CF0077 _0280	Canon EOS 5DS R	Canon EF500mm f/4L IS II USM with Canon Extender EF 2X III	Thousand Oaks Optical Solar filter	100	f/8.0	1/500	11:36:58 AM
2017 USA		20170821 _CF0074 _0253	Canon EOS 5D Mark IV	Canon EF70-200mm f/2.8L IS II USM +2x III	none	100	f/8.0	1/15	11:37:03 AM
2017 USA		20170821 _CF0072 _0072	Canon EOS 6D Mark II	Canon EF100-400mm f/4.5-5.6L IS II USM	none	100	f/8.0	1/60	not synced
2017 USA		20170821 _CF0071 _0066	Canon EOS 5D Mark IV	Canon EF500mm f/4L IS USM +1.4x III	none	100	f/8.0	1/60	not synced
2017 USA		DSC01393	Sony DSC-H55	N/A	none	400	f/5.5	1/60	not synced
2017 USA		20170821 _CF0077 _0281	Canon EOS 5DS R	Canon EF500mm f/4L IS II USM with Canon Extender EF 2X III	none	100	f/8.0	1/8000	11:37:37 AM
2017 USA		20170821 _CF0071 _0067	Canon EOS 5D Mark IV	Canon EF500mm f/4L IS USM +1.4x III	Thousand Oaks Optical Solar filter	100	f/8.0	1/60	not synced

...*Continued*

Eclipse	Photo	File Name	Camera	Lens	Filter	ISO	F-stop	Shutter Speed	Time Stamp
2017 USA	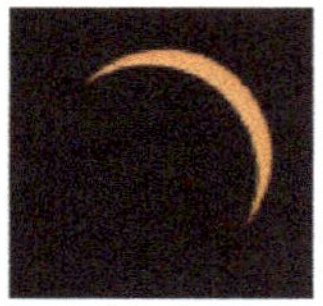	20170821 _CF0077 _0301	Canon EOS 5DS R	Canon EF500mm f/4L IS II USM with Canon Extender EF 2X III	Thousand Oaks Optical Solar filter	100	f/8.0	1/250	11:45:32 AM
2017 USA	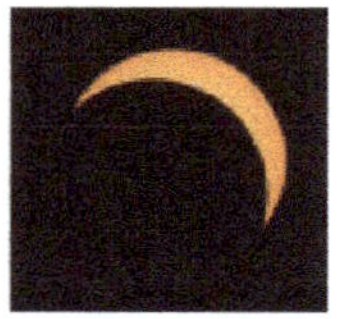	20170821 _CF0077 _0311	Canon EOS 5DS R	Canon EF500mm f/4L IS II USM with Canon Extender EF 2X III	Thousand Oaks Optical Solar filter	100	f/8.0	1/250	11:50:08 AM
2017 USA	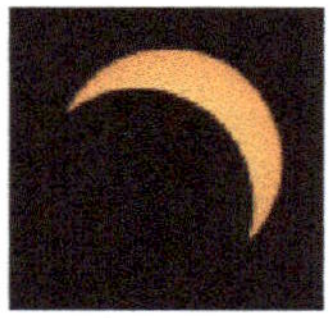	20170821 _CF0077 _0321	Canon EOS 5DS R	Canon EF500mm f/4L IS II USM with Canon Extender EF 2X III	Thousand Oaks Optical Solar filter	100	f/8.0	1/250	11:55:10 AM
2017 USA	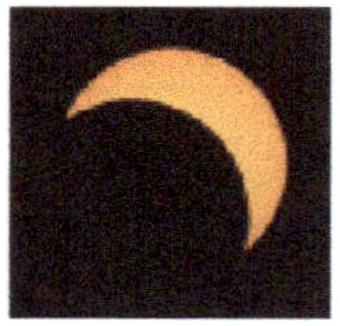	20170821 _CF0077 _0331	Canon EOS 5DS R	Canon EF500mm f/4L IS II USM with Canon Extender EF 2X III	Thousand Oaks Optical Solar filter	100	f/8.0	1/250	12:00:06 PM
2017 USA	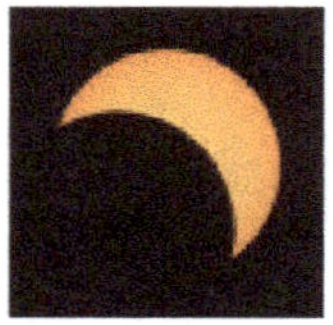	20170821 _CF0077 _0341	Canon EOS 5DS R	Canon EF500mm f/4L IS II USM with Canon Extender EF 2X III	Thousand Oaks Optical Solar filter	100	f/8.0	1/250	12:05:06 PM
2017 USA	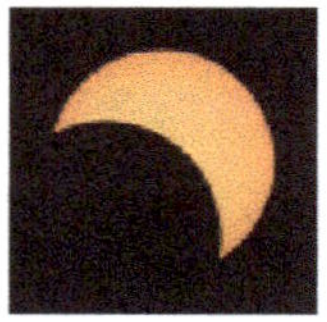	20170821 _CF0077 _0351	Canon EOS 5DS R	Canon EF500mm f/4L IS II USM with Canon Extender EF 2X III	Thousand Oaks Optical Solar filter	100	f/8.0	1/250	12:10:08 PM

2017 USA		20170821 _CF0077 _0356	Canon EOS 5DS R	Canon EF500mm f/4L IS II USM with Canon Extender EF 2X III	Thousand Oaks Optical Solar filter	100	f/8.0	1/250	12:15:02 PM
2017 USA		20170821 _CF0077 _371	Canon EOS 5DS R	Canon EF500mm f/4L IS II USM with Canon Extender EF 2X III	Thousand Oaks Optical Solar filter	100	f/8.0	1/250	12:20:08 PM
2017 USA		20170821 _CF0077 _0381	Canon EOS 5DS R	Canon EF500mm f/4L IS II USM with Canon Extender EF 2X III	Thousand Oaks Optical Solar filter	100	f/8.0	1/250	12:25:07 PM
2017 USA		20170821 _CF0077 _0391	Canon EOS 5DS R	Canon EF500mm f/4L IS II USM with Canon Extender EF 2X III	Thousand Oaks Optical Solar filter	100	f/8.0	1/250	12:30:06 PM
2017 USA		20170821 _CF0077 _0401	Canon EOS 5DS R	Canon EF500mm f/4L IS II USM with Canon Extender EF 2X III	Thousand Oaks Optical Solar filter	100	f/8.0	1/250	12:35:06 PM
2017 USA		20170821 _CF0077 _0411	Canon EOS 5DS R	Canon EF500mm f/4L IS II USM with Canon Extender EF 2X III	Thousand Oaks Optical Solar filter	100	f/8.0	1/250	12:40:07 PM

...Continued

Eclipse	Photo	File Name	Camera	Lens	Filter	ISO	F-stop	Shutter Speed	Time Stamp
2017 USA	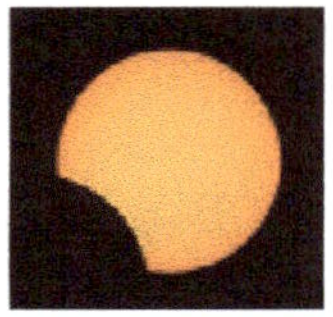	20170821_CF0077_0421	Canon EOS 5DS R	Canon EF500mm f/4L IS II USM with Canon Extender EF 2X III	Thousand Oaks Optical Solar filter	100	f/8.0	1/250	12:45:06 PM
2017 USA	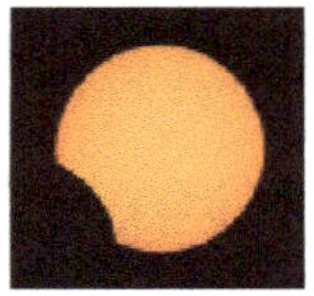	20170821_CF0077_0431	Canon EOS 5DS R	Canon EF500mm f/4L IS II USM with Canon Extender EF 2X III	Thousand Oaks Optical Solar filter	100	f/8.0	1/250	12:50:06 PM
2017 USA	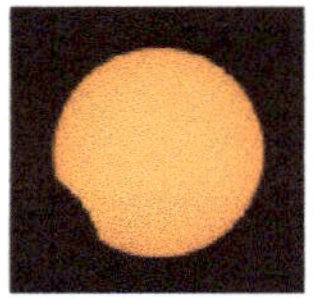	20170821_CF0077_0437	Canon EOS 5DS R	Canon EF500mm f/4L IS II USM with Canon Extender EF 2X III	Thousand Oaks Optical Solar filter	100	f/8.0	1/250	12:55:00 PM
2017 USA	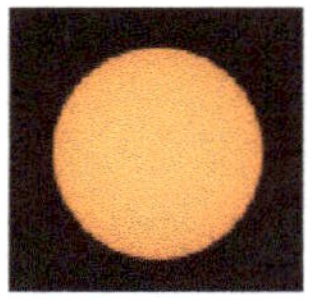	20170821_CF0077_0447	Canon EOS 5DS R	Canon EF500mm f/4L IS II USM with Canon Extender EF 2X III	Thousand Oaks Optical Solar filter	100	f/8.0	1/250	1:00:02 PM
2017 USA	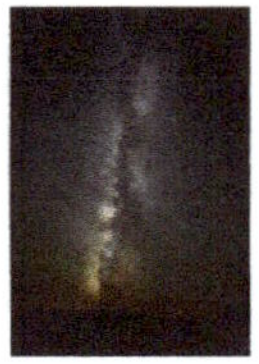	20170822_SD0012_0011	Canon EOS 5D Mark IV	Zeiss Distagon T* 15mm f/2.8 ZE	none	3200	f/2.8	30"	12:09:50 AM

2017 USA	B Roll images of Glenn Sturm in Argentina and Argentina mountains								
PART II									
2019 Chile		20190702 _24mm _MASTER11 _sunset-with-time-lapse COMPOSITE of roughly 40 images	Canon EOS 5DS R (base, corona, partials) & Canon EOS 5D Mark IV (corona, partial)	Sigma 24mm f/1.4 DG HSM Art Lens for Canon EF on Canon 5DS R & Canon EF200mm f/2.8L USM +2x III Extender on Canon 5D Mark IV	Formatt-Hitech Firecrest ND 5.4 / 18-stop during partial phases only None during totality or base sunset image	5DS R at 100 5D Mark IV at 400	f/8.0	Corona: 1/ 1000 - 8" Partials: 1/250, 1/125, 1/60, 1/30, 1/15, 1/4, 1/2 Base images: 1/500, 1/250, 1/15	3:19:17 PM to 5:48:16 PM
2019 Chile		20190630 _SD0118 _0009	Canon EOS 5D Mark IV	Zeiss Distagon T* 15mm f/2.8 ZE	none	6400	f/2.8	20"	10:41:03 PM on June 30, 2019

...Continued

Eclipse	Photo	File Name	Camera	Lens	Filter	ISO	F-stop	Shutter Speed	Time Stamp
2020 Chile	B Roll image of mules near Chungungo, Chile								
2021 Chile	B Roll images of the road to Chungungo, Chungungo, port, and coast								
2019 Chile		03-18-04 _20190702 _SD0119 _0051	Canon EOS 5DS R	Canon EF500mm f/4L IS II USM with Canon Extender EF 2X III	Thousand Oaks Optical Solar filter	100	f/8.0	1/250	3:18:04 PM
2019 Chile		03-23-23 _20190702 _SD0119 _0063	Canon EOS 5DS R	Canon EF500mm f/4L IS II USM with Canon Extender EF 2X III	Thousand Oaks Optical Solar filter	100	f/8.0	1/250	03:23:23 PM
2019 Chile		03-27-29 _20190702 _SD0119 _0068	Canon EOS 5DS R	Canon EF500mm f/4L IS II USM with Canon Extender EF 2X III	Thousand Oaks Optical Solar filter	100	f/8.0	1/250	03:27:29 PM
2019 Chile		03-33-16 _20190702 _SD0119 _0074	Canon EOS 5DS R	Canon EF500mm f/4L IS II USM with Canon Extender EF 2X III	Thousand Oaks Optical Solar filter	100	f/8.0	1/250	03:33:16 PM

2019 Chile		03-38-17 _20190702 _SD0119 _0078	Canon EOS 5DS R	Canon EF500mm f/4L IS II USM with Canon Extender EF 2X III	Thousand Oaks Optical Solar filter	100	f/8.0	1/250	03:38:17 PM
2019 Chile		03-43-18 _20190702 _SD0119 _0085	Canon EOS 5DS R	Canon EF500mm f/4L IS II USM with Canon Extender EF 2X III	Thousand Oaks Optical Solar filter	100	f/8.0	1/250	03:43:18 PM
2019 Chile		03-48-16 _20190702 _SD0119 _0093	Canon EOS 5DS R	Canon EF500mm f/4L IS II USM with Canon Extender EF 2X III	Thousand Oaks Optical Solar filter	100	f/8.0	1/250	03:48:16 PM
2019 Chile		03-53-48 _20190702 _SD0119 _0100	Canon EOS 5DS R	Canon EF500mm f/4L IS II USM with Canon Extender EF 2X III	Thousand Oaks Optical Solar filter	100	f/8.0	1/250	03:53:48 PM
2019 Chile		03-59-15 _20190702 _SD0119 _0107	Canon EOS 5DS R	Canon EF500mm f/4L IS II USM with Canon Extender EF 2X III	Thousand Oaks Optical Solar filter	100	f/8.0	1/250	03:59:15 PM
2019 Chile		04-03-18 _20190702 _SD0119 _0122	Canon EOS 5DS R	Canon EF500mm f/4L IS II USM with Canon Extender EF 2X III	Thousand Oaks Optical Solar filter	100	f/8.0	1/250	04:03:18 PM
2019 Chile		04-08-18 _20190702 _SD0119 _0129	Canon EOS 5DS R	Canon EF500mm f/4L IS II USM with Canon Extender EF 2X III	Thousand Oaks Optical Solar filter	100	f/8.0	1/250	04:08:18 PM

...Continued

Eclipse	Photo	File Name	Camera	Lens	Filter	ISO	F-stop	Shutter Speed	Time Stamp
2019 Chile		04-13-17 _20190702 _SD0119 _0136	Canon EOS 5DS R	Canon EF500mm f/4L IS II USM with Canon Extender EF 2X III	Thousand Oaks Optical Solar filter	100	f/8.0	1/250	04:13:17 PM
2019 Chile		04-18-19 _20190702 _SD0119 _0143	Canon EOS 5DS R	Canon EF500mm f/4L IS II USM with Canon Extender EF 2X III	Thousand Oaks Optical Solar filter	100	f/8.0	1/250	04:18:19 PM
2019 Chile		04-23-17 _20190702 _SD0119 _0151	Canon EOS 5DS R	Canon EF500mm f/4L IS II USM with Canon Extender EF 2X III	Thousand Oaks Optical Solar filter	100	f/8.0	1/250	04:23:17 PM
2019 Chile		04-28-16 _20190702 _SD0119 _0158	Canon EOS 5DS R	Canon EF500mm f/4L IS II USM with Canon Extender EF 2X III	Thousand Oaks Optical Solar filter	100	f/8.0	1/250	04:28:16 PM
2019 Chile		04-33-19 _20190702 _SD0119 _0165	Canon EOS 5DS R	Canon EF500mm f/4L IS II USM with Canon Extender EF 2X III	Thousand Oaks Optical Solar filter	100	f/8.0	1/250	04:33:19 PM
2019 Chile		04-36-18 _20190702 _SD0119 _0173	Canon EOS 5DS R	Canon EF500mm f/4L IS II USM with Canon Extender EF 2X III	Thousand Oaks Optical Solar filter	100	f/8.0	1/250	04:36:18 PM

2019 Chile		20190702 _SD0119 _0176	Canon EOS 5DS R	Canon EF500mm f/4L IS II USM with Canon Extender EF 2X III	none	200	f/8.0	1/4000	4:38:07 PM
2019 Chile		20190702 _SD0118 _0173	Canon EOS 5D Mark IV	Canon EF200mm f/2.8L USM +2x III Extender	none	400	f/8.0	1/60	4:38:20 PM
2019 Chile		20190702 _SD0118 _0174	Canon EOS 5D Mark IV	Canon EF200mm f/2.8L USM +2x III Extender	none	400	f/8.0	1/125	4:38:20 PM
2019 Chile		20190702 _SD0118 _0179	Canon EOS 5D Mark IV	Canon EF200mm f/2.8L USM +2x III Extender	none	400	f/8.0	1/4000	4:38:23 PM
2019 Chile		20190702 _SD0118 _0180	Canon EOS 5D Mark IV	Canon EF200mm f/2.8L USM +2x III Extender	none	400	f/8.0	1/60	4:38:24 PM
2019 Chile		20190702 _SD0119 _0181	Canon EOS 5DS R	Canon EF500mm f/4L IS II USM with Canon Extender EF 2X III	none	200	f/8.0	1/125	4:38:23 PM
2019 Chile		20190702 _SD0119 _0182	Canon EOS 5DS R	Canon EF500mm f/4L IS II USM with Canon Extender EF 2X III	none	200	f/8.0	1/60	4:38:26 PM

...Continued

Eclipse	Photo	File Name	Camera	Lens	Filter	ISO	F-stop	Shutter Speed	Time Stamp
2019 Chile		20190702_SD0119_0184	Canon EOS 5DS R	Canon EF500mm f/4L IS II USM with Canon Extender EF 2X III	none	200	f/8.0	1/2000	4:38:32 PM
2019 Chile		20190702_24mm_MASTER11_totality-only	Canon EOS 5DS R (base, corona) & Canon EOS 5D Mark IV (corona)	Sigma 24mm f/1.4 DG HSM Art Lens for Canon EF on 5DS R & Canon EF200mm f/2.8L USM +2x III Extender on 5D Mark 4	none	5DS R at 100 5D Mark IV at 400	f/8.0	Corona: 1/1000 - 8" Base images: 8", 4", 2"	04:39 PM
2019 Chile		COMPOSITE	Canon EOS 5D Mark IV	Canon EF200mm f/2.8L USM +2x III Extender	none	400	f/8.0	1" 1/4 1/15 1/60	4:39:59 PM to 4:40:12 PM
2019 Chile		20190702_SD0119_0214	Canon EOS 5DS R	Canon EF500mm f/4L IS II USM with Canon Extender EF 2X III	none	200	f/8.0	1/125	4:40:59 PM
2019 Chile		20190702_SD0119_0215	Canon EOS 5DS R	Canon EF500mm f/4L IS II USM with Canon Extender EF 2X III	none	200	f/8.0	1/125	4:41:01 PM

2019 Chile		20190702 _SD0119 _0218	Canon EOS 5DS R	Canon EF500mm f/4L IS II USM with Canon Extender EF 2X III	none	200	f/8.0	1/125	4:41:07 PM
2019 Chile		04-41-58 _20190702 _SD0119 _0233	Canon EOS 5DS R	Canon EF500mm f/4L IS II USM with Canon Extender EF 2X III	Thousand Oaks Optical Solar filter	100	f/8.0	1/250	04:41:58 PM
2019 Chile		04-46-17 _20190702 _SD0119 _0310	Canon EOS 5DS R	Canon EF500mm f/4L IS II USM with Canon Extender EF 2X III	Thousand Oaks Optical Solar filter	100	f/8.0	1/250	04:46:17 PM
2019 Chile		04-51-16 _20190702 _SD0119 _0327	Canon EOS 5DS R	Canon EF500mm f/4L IS II USM with Canon Extender EF 2X III	Thousand Oaks Optical Solar filter	100	f/8.0	1/250	04:51:16 PM
2019 Chile		04-56-19 _20190702 _SD0119 _0334	Canon EOS 5DS R	Canon EF500mm f/4L IS II USM with Canon Extender EF 2X III	Thousand Oaks Optical Solar filter	100	f/8.0	1/250	04:56:19 PM
2019 Chile		05-01-17 _20190702 _SD0119 _0347	Canon EOS 5DS R	Canon EF500mm f/4L IS II USM with Canon Extender EF 2X III	Thousand Oaks Optical Solar filter	100	f/8.0	1/250	05:01:17 PM
2019 Chile		05-06-22 _20190702 _SD0119 _0354	Canon EOS 5DS R	Canon EF500mm f/4L IS II USM with Canon Extender EF 2X III	Thousand Oaks Optical Solar filter	100	f/8.0	1/250	05:06:22 PM

...*Continued*

Eclipse	Photo	File Name	Camera	Lens	Filter	ISO	F-stop	Shutter Speed	Time Stamp
2019 Chile		05-11-19_20190702_SD0119_0361	Canon EOS 5DS R	Canon EF500mm f/4L IS II USM with Canon Extender EF 2X III	Thousand Oaks Optical Solar filter	100	f/8.0	1/250	05:11:19 PM
2019 Chile		05-16-13_20190702_SD0119_0368	Canon EOS 5DS R	Canon EF500mm f/4L IS II USM with Canon Extender EF 2X III	Thousand Oaks Optical Solar filter	100	f/8.0	1/250	05:16:13 PM
2019 Chile		05-23-33_20190702_SD0119_0390	Canon EOS 5DS R	Canon EF500mm f/4L IS II USM with Canon Extender EF 2X III	Thousand Oaks Optical Solar filter	100	f/8.0	1/125	05:23:33 PM
2019 Chile		05-26-33_20190702_SD0119_0396	Canon EOS 5DS R	Canon EF500mm f/4L IS II USM with Canon Extender EF 2X III	Thousand Oaks Optical Solar filter	100	f/8.0	1/125	05:26:33 PM
2019 Chile		05-31-22_20190702_SD0119_0404	Canon EOS 5DS R	Canon EF500mm f/4L IS II USM with Canon Extender EF 2X III	Thousand Oaks Optical Solar filter	100	f/8.0	1/60	05:31:22 PM
2019 Chile		05-36-39_20190702_SD0119_0420	Canon EOS 5DS R	Canon EF500mm f/4L IS II USM with Canon Extender EF 2X III	Thousand Oaks Optical Solar filter	100	f/8.0	1/60	05:36:39 PM

2019 Chile	20190702 _SD0119 _0442	Canon EOS 5DS R	Canon EF500mm f/4L IS II USM with Canon Extender EF 2X III	Thousand Oaks Optical Solar filter	100	f/8.0	1/4	05:39:10
2019 Chile	05-43-08 _20190702 _SD0119 _0490	Canon EOS 5DS R	Canon EF500mm f/4L IS II USM with Canon Extender EF 2X III	Thousand Oaks Optical Solar filter	100	f/8.0	1/15	05:43:08 PM
2019 Chile	05-45-33 _20190702 _SD0119 _0506	Canon EOS 5DS R	Canon EF500mm f/4L IS II USM with Canon Extender EF 2X III	none	100	f/11	1/8000	05:45:33 PM
2019 Chile	20190702 _SD0119 _0553	Canon EOS 5DS R	Canon EF500mm f/4L IS II USM with Canon Extender EF 2X III	none	100	f/11	1/1500	5:53:35 PM
2019 Chile	20190702 _CF0098 _0344	Canon EOS 5D Mark III	Zeiss Distagon T* 15mm f/2.8 ZE	none	100	f/8.0	1/60	5:51:54 PM
2019 Chile	20190702 _SD0119 _0232	Canon EOS 5DS R	Canon EF500mm f/4L IS II USM with Canon Extender EF 2X III	Thousand Oaks Optical Solar filter	200	f/8.0	1/500	4:41:42 PM

...Continued

Eclipse	Photo	File Name	Camera	Lens	Filter	ISO	F-stop	Shutter Speed	Time Stamp
2019 Chile		20190702_20190702_15mmcomposite_2023.11.14b COMPOSITE of roughly 40 images	Canon EOS 5D Mark III (base, partials), Canon EOS 5DS R (corona, partials), Canon EOS 5D Mark IV (corona)	Zeiss Distagon T* 15mm f/2.8 ZE on Canon 5D Mark III, Sigma 24mm f/1.4 DG HSM Art Lens for Canon EF on Canon 5DS R, Canon EF200mm f/2.8L USM +2x III Extender on Canon 5D Mark IV	Formatt-Hitech Firecrest ND 5.4 / 18-stop during partial phases only None during totality or base sunset image	5D Mark III at 100-200 5DS R at 100 5D Mark IV at 400	f/8.0	Corona: 1/1000 - 8" Partials: 1/250, 1/125, 1/60, 1/30, 1/8, 1/4 Base images: 1/250, 1/15	03:19:17 PM to 05:51:56 PM

2019 Chile		chile2019-vert COMPOSITE of roughly 40 images	Canon EOS 5DS R (base, corona, partials) & Canon EOS 5D Mark IV (corona, partial)	Sigma 24mm f/1.4 DG HSM Art Lens for Canon EF on Canon 5DS R & Canon EF200mm f/2.8L USM +2x III Extender on Canon 5D Mark IV	Formatt-Hitech Firecrest ND 5.4 / 18-stop during partial phases only None during totality or base sunset image	5DS R at 100 5D Mark IV at 200 for partials, 400 for corona	f/8.0	Corona: 1/1000 - 8" Partials: 1/250, 1/125, 1/60, 1/30, 1/15, 1/4, 1/2 Base images: 1/500, 1/250, 1/15	03:19:17 PM to 05:48:16 PM
2019 Chile		20190702_SD0118_0520	Canon EOS 5D Mark IV	Zeiss Distagon T* 15mm f/2.8 ZE	none	6400	f/2.8	20"	09:41:41 PM on July 2, 2019
2019 Chile	B Roll images of individuals who helpd us in Chile								

...Continued

Eclipse	Photo	File Name	Camera	Lens	Filter	ISO	F-stop	Shutter Speed	Time Stamp
PART III									
2023 Australia		DSCF2700	Fuji GFX 100S	GF30mm F3.5 R WR	none	100	f/9.0	1/5	Sunset April 19, 2023
Various eclipses	6 images of examples of total eclipse, partial eclipse, and annular eclipse								
2023 Australia	B Roll images of Glenn, Brit, and partial equipment setup								
2023 Australia		10-03-28 _20230420 _SD0158 _0008	Canon EOS 5D Mark IV	Canon EF500mm f/4L IS II USM with Canon Extender EF 2X III	Thousand Oaks Optical Solar filter	100	f/8.0	1/250	10:03:28 AM
2023 Australia		10-17-40 _20230420 _SD0158 _0013	Canon EOS 5D Mark IV	Canon EF500mm f/4L IS II USM with Canon Extender EF 2X III	Thousand Oaks Optical Solar filter	100	f/8.0	1/250	10:17:40 AM

Metadata for all Images in the Book

145

2023 Australia		10-13-21 _20230420 _SD0158 _0018	Canon EOS 5D Mark IV	Canon EF500mm f/4L IS II USM with Canon Extender EF 2X III	Thousand Oaks Optical Solar filter	100	f/8.0	1/250	10:13:21 AM
2023 Australia		10-17-51 _20230420 _SD0158 _0023	Canon EOS 5D Mark IV	Canon EF500mm f/4L IS II USM with Canon Extender EF 2X III	Thousand Oaks Optical Solar filter	100	f/8.0	1/250	10:17:51 AM
2023 Australia		10-22-56 _20230420 _SD0158 _0028	Canon EOS 5D Mark IV	Canon EF500mm f/4L IS II USM with Canon Extender EF 2X III	Thousand Oaks Optical Solar filter	100	f/8.0	1/250	10:22:56 AM
2023 Australia		10-27-51 _20230420 _SD0158 _0033	Canon EOS 5D Mark IV	Canon EF500mm f/4L IS II USM with Canon Extender EF 2X III	Thousand Oaks Optical Solar filter	100	f/8.0	1/250	10:27:51 AM
2023 Australia		10-33-06 _20230420 _SD0158 _0038	Canon EOS 5D Mark IV	Canon EF500mm f/4L IS II USM with Canon Extender EF 2X III	Thousand Oaks Optical Solar filter	100	f/8.0	1/250	10:33:06 AM
2023 Australia		10-38-14 _20230420 _SD0158 _0043	Canon EOS 5D Mark IV	Canon EF500mm f/4L IS II USM with Canon Extender EF 2X III	Thousand Oaks Optical Solar filter	100	f/8.0	1/250	10:38:14 AM
2023 Australia		10-43-04 _20230420 _SD0158 _0048	Canon EOS 5D Mark IV	Canon EF500mm f/4L IS II USM with Canon Extender EF 2X III	Thousand Oaks Optical Solar filter	100	f/8.0	1/250	10:43:04 AM

...Continued

Eclipse	Photo	File Name	Camera	Lens	Filter	ISO	F-stop	Shutter Speed	Time Stamp
2023 Australia		10-48-09_20230420_SD0158_0053	Canon EOS 5D Mark IV	Canon EF500mm f/4L IS II USM with Canon Extender EF 2X III	Thousand Oaks Optical Solar filter	100	f/8.0	1/250	10:48:09 AM
2023 Australia		10-53-07_20230420_SD0158_0058	Canon EOS 5D Mark IV	Canon EF500mm f/4L IS II USM with Canon Extender EF 2X III	Thousand Oaks Optical Solar filter	100	f/8.0	1/250	10:53:07 AM
2023 Australia		10-58-01_20230420_SD0158_0063	Canon EOS 5D Mark IV	Canon EF500mm f/4L IS II USM with Canon Extender EF 2X III	Thousand Oaks Optical Solar filter	100	f/8.0	1/250	10:58:01 AM
2023 Australia		11-03-19_20230420_SD0158_0068	Canon EOS 5D Mark IV	Canon EF500mm f/4L IS II USM with Canon Extender EF 2X III	Thousand Oaks Optical Solar filter	100	f/8.0	1/250	11:03:19 AM
2023 Australia		11-08-02_20230420_SD0158_0073	Canon EOS 5D Mark IV	Canon EF500mm f/4L IS II USM with Canon Extender EF 2X III	Thousand Oaks Optical Solar filter	100	f/8.0	1/250	11:08:02 AM
2023 Australia		11-13-04_20230420_SD0158_0078	Canon EOS 5D Mark IV	Canon EF500mm f/4L IS II USM with Canon Extender EF 2X III	Thousand Oaks Optical Solar filter	100	f/8.0	1/250	11:13:04 AM

2023 Australia		11-18-02 _20230420 _SD0158 _0083	Canon EOS 5D Mark IV	Canon EF500mm f/4L IS II USM with Canon Extender EF 2X III	Thousand Oaks Optical Solar filter	100	f/8.0	1/250	11:18:02 AM
2023 Australia		11-23-07 _20230420 _SD0158 _0088	Canon EOS 5D Mark IV	Canon EF500mm f/4L IS II USM with Canon Extender EF 2X III	Thousand Oaks Optical Solar filter	100	f/8.0	1/250	11:23:07 AM
2023 Australia		20230420 _SD0154 _0306	Canon EOS R5	Canon EF600mm f/4L IS II USM with Canon Extender EF 2X III	none	400	f/8.0	1/8000	11:28:11 AM
2023 Australia		20230420 _SD0154 _0327	Canon EOS R5	Canon EF600mm f/4L IS II USM with Canon Extender EF 2X III	none	400	f/8.0	1/8000	11:28:33 AM
2023 Australia		20230420 _SD0154 _0335	Canon EOS R5	Canon EF600mm f/4L IS II USM with Canon Extender EF 2X III	none	400	f/8.0	1/4000	11:28:37 AM
2023 Australia		20230420 _SD0158 _composite	Canon EOS 5D Mark IV	Canon EF500mm f/4L IS II USM with Canon Extender EF 2X III	none	400	f/8.0	1/125, 1/60, 1/30, 1/15, 1/8	11:29:01 AM to 11:29:05 AM

...*Continued*

Eclipse	Photo	File Name	Camera	Lens	Filter	ISO	F-stop	Shutter Speed	Time Stamp
2023 Australia		11-29-05 _20230420 _SD0158 _0131	Canon EOS 5D Mark IV	Canon EF500mm f/4L IS II USM with Canon Extender EF 2X III	none	400	f/8.0	1/125	11:29:05 AM
2023 Australia		11-29-01 _20230420 _SD0158 _0122	Canon EOS 5D Mark IV	Canon EF500mm f/4L IS II USM with Canon Extender EF 2X III	none	400	f/8.0	1/60	11:29:01 AM
2023 Australia		11-29-01 _20230420 _SD0158 _0123	Canon EOS 5D Mark IV	Canon EF500mm f/4L IS II USM with Canon Extender EF 2X III	none	400	f/8.0	1/30	11:29:01 AM
2023 Australia		11-29-01 _20230420 _SD0158 _0124	Canon EOS 5D Mark IV	Canon EF500mm f/4L IS II USM with Canon Extender EF 2X III	none	400	f/8.0	1/15	11:29:01 AM
2023 Australia		11-29-01 _20230420 _SD0158 _0125	Canon EOS 5D Mark IV	Canon EF500mm f/4L IS II USM with Canon Extender EF 2X III	none	400	f/8.0	1/8	11:29:01 AM
2023 Australia		20230420 _SD0154 _0383	Canon EOS R5	Canon EF600mm f/4L IS II USM with Canon Extender EF 2X III	none	400	f/8.0	1/8000	11:28:59 AM

2023 Australia		20230420 _SD0161 _Enhanced _composite	Fuji GFX 100S	GF23mmF4 R LM WR	none	200	f/8.0	base image: 1" Corona: 1/500 1/250 1/125 1/60 1/30 1/4 1/2 1" 2"	11:28:48 AM to 11:29:06 AM
2023 Australia		20230420 _SD0154 _0467	Canon EOS R5	Canon EF600mm f/4L IS II USM with Canon Extender EF 2X III	none	400	f/8.0	1/8000	11:29:34 AM
2023 Australia		20230420 _SD0154 _0474	Canon EOS R5	Canon EF600mm f/4L IS II USM with Canon Extender EF 2X III	none	400	f/8.0	1/8000	11:29:41 AM
2023 Australia		20230420 _SD0154 _0475	Canon EOS R5	Canon EF600mm f/4L IS II USM with Canon Extender EF 2X III	none	400	f/8.0	1/4000	11:29:42 AM
2023 Australia		20230420 _SD0154 _0485	Canon EOS R5	Canon EF600mm f/4L IS II USM with Canon Extender EF 2X III	none	400	f/8.0	1/500	11:29:49 AM

...Continued

Eclipse	Photo	File Name	Camera	Lens	Filter	ISO	F-stop	Shutter Speed	Time Stamp
2023 Australia		11-41-02 _20230420 _SD0154 _0814	Canon EOS R5	Canon EF600mm f/4L IS II USM with Canon Extender EF 2X III	Thousand Oaks Optical Solar filter	400	f/8.0	1/250	11:41:02 AM
2023 Australia		11-46-02 _20230420 _SD0154 _0832	Canon EOS R5	Canon EF600mm f/4L IS II USM with Canon Extender EF 2X III	Thousand Oaks Optical Solar filter	400	f/8.0	1/250	11:46:02 AM
2023 Australia		11-51-00 _20230420 _SD0154 _0846	Canon EOS R5	Canon EF600mm f/4L IS II USM with Canon Extender EF 2X III	Thousand Oaks Optical Solar filter	400	f/8.0	1/250	11:51:00 AM
2023 Australia		11-56-00 _20230420 _SD0154 _0869	Canon EOS R5	Canon EF600mm f/4L IS II USM with Canon Extender EF 2X III	Thousand Oaks Optical Solar filter	400	f/8.0	1/250	11:56:00 AM
2023 Australia		12-01-13 _20230420 _SD0154 _0877	Canon EOS R5	Canon EF600mm f/4L IS II USM with Canon Extender EF 2X III	Thousand Oaks Optical Solar filter	400	f/8.0	1/250	12:01:13 PM
2023 Australia		12-06-31 _20230420 _SD0154 _0891	Canon EOS R5	Canon EF600mm f/4L IS II USM with Canon Extender EF 2X III	Thousand Oaks Optical Solar filter	400	f/8.0	1/250	12:06:31 PM

2023 Australia		12-11-02 _20230420 _SD0154 _0905	Canon EOS R5	Canon EF600mm f/4L IS II USM with Canon Extender EF 2X III	Thousand Oaks Optical Solar filter	400	f/8.0	1/250	12:11:02 PM
2023 Australia		12-16-16 _20230420 _SD0154 _0919	Canon EOS R5	Canon EF600mm f/4L IS II USM with Canon Extender EF 2X III	Thousand Oaks Optical Solar filter	400	f/8.0	1/250	12:16:16 PM
2023 Australia		12-21-06 _20230420 _SD0154 _0933	Canon EOS R5	Canon EF600mm f/4L IS II USM with Canon Extender EF 2X III	Thousand Oaks Optical Solar filter	400	f/8.0	1/250	12:21:06 PM
2023 Australia		12-26-01 _20230420 _SD0154 _0954	Canon EOS R5	Canon EF600mm f/4L IS II USM with Canon Extender EF 2X III	Thousand Oaks Optical Solar filter	400	f/8.0	1/250	12:26:01 PM
2023 Australia		12-31-05 _20230420 _SD0158 _0383	Canon EOS 5D Mark IV	Canon EF500mm f/4L IS II USM with Canon Extender EF 2X III	Thousand Oaks Optical Solar filter	100	f/8.0	1/250	12:31:05 PM
2023 Australia		12-35-56 _20230420 _SD0158 _0388	Canon EOS 5D Mark IV	Canon EF500mm f/4L IS II USM with Canon Extender EF 2X III	Thousand Oaks Optical Solar filter	100	f/8.0	1/250	12:35:56 PM
2023 Australia		12-41-01 _20230420 _SD0158 _0393	Canon EOS 5D Mark IV	Canon EF500mm f/4L IS II USM with Canon Extender EF 2X III	Thousand Oaks Optical Solar filter	100	f/8.0	1/250	12:41:01 PM

...*Continued*

Eclipse	Photo	File Name	Camera	Lens	Filter	ISO	F-stop	Shutter Speed	Time Stamp
2023 Australia		12-46-12 _20230420 _SD0158 _0398	Canon EOS 5D Mark IV	Canon EF500mm f/4L IS II USM with Canon Extender EF 2X III	Thousand Oaks Optical Solar filter	100	f/8.0	1/250	12:46:12 PM
2023 Australia		12-51-04 _20230420 _SD0158 _0403	Canon EOS 5D Mark IV	Canon EF500mm f/4L IS II USM with Canon Extender EF 2X III	Thousand Oaks Optical Solar filter	100	f/8.0	1/250	12:51:04 PM
2023 Australia		12-56-08 _20230420 _SD0158 _0408	Canon EOS 5D Mark IV	Canon EF500mm f/4L IS II USM with Canon Extender EF 2X III	Thousand Oaks Optical Solar filter	100	f/8.0	1/250	12:56:08 PM
2023 Australia		13-01-01 _20230420 _SD0158 _0413	Canon EOS 5D Mark IV	Canon EF500mm f/4L IS II USM with Canon Extender EF 2X III	Thousand Oaks Optical Solar filter	100	f/8.0	1/250	1:01:01 PM
2023 Australia		20230420 _SD0156 _0291	Fuji GFX 100S	GF23mmF4 R LM WR	none	200	f/8.0	1/1250	1:14:52 PM

2023 Australia		20230420 _SD0156 _Enhanced-composite	Canon EOS 5DS R	Zeiss Distagon T* 15mm f/2.8 ZE	Formatt Hi-Tech ND 5.4	200	f/8.0	partials: 1/500 corona: 1/500, 1/250, 1/125, 1/60, 1/30, 1/4, 1/2 sky: 1/4 fore ground: 1/2	11:28-11:29 AM
2023 NM		20231003 _CF0204 _0060	Canon EOS 5D Mark IV	Sigma 35mm f/1.4 DG HSM ART	none	100	f/11.0	1/250	N/A
2023 NM		20231014 _SD0210 _0256	Canon EOS R5	EF1200mm F8 L IS USM + EXTENDER 1.4x	Thousand Oaks Optical Solar filter	800	f/11.0	1/125	10:30:03 AM
2023 NM		20231014 _SD0210 _0970	Canon EOS R5	EF1200mm F8 L IS USM + EXTENDER 1.4x	Thousand Oaks Optical Solar filter	800	f/11.0	1/125	10:35:17 AM
2023 NM		20231014 _SD0210 _1971	Canon EOS R5	EF1200mm F8 L IS USM + EXTENDER 1.4x	Thousand Oaks Optical Solar filter	800	f/11.0	1/125	10:40:17 AM

For more images and information and to stay informed about the proceeding Syzygies books visit Syzygies.com or scan the QR Code.

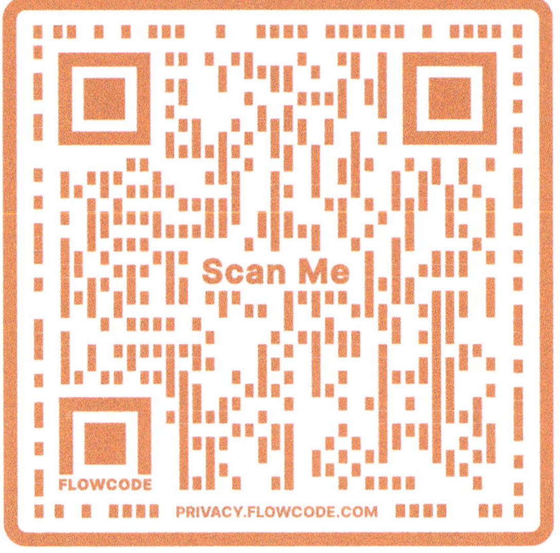

www.ingramcontent.com/pod-product-compliance
Lightning Source LLC
LaVergne TN
LVHW060639110826
845147LV00018B/1009
9781945674969